JOHN ALDRIDGE

MY STORY

G000231599

JOHN ALDRIDGE

MY STORY

John Aldridge

with Hyder Jawad

CORONET BOOKS

Hodder & Stoughton

Copyright © 1999 by John Aldridge

The right of John Aldridge to be identified as the Author of
the Work has been asserted by him in accordance with the
Copyright, Designs and Patents Act 1988.

First published in Great Britain in 1999 by Hodder and Stoughton
First published in paperback in 2000 by Hodder and Stoughton
A division of Hodder Headline

A Coronet paperback

10 9 8 7 6 5 4 3 2 1

A CIP catalogue record for this title
is available from the British Library

ISBN 0 340 73952 5

Typeset by Palimpsest Book Production Limited,
Polmont, Stirlingshire
Printed and bound in Great Britain by
Clays Ltd, St Ives plc

Hodder and Stoughton
A division of Hodder Headline
338 Euston Road
London NW1 3BH

CONTENTS

	Acknowledgements	vii
	Foreword by Jack Charlton	ix
1	Thicker than water	1
2	Dreamer's ball	23
3	Maxwell house	41
4	When we were kings	65
5	'They only came to watch football'	91
6	Brave new world	115
7	The team that Jack built	145
8	King's court	177
9	Forever young	203
10	I think I'll manage	233
11	In the name of the father	247
	Postscript	253
	Appendix: John Aldridge career details	261
	Index	263

Photographic Acknowledgements

The author and the publisher would like to thank the following for the permission to produce their copyright photographs: Associated Sports Photography, Bob Thomas Sports Photography, Empics, Fotosports International, Gordon Whiting, Jim Larkin Fotos, *Liverpool Daily Post & Echo*, Lloyd Wright, Mercury Press Agency, The Press Association Ltd, Sport & Politics in Focus, Sportsphoto Agency.

ACKNOWLEDGEMENTS

John Aldridge: Work on this book began on 16 August 1998 and ended on 16 November, exactly three months later. Keeping to such a tight deadline might have been impossible had it not been for the help of a host of people. My warm thanks, therefore, to the following who, in one way or another, contributed to making this book possible: Hyder Jawad, my ghost writer; Roddy Bloomfield, my publisher; my mother, Betty McNamara, for helping me remember the early days and for being a constant source of encouragement; Joan, my wife, for her love and support and her ability to remember the things I couldn't; Paul and Joanne, my son and daughter, just for existing; and my late father Bill whose memory still inspires me. Thanks also to the managers and players who, over the years, have made my days in professional football so exciting, and to all my friends who keep me laughing.

Hyder Jawad: I would like to thank the following for their help and support: Mum, Dad, Amer and Natasha; Christine Jones; Tim Bown; Garry Doolan; Paul Dove; Eric Stokes; Richard Williamson; Angela Hall; Tony at the Gardener's Arms; Graham Bell; Alan Bartlam; Richard Shepherd; Brian Miller; Roddy, his editorial assistant Nicola Lintern, copy-editor Marion Paull, and John Burke. Finally, many thanks to John Aldridge for the hospitality, the gallons of mineral water, and the conversations which produced sixteen C90 cassettes of priceless material.

*This book is dedicated to the memory of my father
and to the memory of the ninety-six people who died
as a result of the Hillsborough tragedy.*

FOREWORD
by Jack Charlton

I credit John Aldridge with being one of my main men during my decade as manager of the Republic of Ireland. He played in my first match against Wales in Dublin in 1986 and in my last against Holland in Liverpool in 1995. In between he emerged as one of international football's most respected strikers. Little wonder the Irish public adore him. He was as honest a professional as you could wish to meet, while his hard work and goalscoring ability helped to make Ireland one of the most feared teams in world football.

It took John twenty games to score for Ireland but that never worried me. My policy was for Ireland to do their defending in the opponents' half of the field, which meant a lot of work for John. He was doing the work I'd asked him, something the supporters appreciated. When his first international goal did come – against Tunisia in 1988 – it was worth the wait. The statisticians tell me it was 1,738 minutes of action before John broke his international duck.

Even before he had kicked a ball for Ireland, John was important to me. When I asked him if he fancied playing for Ireland he not only expressed an interest, he told me about Ray Houghton. 'He's more Irish than me,' John said. So on a cold night in March 1986 I acquired, thanks to John Aldridge, two of the greatest players in Irish football history.

Jack Charlton
December 1998

— 1 —

THICKER THAN WATER

W<small>HEN</small> you spent your childhood days in a tiny two-bedroomed house that had an outside toilet, you don't find it hard to appreciate first-class travel and five-star hotels. Sometimes the contrasts between childhood and adulthood are so great that you cannot easily analyse the intervening years. But one thing I know is this: the working classes rarely see reason to forget their roots. In moments of introspection, I sit in the Gardener's Arms in Woolton, Liverpool, and cast my mind back to the days when life was simpler and everything seemed possible. I think about my father and his successful, if often unorthodox, efforts to keep our family above the poverty line. I think about my mother; a wonderful woman who worried for the future but always made sure we had enough for the present.

Yes, I've been lucky. Our early struggles shaped me for the career I chose and strengthened me in times of despair. If I have a regret it is that my father is no longer a phone-call away. His death, in March 1998, still hurts.

Hailing from Dingle, one of Liverpool's more deprived areas in the immediate post-War years, Bill Aldridge earned money whichever way he could. He had spells on the buses and spent most of his time working as a roof contractor. But he had his fingers in many pies and there were few money-making schemes he never embraced. Stories of my father's shady deals were well discussed at family get-togethers, though his instincts

1

for survival in a tough environment were to be admired. I think the character that most resembles my father is the Artful Dodger in Charles Dickens' *Oliver Twist*. Being shrewd, intelligent, and hard-working came with the territory, as did the gift of the gab. My father could talk people into doing anything for him and when he turned on the charm he was difficult to resist. And that is how Betty McNamara, my mother, remembers him.

Bill and Betty had other partners when they met for the first time. It was at a dance hall in Dingle. Quite what they were thinking at the time is a mystery to me – I accepted the story, like I accepted all things in which my father was involved – but once their eyes strayed there was only one outcome. They began living together soon after and that was how it stayed for nearly half a century. For sure, it wasn't morally correct, but I have to be grateful for such a twist of fate.

I was born John William Aldridge on 18 September 1958. Our address was Vulcan Street, Garston, which was three miles to the south of Dingle. Under the bridge in Garston, where I lived, was a tough area. We lived in the shadow of the gasworks, not far from Garston Docks, which was our gateway to the River Mersey. To us, the Mersey was always the sea.

I had half-sisters from both sides of the family. I was particularly close to Jean and Anne, my mother's daughters. They may have had a different dad but they were like real sisters to me. Alfie, their father, lived round the corner from us and was a lovely fellow. I had so much respect for the way he handled a difficult situation. Alfie was a typical Garstonian. In those days, the local populace was the salt of the earth. If you were in a pub in Garston and it was obvious you were short of money, someone would usually give you a quid to make sure you could get a few drinks. People were always looking out for each other, creating a unique family-like community.

I spent a lot of my time playing on the pavement outside our house with other young scamps from the neighbourhood. It was a street education, the kind that gives kids the greatest insights into what growing up means. We learned quickly,

2

developed sharp minds, and cultivated the circumstances in which our skills flourished.

Though we were far from well-off, my childhood memories are all sweet; I wanted for nothing. I suppose I was spoiled – well, as spoiled as a working-class kid could be. My father was always coming home with money for me, always giving me things. He was very generous to me and was pleased I appreciated it. So whenever there was an opportunity for me to work for him, he got me involved. I remember mixing cement for him when he was working on a house. I did all kinds of things. It didn't really matter what; I appreciated the involvement, the chance to be significant. And while I worked, my father was able to watch me grow up and develop. I do believe it gave him pleasure to see how much his wide-eyed son looked up to him.

My father's routine was the same for years. He went to work in the daytime, made sure he had enough for my mother and myself, and went off to the pub for a drinking session at the Victoria Arms with his pals. He always went out at around seven o'clock and would be back for around quarter to eleven. Then it was up for the work the next day and so the cycle went on. He really did live for today; tomorrow was too far in the future.

It's hard to say what effect this was having on my mother. I didn't think too deeply about it when I was a child yet now I can see what the relationship between my father and mother was like. They often fought, like cat and dog. You know the sort of thing – can't live with each other, can't live without each other. They were able to absorb their disagreements like sunlight and photosynthesize them into energy. In the final analysis, they needed each other. That is why, now that my father has been laid to rest, my mother talks of his virtues and little else.

I went to Banks Road School, which was a short walk away from Vulcan Street, and found that my inability to conform often landed me in trouble. I had a major problem from day one: I was Catholic and Banks Road School was Protestant. But this was a peripheral issue compared to my refusal to accept authority. I argued with schoolteachers habitually. My parents were regularly called to the school to be told of my latest misdemeanours, which did nothing other than inspire me to greater levels of bad behaviour. My father didn't approve but he insisted I stand up for myself – especially where the cane was concerned.

To a proud man such as Bill Aldridge, the cane was an indignity our family could do without. My father couldn't entertain the thought of anyone hitting me. Neither he nor my mother ever hit me and they certainly were not going to allow a schoolteacher to give me the cane. My father was clear on this issue; I was to avoid it at all costs. I remember his words to this day: 'John, son, if they are going to give you the cane, you run out of school and come home, and I'll sort them out.'

I ran home once too often, however, and the school expelled me. This was no surprise as I had been suspended on one previous occasion. My father, bless him, went straight up to the school to plead with the headmaster to allow me back into the fold. The oratory skills worked yet again; reluctantly, the head-master offered me the chance to start afresh. The greater issue, of course, was that I lacked an outlet for my energy. Though not without intelligence, I wasn't cut out for the disciplines of school. Formal education bored me. Trouble, on the other hand, followed me round like a bad penny and the situation might have been worse had I not been introduced to football.

Football in the early 1960s had not yet been claimed by the middle classes. It was then essentially the game for the masses. You could not avoid it, especially if you lived in the highly populated inner-cities of Liverpool. Either you played it or you watched it; or you did both. Football was the right shaped sport for kids my age. All you needed was a ball and an open space and you had something that would occupy you for hours. At last I had a purpose in life; something to dream about.

Behind our house there was a tiny space of uneven concrete – a back entry, as we called it – which was perfect for playing three-a-side football. That walled area became my entire world as friends would come and play and help turn our little matches into epics that consumed my thoughts for hours. Even without the company of my friends, the ball was enough. In the comfort of my solitude, I would constantly head the ball against the wall – I once did it 365 times without the ball hitting the floor – and shoot into a goal I created out of two pillars. Little wonder these are my happiest childhood memories.

The neighbours didn't approve, of course. I lost count of the number of times windows at the back of their houses were flung open in annoyance; the greetings were always less than complimentary. And did we care? Not one jot. It's funny that when you have found your personal Utopia, the feelings of others become irrelevant.

I learned more about football in those few years, playing in that humble backyard, than at any other time since. I believe my ability to score goals at the highest level in later years was formed in those games with friends. Even at the age of seven, I found it easier than most of my contemporaries to find space and time in confined areas to get clean shots at goal. I owe that back entry a lot. I often think about it as being my own gym, which is perhaps why, once the good times came, I always had a gym in my house.

We played football as often as we could in school; break time, dinner time – it didn't matter. And, typically, my father always made sure I had a ball. If I lost one he'd get me another. My parents understood my love of the game and always came to watch me when I played for the school team. It was no big deal if my father had work on a Saturday morning because he'd still drop everything and drive to the school field to join my mother while I tried to impress them. At half-past ten every Saturday morning I could guarantee they would be there, cheering me on from the line, giving me constant encouragement.

That car served my father well. It was only years later that I found out he'd never passed his driving test. He considered the lack of a licence to be a risk only on the motorway; or perhaps he didn't like the idea of travelling at speed. Either way, long-distance drives were avoided.

What my parents must have thought of my first game for the school is anyone's guess. I was terrible. I played right-half and contrived to hit my own post. Nothing serious but enough to make me realise right-half wasn't my position. I was moved further upfield in the next match, with favourable results. I scored sixty-odd goals in one season and we soon became the best team of our age group in Liverpool. We won all the cup competitions we entered, though in one final I remember missing an easy scoring chance and bursting into tears. That is how much the game meant to me. The price of failure, even then, seemed high.

Not that football was considered a possible profession for the future. It took a major event in my life before I could begin dreaming of what it might be like to earn a living as a footballer.

Anfield was always my ready symbol of a place more beautiful than heaven. Cut like a canyon into a multitude of terraced streets, Liverpool's largest soccer stadium is at first almost difficult to detect. On matchdays, however, it is a powerful magnet, attracting some of the game's most unusual and colourful supporters. Only then, when the atmosphere is fully charged, does it help provide a life-changing experience.

My love affair with Liverpool Football Club began on 21 January 1967. I was an impressionable eight-year-old when my father and uncle, Denny McNamara, took me to Anfield to see champions Liverpool play newly promoted Southampton in a first-division match. I recall walking the cobbled streets towards the stadium, looking up at people and wondering if they were enjoying the same feeling of anticipation. My spirits rose further once inside the stadium. Though we were in the paddock in front of the old Main Stand, the sight of the Spion Kop, with sea upon sea of smiling faces, will live with me for as long as I am sane. Liverpool won 2–1 in front of around 42,000 people. Chris Lawler and Alf Arrowsmith scored the goals.

My father, himself a Liverpool fan, put me on a box to make sure I got a good view of the match, and that in turn gave me the opportunity to watch Roger Hunt in action for the first time. A dynamic centre-forward of versatility, Hunt had won a

World Cup winners' medal with England the previous summer. I identified with him instantly. He did the things I wanted to do. He inspired those around him, he aroused the interest of the fans, and, most significantly, he scored goals. My love for scoring goals – some would call it an obsession – stems from watching Roger Hunt that winter's day. And, with one of the ironies that seem to have littered my life, it was almost twenty years later to the day that I scored my first goal for Liverpool. It was also at Anfield and also against Southampton.

To be at Anfield when it was empty was enough to send shivers down my spine, so imagine what it did to my under-developed emotions when it was packed with fifty-odd thousand people in the late 1960s. The Kop, often as frightening as it was exciting, was the focal point and I went there as often as possible, firstly in the boys' pen before graduating to the main terracing when my father felt I was old enough. I was regularly to be found in the Kop right up to the late 1970s, swaying with the masses, singing songs of such insidious charm that I, along with everyone else, felt a special kind of involvement with what was happening on the pitch. At Liverpool, the fans participated as much as the players.

Football seemed to bring acclaim, something I craved as a ten-year-old. It would be years before I got the acclaim, but at least there was some money knocking around. At the time, my father was secretary of the Blue Union club in Garston, which took up a lot of effort. He often let me into the club, allowing me the opportunity to see another world and to meet people older than myself. I got a lot of attention from my father's friends and this made for a memorable atmosphere. I particularly recall the times a man would come to empty the money from the one-armed bandit. I got to know this chap very well and before long he would arrange to 'drop' the £50 jackpot for me. 'Just put in a couple of coins and it's yours,' I remember him telling me. 'We'll go halves on it, twenty-five quid each.' In 1968, £25 bought a lot of lemonade and crisps.

Christmases were the same; I always got what I wanted. I would start hinting for things from the moment my birthday presents had lost their novelty and, come 25 December, my father and mother had arranged things with military precision. My reward was a feast of presents; their reward was the sight of my beaming face.

Summertime usually meant a trip to Butlin's or to the Isle of Man. The Isle of Man holidays are the ones that stick out because it was there my father taught me to fish. Nothing complicated, just an old-fashioned system he had used as a child. Once the sea had gone out, we would lay out a line and put hooks on it. We would then tie the line to rocks and go to the arcade to wait for the sea to come back in, returning eagerly to see what, if anything, was on the line. Often there would be an abundance of fish, which was a great thrill to me. Perhaps there is a link between catching fish and scoring goals!

After Banks Road, I went to New Heys School, which involved a short bus journey to where Garston and the slightly more upmarket Allerton met. The change of scene did nothing to improve my behaviour, however. But as I've said, formal education wasn't designed to bring out the best in John Aldridge. Football, at least, was encouraged. I continued to make progress, even if most of the school's matches were on a friendly basis. There was no school league in those days, just the Echo Cup and the Martindale Cup as we got older. I remember playing against one school who had a brilliant player conducting everything from midfield. Small but strong, this boy seemed to be able to do anything with a ball. 'Oh, that's Sammy Lee,' I was told. Sammy would go on to win a host of honours with Liverpool.

Much to my disappointment, I failed to make the Liverpool schoolboys team. Strangely, I did make the Liverpool schoolboys cricket team, but my father thought it was better if I stuck to football. The Liverpool schoolboys football failure and the lack of competition with the New Heys team frustrated me for a time and made me desperate for a lucky break. The break came in the shape of the gas man. His name was Johnny Bennison, a clean-cut former South Liverpool player who read meters in the area and scouted for Liverpool in his spare time. He was in our house one day and noticed my football medals on top of the mantelpiece. My mother explained to him that I was anxious to be a professional footballer and he suggested to her that I might be interested in going to Liverpool for a trial. That night I asked myself if a fourteen-year-old really deserved to be so happy. I couldn't sleep.

In my first trial match I scored in a 7–1 defeat against Liverpool's youth team. I did enough for Liverpool to invite me back for twice-weekly training sessions so they could take a closer look at me. And so it went on, every Tuesday and Thursday, until Tom Saunders, one of the club's most well-known coaches, asked to see me. He was brief and straight to the point: 'You've done very well but we can't take you on at the moment. Keep in touch.' In the time it takes to mutter a single sentence, my whole world had caved in.

No logical explanation will console you in a situation like that. I knew all the stories of soccer stars who had failed their first trial and bounced back but, believing my one and only chance was gone, I chose to sulk and be negative. My father was equally disappointed and, a year later, he wrote to Liverpool, telling them that I was a natural goalscorer and that they would save themselves a lot of money if they signed me. Liverpool's response was to offer me another trial, this time a one-off on a Sunday morning. It was one of those matches when you work so hard and put so much effort into it that everything goes right. I had a tremendous game and scored five goals in a 6–3 win for our team. If I'd farted that day it would have smelt of a rose garden. My father was on the touchline and I remember his words afterwards: 'They've got to take you on now, son.' So I waited for the call. I waited and waited. Nothing. I'd just had the game of my life in a trial at Liverpool and still they were not interested.

Looking back on it, I don't believe they had anyone watching the game. How else do you explain it? I was as low as I'd ever been up to that point, though now I can look back on it and say it made me stronger. The thought of failure scared me so much that I acquired the determination to succeed. Fourteen years later, Liverpool paid Oxford United £750,000 to sign me.

They never admitted it themselves, but their desire to take me to Anfield in 1987 showed that my father was right all along. They would have saved themselves a fortune had they made the telephone call in the early 1970s instead of making one that cost £750,000 years later.

Soon after the second trial, a girl called Joan Corlan came bouncing into my life. She had all the fizz of a bottle of champagne and much the same attraction. I first met her when I was thirteen, in the second year at New Heys. We were in the French class together – she sat directly behind me – but not many people were learning the subject. The teacher was a nightmare. There were a lot of teachers at Banks Road and New Heys who played a fair game. I didn't necessarily like them all but I was at least able to appreciate their ability. And then there was this French teacher. She had neither charm nor personality and served only to deprive us of interest in the language.

After weeks of deliberation, I decided to lock her in the class storeroom. I did it primarily to relieve the boredom of the lesson, but there was the added incentive of inflicting revenge upon someone who was giving us such a miserable time. It was one of the funniest things I've seen – and, best of all, I never did get into trouble for it. Apparently it was some time before someone with a key to the room could be located. She could have stayed locked up forever as far as I was concerned.

Joan often tells me I went up in her estimation after that incident. So many people wanted to lock the teacher in the room, she says, yet I was the only one with the balls to do it. I was secretly pleased Joan admired me for it. We got on well from that day on. Three years later, I talked a friend, Mark Dysart, into convincing her she should date me. To my delight, she agreed. I met Joan as she got off the bus and we spent most of the evening sitting on a wall outside Garston market, eating chips and talking about the trials and tribulations of two adolescent lives. I'd had a lot of girlfriends before then but Joan was the first one to mean anything to me. She had a brilliant personality and great character and I am pleased our daughter, Joanne, has inherited the same traits.

Only at the end of that first night did I get a kiss but, though we were only sixteen, we both knew where the relationship was heading. On that day, 2 December 1974, I was beginning to fall in love, which is why the date holds special significance for us. We never looked back from that night on and we married five-and-a-half years later. With perfect symmetry, our son, Paul, was born on 2 December 1981.

But while my football career was on ice, and my romance was flourishing, my education was dying a death. Two months before our Certificate of Secondary Education exams, I was expelled from New Heys. I remember the day well. It was pouring down outside and four of us – myself, my cousin and two friends – decided we would hide in the school hall, which was strictly against the rules. The headboy, an eighteen-year-old who was about six foot two and had a moustache, found out and came over to break up our badly concealed, four-man revolution. He marched us unceremoniously out of the building. He let my cousin and friends go but insisted on keeping me in his presence. That was when the situation deteriorated. In front of everyone, he picked me up by the scruff of my neck, making me look foolish, and held me up against a wall while the school prefects let out exaggerated howls of laughter. I was angry – I've never liked people belittling me – but I really flipped when I saw that Joan was among the gathering crowd.

Her presence spurred me into action. When the headboy refused to release his grip, I leaned back and head-butted him, drawing blood from his nose. It was a personal triumph. I'd been brought up to stick up for myself, something Garstonians regarded as second nature. It was a kind of survival-of-the-fittest mentality, yet it was essential. You lived or died by your ability to fight. Rightly or wrongly, that was how my father told me to settle my differences.

The headmaster never asked for my side of the story. I was thrown out of school. And this time there was no need for my father to intervene.

The whole episode left a bad taste and it was twenty-three years before I could face going back to New Heys for a visit.

On the positive side, the fifth-year head, Mr Leeson, found out the true story and said he was disgusted with the circumstances surrounding my expulsion. He was one of the few to take my side, even if he had no power to reverse the headmaster's decision. 'If you need a reference for a job,' he said, 'make sure they write to me, not the school.' That won back a little of the faith I'd lost in authority.

If it was any consolation, the school allowed me to come back for my exams. I didn't do too badly considering my lack of interest in education. I emerged with six CSE passes. Nothing special, but good enough to gain an apprenticeship in toolmaking at the Standard-Triumph car factory. My father had wanted me to go into welding. He believed welders would soon be in demand and that the industry would provide a safe career, not to mention a steady income. There was only one career I really wanted, however. I still believed I was going to make it as a footballer. Too many people were praising my ability for me to dismiss the possibility that I might make the grade and, in any case, I had confidence in what I could do on the football field. The ambition sparked by my earliest football memories still burned brightly.

Unlike some of my pals, my love for football didn't diminish in all the years at secondary school. I stood on the Kop for most Liverpool matches in the early to mid 1970s, rarely missing an important triumph. I was there the day the Reds drew 0–0 with Leicester City at Anfield to clinch the 1972–73 League Championship. Bill Shankly's lap of honour that day is a memory that will stay with me for life. We cheered on the Kop for fifteen minutes, hoping Shanks would give us an appearance. When he emerged from the players' tunnel we screamed with delight, perhaps hoping our enthusiasm would somehow make him come over to shake our hands individually. We knew him so well; we couldn't believe he didn't know us. It was always a regret of mine that I never got to meet him. The legendary former manager of Liverpool died in September 1981.

An even clearer memory is the night Liverpool overturned a two-goal deficit to beat FC Bruges 3–2 in the UEFA Cup final first leg at Anfield in May 1976. Kevin Keegan, who became my new hero following the retirement of Roger Hunt, scored the winning goal with a penalty. The following season, 1976–77, I only missed two Liverpool away matches. It was the season Bob Paisley's men won the League Championship and the European Cup, and finished runners-up in the FA Cup. What sticks out most is being on the Kop for Liverpool's 3–1 win against St Etienne in March 1977. The sight of David Fairclough sliding home Liverpool's crucial third goal remains an inspiring moment to this day. And I know I am not alone; David is still asked about that moment. That season was Kevin Keegan's last before his move to SV Hamburg of West Germany.

How I wanted to emulate him. I was making reasonable progress in my own playing career. I was in the South Liverpool team that lost to Manchester City at Maine Road in the FA Youth Cup in 1976. It was the first time I'd played at a big stadium and the lack of a crowd did nothing to take away the thrill. There is something special about a football ground and I've always believed the best ones look just as good when they are empty. Maine Road was beautiful that night. I played regular Sunday League football, firstly with Blue Union, and then with Garston Woodcutters. It was with the Union that I heard how a win-at-all-costs attitude was good for morale.

A few years before I joined them, the Union went to the Isle of Man for a tournament. They reached the final against a German team and, fancying their chances of winning, didn't see the need for elaborate preparation the night before the match. Besides, the bright lights of Douglas were calling, so they went out drinking. Worse, they stayed out all night in a casino and it was around five o'clock in the morning before they finally emerged. They were so drunk not one of them could walk in a straight line. They were stumbling along the promenade as the sun started to rise, which was when one of the players cast his eyes towards the beach and saw the German squad doing what looked like an aerobics session. Their early morning stretches provided a comical contrast to the Union's situation. They didn't know whether to laugh or cry. So they cried with laughter.

In the final later that day, the Union were 1–0 down with the game going into stoppage time. It was then their captain approached the referee and told him to fear the worst if the final whistle blew before the equaliser was scored. I think the referee had played eight minutes of stoppage time when the Union scored and, of course, they won in extra time. Either the referee had taken the threat seriously or his watch had stopped.

The Union were the best Sunday League side in Liverpool before I joined them. They had some great players for that level. Tosh Jones, a friend of mine, was tremendous and never got the credit he deserved. The same could be said for a guy called Johnny Moore. But their best player was Jimmy Case, a youngster who had a full range of skills and a remarkable shot. It was never in doubt that he would make it as a professional and we were pleased when, after a spell with South Liverpool, he signed for Liverpool. He later won two European Cup winners' medals with the Reds and scored in the 1977 FA Cup final in Liverpool's 2–1 defeat against Manchester United. Even after he left Liverpool, Jimmy remained a credit to football, playing well into his late thirties. He is a nice fellow, too.

So much happened to me around the time I was with the Blue Union that I put it among the happiest periods of my life. I had my first taste of what going out with the lads meant. One night I'd had more drink than I could handle and ended up being taken home and put into bed by a fireman. I made friends on a massive scale, for a time keeping the company of some very humorous people. All this while the team won trophies in front of a regular support of around 300 people. Happy days.

The Isle of Man continued to play an important part in my early life. I was always guaranteed a good time there. After I'd stopped sailing to Douglas with my father and mother, I went there with my friends a couple of times. We did everything from watching Showaddywaddy in concert to gambling in the casinos. And all the time we were drinking just about as much as we could.

After the Union, I signed for Garston Woodcutters, who played in the Liverpool Sunday League. Strangely, my first game for them was under someone else's name. I was a 'ringer'. Prior to their third division match against Broadway on a cold morning in 1977, the Woodcutters were a man short. That was when I got a knock at the door from a guy called Kevin Harnan. He explained he was the manager of the team and heard I might fancy a game for them. I threw on my tracksuit and went with him to the Long Lane recreation ground on Garston Park. I didn't score but I did enough to suggest I could do a job for the Woodcutters. They signed me on. It was a successful spell for the club and for me. In one match I scored nine goals, while more significantly, I was scoring goals regularly.

By this time, I was also playing on a Saturday, for Cheshire Lines. Their manager, Joby Humphries, was involved with South Liverpool, for whom I'd played in the FA Youth Cup two years before. It was only natural, with the success I was having at amateur level, that I should move up to semi-professional football.

South Liverpool, an ailing Northern Premier League club, signed me in the summer of 1978. Russ Perkins, the player-manager, paid Cheshire Lines £11 for my registration and that was how much per game they were paying me. Along with the £82 per week I was earning with British Leyland, I wasn't too far off the £100-per-week mark. I felt rich.

Not that South Liverpool was easy at the start. Russ, who had a unique personality, was a footballing romantic who would rather see his team lose 4–3 than draw 0–0. 'Better for the watching public,' he used to say. The problem was, Russ would occasionally get his wish. We never did as well as we should have done, though we had some very good players.

Phil McFerran, a midfielder, was one who could easily have made the grade as a professional but, for whatever reason, failed to do so. Sometimes a player prefers the security of a career outside the game; sometimes the lack of hunger for professional football is the factor. I don't know why Phil never made it big but it was an injustice he didn't progress beyond non-League football. Even before Phil and I played together for South Liverpool we were denied a place in a Liverpool County FA team that played a cup final at Anfield. Phil and I played together for a number of teams and he is one of the many people from my formative days with whom I am still in touch. Phil even went on to manage South Liverpool for a time.

No doubt he was able to put into practice the lessons he picked up from playing under Russ Perkins. Russ was a fine example as a player-manager. I learned so much from him about striking partnerships and movement off the ball, skills which became essential later on. Russ had so much experience that you couldn't help but admire him. I would sometimes laugh at the way he would throw himself forward to win a free kick when he had barely been touched by the opposing defender. I also learned a lot from a centre-back called John King (not the former Tranmere Rovers manager of the same name), who had won an FA Trophy winners' medal with Altrincham at Wembley the previous May. Ominously hard but fair, he had more skill than he was given credit for. I recall having a tremendous battle with him in one match and I knew I'd had an education.

It was autumn 1978 before I won a regular place in the South Liverpool first team and the turn of the year before I started scoring goals on a regular basis. At the beginning of the season, I was described in the club's official pen pictures as 'a local youngster who shows great potential with his flair for attack'. By the middle of the season, the pen pictures called me 'an exciting goalscorer'. I had clearly made progress. My first goal for the club was in a Northern Premier League Cup tie against Southport, which we won 4–2. Southport had just been demoted from the Football League so were still a decent team.

I recall playing against leaders Goole Town at Holly Park on a Saturday in December 1978, during the big freeze. I'd hurt my thumb when falling over the night before but it didn't affect my performance because I scored in a 2–1 win. The following Monday, I went to the first-aid room at work and it was there I found out the thumb was broken. I told everyone in work and expected sympathy, but they laughed at me. They wondered why I didn't say the injury was sustained in work, thus allowing me to push for a healthy compensation payment.

In any case, I didn't have time to fill in a claim form. I was working a fifty-hour week and playing at least eight matches a month. On top of that, South Liverpool trained regularly. It wasn't high-tech training but it was amusing. The club could only afford to put on their Holly Park floodlights for matches so our twice-weekly training sessions took place on the central reservation in Springwood Lane, Allerton, where there was at least enough light to see what was going on. Footballs would be flying everywhere, rolling into the road, hitting cars, getting stuck in trees, all while we were trying to get fit for our Northern Premier League challenge.

Scoring goals in non-league football had satisfying rewards; suddenly, I was in a new world. Talent scouts were everywhere – and one of them was my friend. Robin Ashurst worked with me at British Leyland. His brother was Len Ashurst, the former Sunderland player who was manager of Newport County. Robin and I had one thing in common: we both loved football. We talked of nothing else while we worked and he decided to come and see me play for South Liverpool against Runcorn one Saturday in April 1979. That game was during a good spell for me so it was no surprise that I should score and impress the 400 or so watching spectators. Though he didn't say anything to me, Robin was clearly enthused by my performance and told his brother about the skinny South Liverpool centre-forward called John Aldridge.

Len came to watch me play for South against Frickley Athletic at Holly Park the following week. Again I had a good game, though this time I scored a hat-trick in our 3–0 win. After my second goal we won a penalty, which someone else was about to take. 'No,' shouted Jack Tait, Russ Perkins' assistant, 'give it to John for his hat-trick.' I duly crashed the ball into the goal.

I didn't know it at the time, but there were other Football League club managers there to watch me. John King (not the former Altrincham player), who was in his first spell at Tranmere

17

Rovers, was one of them. I played for South against Tranmere in the Liverpool Senior Cup semi-final that month. Tranmere had Gordon West, the former Everton goalkeeper, in their side so I was pleased to score in our 2–1 victory. John King tried hard to sign me but either his club couldn't afford to pay the £3,000 asking price or their chairman didn't think I was worth it. Still, John agreed with the South Liverpool programme's assessment of me: 'On current form, John Aldridge must be one of the best strikers in the Northern Premier League.'

Len Ashurst, however, could come up with the £3,000. And, like John King, he was impressed. The Newport manager asked me to meet him for a chat about a possible move. I was suddenly faced with a very real dilemma. I was, at the age of twenty, confronted with the biggest decision of my life up to that point. My mind raced. Should I leave my home in Liverpool, my job at British Leyland, to play professional football at Newport? Or do I take the risk and wait in the hope a bigger club shows interest in me?

To make the problem even more complicated, I was now engaged to Joan. The thought of leaving her behind scared me. The three-and-a-half-hour train journey between Liverpool and Newport, via Crewe, seemed a mighty chasm. As usual, I turned to my father. 'Forget it, son, you're not going,' was his response. He felt I should stay in the Liverpool area. He really did believe I would make it as a professional footballer in my home town. Why, he asked, did I have to go so far away to fulfil my ambitions? He told me to telephone Len Ashurst and say our scheduled meeting was off. Joan was equally determined to talk me out of going to Newport.

Russ Perkins was more positive. He said the chance to make it at Newport was a good one. But he also believed I would get the opportunity to sign for a club closer to home. Either way, he reckoned, I couldn't lose. The South Liverpool manager remained convinced I was set for a long career in the game, whether I moved away or not. Robin Ashurst's advice was welcome but hardly impartial. He told me Newport were a club with the potential to rise quickly up the football ladder.

In fact, he built them up to be so big that I considered it would be foolish not to play for them.

And all along, rumours were flying round like dead leaves in the autumn wind. Aston Villa were going to sign me. Everton manager Gordon Lee wanted me on a loan basis. Tranmere were now trying to raise the £3,000 asking price. I couldn't distinguish fact from fiction. So I ignored my father's advice and decided to accept the only concrete offer on the table. I travelled to meet with Len in a Manchester hotel and discuss my first contract as a footballer.

I saw Newport lose 1–0 at Rochdale in a Football League division four match on 23 April 1979, before I got down to serious business with the Welsh club's manager. I was at a disadvantage from the start. Through Robin, Len found out my salary at British Leyland. I naturally assumed I would be getting more than the £82 per week I earned as a toolmaker. I was not prepared to be offered less, but Len was a master of psychology. 'We'll pay you £78 a week,' he said. As I thought he was joking, I said nothing; I merely offered him a sickly smile. But the silence of about ten seconds seemed like an eternity. It was then I realised he wasn't joking. The blow was cushioned by the bonus schemes he was offering: £10 per appearance, £20 per league point gained in the fourth division.

Years later I realised Len could have given me more money but deliberately offered me less than the £82 per week I was earning at British Leyland. It was to test my hunger. He needed to know how badly I wanted professional football. He also felt his bonus scheme would be an incentive for me to work harder. Though I understood his mind games regarding my salary, he needn't have bothered playing them with me. I was as hungry for football as anyone. And incentive? I didn't need any. I'd spent years jogging up and down Speke Boulevard in Liverpool in an effort to keep fit. I trained like a man on fire. I played football as often as I could.

I agreed to sign for Newport County that night. It was a difficult decision and, yes, there were doubts in my mind. I wasn't jumping for joy when I handed in a week's notice at British

Leyland. And I was full of emotion when my workmates came to say goodbye to me. The sense of loss consumed me for a time.

It was sad to leave South Liverpool, too. I'd only been there eight months yet I felt an affinity for the place. I scored fifteen goals in thirty-nine appearances. Newport eventually paid the non-league club £2,500 for me with a stipulation in the contract that South would receive an extra £1,000 if I played a certain number of games. I believe they spent the money on improving their pitch.

Having never got to grips with the depression that enveloped Merseyside in the late 1970s and the whole of the 1980s, South Liverpool deteriorated badly. Non-league football had progressed in the same period so it was no surprise when the club folded up in 1991. Having left Holly Park, fewer than 100 people were watching their home matches at Bootle in their final season, which was a far cry from the attendances that had watched us thirteen or so years before. The people running the club deserved better.

When I see Holly Park now I become disillusioned, angry even. It was bulldozed to the ground while I was playing in the 1990 World Cup for the Republic of Ireland. I did not appreciate the irony of that. Where there was once a quaint football stadium, there is only wasteland. Dogs now piss on the pitch, except it doesn't look like a pitch any more. Overgrown weeds conceal all evidence to suggest football was ever played there. Holly Park, which was so much a part of my life and remains in my affections, has become one of the saddest sights in Liverpool.

But football can affect your emotions like that. When I told my father I was going to sign for Newport County, he was genuinely annoyed. By the time it came to seeing me off at Lime Street train station, however, he had mellowed. He was noticeably upset. He helped carry my suitcases on to the train and I could see he had tears in his eyes. His twenty-year-old son was leaving home, going to Newport to be a footballer, yet he wanted me to stay in Garston. It was the end of an era for him.

A week before, I had fallen out with my father for the first time. Now, as he waved me off, I valued him so much it hurt. The train began its journey to Crewe and I could see my father disappearing into the distance. I did something for the first time in many years: I locked myself in the toilet and cried.

— 2 —

DREAMER'S BALL

THE belief that my background had matured me ahead of my years was cruelly shattered during the forty-five-minute journey between Liverpool and Crewe. The train was full of businessmen, students and old people, yet a casual glance in my direction was enough to know I was lonely. I could cope with the depression – that was easy. It was the feeling of emptiness that screwed me up. The twenty-year-old man who had survived effortlessly on the streets of Garston was forced to face one inescapable fact: he was still a boy. Still raw. Still with much to learn.

The first night in digs in Newport was the longest of my life. I wanted morning to come quickly, though it's difficult to know why. Perhaps I believed daylight would somehow ease the uncertainty. Perhaps I simply needed a game of football to boost my confidence. Luckily, I had a game the following afternoon, a reserve-team clash against Llanelli in the Welsh League. A good performance would help to settle me down, by which time I would have met some of my new team-mates. At least, that was the plan. In reality, I had the worst game of my career. Brian Clark, the reserve-team manager, afterwards gave me a quiet word of encouragement but I wasn't fooled – I knew my performance offered no suggestion that I could play football. The move from Liverpool – the upheaval and the thousand natural shocks that seemed to come with it –

affected me more than I thought possible. Nothing can prepare you for it.

Months later, when life was easier and I could afford to smile, Brian was less protective. 'John,' he told me, 'I wondered what we had bought when I saw you for the first time. You were terrible and didn't seem to know what to do.' Not usually given to hyperbole, Brian's words struck a chord. I valued his honesty and, as I grew in stature, came to appreciate his advice and constructive criticism. He was as nice a guy as you could wish to meet. Having played up front with John Toshack at Cardiff City a decade before, Brian knew all the aspects of being a centre-forward. So keeping an eye on me was added to his ever-growing list of tasks.

That calamitous first game made me realise what a risk Len Ashurst had taken by signing me. Suddenly, the initial one-year contract seemed generous. With disturbing clarity, I could see that football offered no easy ride to success. To make the grade, I needed to work hard and be lucky at the same time. Only then would my talent in front of goal shine through.

But settling down was the major problem in those depressing early weeks in South Wales. After a spell staying with a friend, Steve Warriner, I lived at 49 Cromwell Road, Newport, in the home of Dolly Horner. She did her best to ease the boredom but there was no helping me. Only success on the football field would help.

My second reserve match, three days after the first, went better and made me feel part of life at Somerton Park. My third reserve match went even better. Yet it was after a night out with the players in Cwmbran that the homesickness really set in. There I was, at six o'clock in the morning, trying to hitch a lift back to Newport. All alone save for the singing sparrows, I shouted out aloud: 'What the hell am I doing here?' I ended up walking back to my digs, which seemed to take forever, and vowed to go back to toolmaking and the simplicity that went with it. How I didn't go back to Liverpool that morning I will never know. British Leyland had already said they would take me back if things didn't work out at Newport. Life in Garston seemed so attractive and I was beginning to crave even the mundane aspects of my days there. Newport, on the other hand, was providing one problem after another.

I also cursed the fact that I couldn't play in any first-team matches. Having signed after the transfer deadline, I was ineligible for Football League games, which meant Len wasn't allowed the luxury of seeing me at a higher level. I believe he would have given me the chance in our last game of the 1978–79 season, away at Halifax Town on 5 May. Len, however, had other plans for me. After that game against Halifax – Newport won 2–1 – the manager called me into his office and calmly told me I must remain in South Wales over the summer to build up my physique. This was yet another blow; my enthusiasm for Newport was diminishing by the minute. With a last throw of the dice, I suggested the compromise of a crash course in weight training in Liverpool. Len agreed; I breathed a sigh of relief.

So it was off to Liverpool to see my parents; to see Joan. It was like a black cloud had lifted from above my head and I was able to see clearly, thankful for the chance to assess my life in a more logical manner.

No longer content with the body nature had given me, I set to work on trying to create something more befitting a professional footballer. My plan was simple. Up early to help my father work on a house, then to the gym for a three-hour workout, a generous plate of steak and eggs, and then a light jog across south Liverpool to see Joan. Day after day it was the same, yet the routine provided a kind of refuge for me. The work was hard but rewarding and within days I could feel the difference. I began to develop muscles in places I didn't know existed, while the jogging became less of an effort as the summer wore on. By the middle of July I was running as if on air.

I enjoyed the summer of 1979 so much that I almost forgot I was due to return to Newport for pre-season training. The time went by so quickly. When it was time for me to leave, Joan was particularly upset, more so than the first time I left. Deep down, she knew her hopes of keeping me in Liverpool were rendered futile by my desire to succeed. I had a new determination which in turn boosted my confidence. Whereas before the summer I was fearful, now I knew becoming a professional footballer was the right decision. There was no turning back and those with whom I came into contact saw a change. The boy who felt sorry for himself had been replaced by a man so sure of himself he felt he could achieve all those childhood dreams.

Neither Len Ashurst nor the players could believe it when I appeared for the first training session. When last they'd set eyes on me, I was a waif; now I was fit, strong and confident. We went to a running track for what Len called a mini-Olympics, and I proceeded to win the tournament. Coming second to a big defender in the shot-put contest provided the best evidence of my reincarnation. I went up in Len's estimation after that. Managers like it when footballers respond to orders. When I became manager of Tranmere Rovers in later years, I always had more respect for those players who listened to me and acted on my advice. I now know how pleased Len must have felt.

But when Newport County played at home to Port Vale on the opening day of the 1979–80 season, my name was not on the team sheet. I always knew I would have to wait. Len had an abundance of striking talent at the club and I was merely one of a handful of centre-forwards at his disposal. Why should he take a risk on me when there were tried and trusted players available to him? Who the hell was I anyway?

For his attractive brand of football, Len needed all kinds of centre-forward. Tommy Tynan and Howard Goddard were the pair in favour and it wasn't difficult to see why. Both were strong, skilful and impressive in front of goal. Tommy was from Liverpool and had managed to sign professional forms with the Anfield club at the start of his career without making the first team. Howard, by contrast, had begun at Bournemouth and he was averaging around a goal every other game at Newport. Behind Tommy and Howard, there was a rivalry between myself and Mike Bruton, a new arrival from Gloucester, to make the breakthrough into the first team. Disappointingly for me, Mike was offered his chance first.

With Newport winning more games than they were losing, I

couldn't see how I was going to make the breakthrough. So I was surprised to find myself on the substitutes' bench for our home game against Lincoln City on 29 September 1979. I was given my debut at half-time, replacing Howard, who was our leading scorer up to that point. I did well and was involved in the move which brought an own goal in our favour. I could hear the Newport fans chanting my name, which was a thrill for me. Alas, Mick Harford – who has since become a friend, but was always a player I rated – equalised for Lincoln late on for a 1–1 draw. Len wasn't happy with letting the lead slip; he ordered us in for extra training the following morning.

From a personal point of view, things must have gone well because Hugh Johns, the HTV football commentator, asked if he could interview me in front of the cameras. Afterwards, the journalist told me he thought I was a good prospect. I was pleased the man who had covered the previous three World Cup finals for ITV rated me. Journalists can be influential, especially to a young player, and this was an example of one putting his experience to good use.

I kept my place in the team for the following game, away at Northampton Town. I didn't have a great game and Newport lost 3–2. Perhaps the occasion got to me a little. It was, after all, my first away game in the Football League. To make matters worse, Northampton's first goal was deflected into the net off my head. My Football League career began with an own goal!

Still, I was moving in the right direction, finally making my mark by scoring twice in the 4–2 win over Aldershot at Somerton Park on 9 October. That set me on a run of scoring nine goals in eight games, culminating in a hat-trick in a 5–0 win over Stockport County on 17 November. The performance of Tommy Tynan sticks most in my mind about that Stockport game. Though he didn't score, his movement off the ball was terrific and helped me get the three goals. As a pair, we were devastating that day, yet I knew Tommy was hurt he didn't score. I made a point of talking to him after the match, telling him I appreciated his efforts. Like all good strikers, Tommy preferred to score goals rather than make them. I laugh when

I hear some strikers say they don't care who scores so long as the team wins. It always bothered me when I didn't score, even if my team won. That is the natural striking instinct that can't be created; the player has to have it.

Tommy had put on a bit of weight round about the time I joined Newport but was back to his physical peak by the time we forged that striking partnership. It was a partnership which might never have seen the light of day had Howard Goddard not broken his leg against Portsmouth the month before. In front of more than 20,000 people, we won 2–0, ending their run of ten successive wins at Fratton Park. But though Howard did come back eighteen months later, he was never the same player. Fate can be cruel. I always thought Howard was too good for the fourth division – I put Tommy Tynan in the same category – yet he barely had the chance to prove it. I believe ability can only take you so far in life. Apart from graft, you need the breaks. Luck plays a huge part.

But when the bad times come it's important you deal with them with a positive attitude. And that is what I was thinking when, after my run of good form, I went seven games without scoring. For sure, it hurt; but what hurt more was the headline in the *South Wales Argus* when I ended that barren run by scoring against York on 12 January 1980. The large letters jumped up at me: 'Aldridge scores at last'. How patronising.

More welcome was the offer of a new contract, with a £40-a-week wage rise and a £2,500 signing-on fee to match my dramatic improvement. It was a two-and-a-half-year deal with a salary of £6,240 plus bonuses. It was a good deal yet I felt confident enough to tell Len Ashurst I would think about his offer. I asked my father for his advice and, as usual, he took a rebellious stance: 'Don't sign anything until you get what you want.' I went back to Len to ask for a deal that involved a payment for every goal I scored. It was probably a mistake. Len flew into a rage and screamed at me.

'You cheeky bastard.'

'That's what I was told to ask for, Boss.'

I eventually accepted the original offer and walked sheepishly out of the manager's office. It was just as well the club never paid me per goal for that would surely have bankrupted them. Money was tight at Somerton Park but by the end of the season, the club's financial troubles were eased. We gained promotion and won the Welsh Cup, all in one memorable ten-day period in May. Newport went into the last two games needing two points to secure a place in the top four of the fourth division. We went to Rochdale on 29 April and played poorly, losing 2–0. Perhaps in our arrogance we relaxed, thinking it would be a stroll. Afterwards, in a motorway café during our trip back to Newport, a few of the club's supporters shouted abuse at us, mocking us for our ineptitude. Football fans always have their own way of deciding what is an acceptable performance, and as they indirectly pay our wages, we have to consider their sentiments.

Defeat against Walsall in the final game of the season, at Fellows Park, was unthinkable. Fortunately, we were in good form and won 4–2. I scored two goals, with David Gwyther – another talented striker – and Tommy Tynan scoring the others. My first was a left-footed shot which flew into the top corner. The second had less to commend it; my weak shot somehow crawled under the body of the Walsall goalkeeper. It didn't matter. As our supporters spilled on to the pitch to express their delight, I couldn't help thinking that it must have been the greatest day in the club's history.

The after-match celebrations were equally memorable. A seemingly endless supply of champagne was passed around the dressing-room and it was then I met comedian Frank Carson for the first time. He was an honorary president of the club and was as pleased as the players with the success. We went on to a nightclub afterwards, letting our delight show by drinking as much alcohol as the body would take. Funnily enough, though I was drunk out of my mind, I remember everything about that night; like the moment I was confronted by a delighted Newport fan as the taxi dropped me off at Cromwell Street. The supporter, who was only young, threw his arms around me and mumbled words to the effect of: 'Thanks for everything, John, how are you?' I was about to tell him how rough I felt when I released the entire contents of my stomach on to his shirt.

'I'm sorry, mate, I'll get it washed for you,' I said.

'Don't be sorry, John, I am putting this shirt on my bedroom wall.'

It is quite possible that, somewhere in a South Wales mining town, there is a respectably married man who has grown bored of explaining to visitors why he has a stinking shirt with hardened vomit hanging on his wall.

I was still drunk the next morning when I went in for a training session. Len had us in for work because we had a two-legged Welsh Cup final with Shrewsbury Town on the Wednesday. As Shrewsbury were the wrong side of the border with England, we'd already qualified to represent Wales in the European Cup-Winners' Cup for the following season, but that didn't take away the hunger for success. The Welsh Cup meant a lot in Wales at that time. We won the first leg 2–1 at Somerton Park on 6 May. I didn't play well and neither did I score. The return leg saw us win 3–0 at Gay Meadow. Again, I didn't score, but this time I had a good game. So when the final whistle went I was able to celebrate my first full season as a professional footballer with a trophy. I finished the season with fourteen league goals and two in the Welsh Cup competition.

Joan and I were married on 21 June 1980 and went to Malta for our honeymoon. Len Ashurst allowed me an extra few days off providing I agreed to train while I was away. He was concerned that I shouldn't lose my fitness. I knew better than to argue, yet found it strange that my first two weeks of married life were to be dominated by obsessive running in the Mediterranean heat. To onlookers I was clearly a mad dog.

Joan had provided me with a tremendous amount of security, especially during that first year in Cromwell Street. She wrote to me regularly and came to my digs at least once a fortnight. We were on the telephone constantly. This would have taken up much of her earnings as a typist had I not paid the telephone bills. When she was not around, I would go to the cinema with some of the Newport players. It was pleasant but often boring; nothing like the rollercoaster life I enjoyed in Liverpool. So armed with a new wife, a Welsh Cup winners' medal, and renewed enthusiasm, I looked forward to our return to Newport for the 1980–81 season. We rented a house in the Croserciliog area of Gwent, which allowed us to enjoy a more settled existence. I was maturing quickly.

Life in the third division was never going to be easy for Newport, though we did begin with a creditable 1–1 draw away at Burnley. I scored that day but Len would never let me relax. Having so many talented strikers at his disposal allowed him much flexibility. We were constantly on edge as a result. We knew by the end of September that promotion was not on the cards. In Europe, however, we more than made our mark. On 1 October 1980, we drew 0–0 against Crusaders of Northern Ireland in Belfast to complete a 4–0 aggregate victory. In the following round, we beat SK Haugar Haugesund of Norway 6–0 on aggregate. I played in all four matches and enjoyed the feel of football against teams from outside the British mainland.

But I fell out with Len Ashurst in the middle of December. After a spell when I didn't seem to be trying too hard in matches, I picked up a niggling knee injury. I didn't tell anybody; I thought I could hide it. Len, of course, knew better. Though mild-mannered, he could get angry when circumstances demanded such a reaction. I needn't have bothered arguing. He flew into such a rage that I thought he was going to hit me.

'What's wrong with you, lad?' he bellowed. 'You're married now, you've got a lovely house. You're not in that shit-hole in Garston with your outside toilet.'

This was an insult of the lowest kind. Criticising me was one thing, but bringing my family into it was way out of order. My parents' house was always clean and was a credit to my mother. Regardless of where you live, the best you can do is keep your house tidy and make guests welcome. My parents accomplished this, yet Len chose to exaggerate the worst aspects of working-class life. Why, I don't know. I expected him to respect my roots, especially as he had come from Liverpool himself. On the whole, Len was good for me. He taught me ways of dealing with professional football, he toughened me up, he helped me become a better player. He was a lovely man. But, like us all, he had a dark side. I'll never understand the reasons for this verbal attack. It's fortunate for him my father never got hold of him.

My injury was diagnosed as tendonitis, the cure for which is rest. An operation was no substitute for allowing the damage to heal naturally, so I spent a frustrating three-month period sitting on my backside. I missed fifteen league matches and, worst of all, the two European Cup-Winners' Cup quarter-final ties against Carl Zeiss Jena of East Germany in March 1981.

Len was trying to get me fit in time for the trip to East Germany – we'd read in a newspaper that the Carl Zeiss Jena manager was fearing the possibility that I might play – but I didn't quite make it. It would have been nice for Newport to invite me over as a non-playing member of the squad, but they never asked me. I listened to the match on the radio and was delighted to hear Tommy Tynan score twice in a 2–2 draw. It meant we only needed to keep a clean sheet in the return leg at Somerton Park to go through to the semi-final.

After two reserve games, I was declared fit to play against the Germans two weeks later. Len considered his options and gave me a place on the substitutes' bench. I felt confident of getting into the action at some point, however, and watched Newport turn in one of the bravest displays I'd seen. We conceded a goal but, as a 1–1 draw would still have been good enough, we didn't worry. We attacked the goal, hit the bar, the post, had shots cleared off the line. The ball wouldn't go in. And all along, I was sitting on the bench, desperate to get into the action. As the minutes ticked away, it dawned on me that I was going to end the game where I'd begun it: sitting next to the manager. To cap a disappointing night, Carl Zeiss Jena held on to their lead and moved into the semi-final.

I played seven out of the last eight games in the 1980–81 season, finishing it with seven league goals, two League Cup goals, and two goals in the European Cup-Winners' Cup. Newport finished twelfth in division three. From a personal point of view, it was an anti-climax compared with the previous season. Our European exploits were deservedly applauded throughout Britain, yet as I'd played no part in our near-miss against Carl Zeiss Jena, I felt like an outsider.

We went back to Merseyside for the summer, staying with Joan's parents, Tommy and Nell, in Hunts Cross. I liked both my in-laws. They were hospitable and, like their daughter, had great personalities. It was a shock to me when Tommy died suddenly in the summer of 1996, not long after my testimonial match at Tranmere Rovers. He seemed so fit and healthy.

That summer of 1981 in Hunts Cross, Tommy and Nell gave us the use of a downstairs room and a couch to sleep on. It was no reflection of the progress I'd made in my career but we were not snobs. I welcomed the simple pleasures of my youth and never lost touch with the friends who delighted me so much in the 1960s and 1970s.

The following season, 1981–82, saw a welcome arrival and a sad departure. Our first child, Paul, was born on 2 December 1981 in Liverpool. Nothing against Wales, but I wanted our son to be born on Merseyside. Joan and I were delighted when we saw him force his way into the world, kicking and screaming. But if Paul's arrival was a miracle of nature, my presence at the birth was a miracle of timing. Joan and I had rowed the night before. Being heavily pregnant, my wife was acting strangely and we'd been niggling each other. It got to the point where she kicked me out of her parents' house and, with my head ready to explode, I duly drove back to Newport. The problem was we didn't have a telephone in our house in Gwent, so when Joan's waters broke there was no way for anyone to contact me directly. Incredibly, someone managed to get a message to Newport player Terry Lees who in turn passed on the news. These are the times when your body reacts quicker than your mind. Though barely dressed – all I had on was a pair of tracksuit bottoms and a pair of slippers – I put on an overcoat and drove back to Liverpool. Breaking every existing speed record, and delighted that no policeman witnessed my illegal motorway dash, I got to Mill Road Hospital in time to see Paul arrive. It was an amazing experience.

Three months later, in March 1982, Len Ashurst vacated his position at Newport County. We had not been adapting to life in the third division as well as we expected. Winning only two matches in thirteen weeks turned the fans against us and, for a time, the spectre of relegation hovered over our collective head. Len took over at struggling Cardiff City – they had their own fight against relegation, a fight they subsequently lost – and we wished him well. I was sorry to see Len go. He'd been a major influence in my life and was among the greatest figures in Newport's history. It wasn't the last I saw of him, as we will see.

Len's replacement was Colin Addison, a former Hereford United player who appeared none the worse for his tough spell managing Derby County. Colin had experience managing in South Africa and was rated among the country's top young coaches. It was his second spell at Newport; he'd managed the club in the late 1970s when much less was expected of him. Colin didn't make too many immediate changes but his arrival either caused, or coincided with, a run of six wins in our final eleven matches of the season. We finished in sixteenth place, avoiding relegation with more comfort than we thought possible two months before.

The end of the season gave me the chance to consider my future. I was aware my two-and-a-half-year contract with Newport was coming to a close. And this time I was determined to entertain the possibility of playing elsewhere. The birth of Paul had brought home the realities of family life and the financial pressures that came with it. We weren't poor but neither were we rich. I think we had a few grand in the bank, that's all. Security was paramount and I knew Newport could never pay enough to ease those fears.

While Newport and I fell into dispute over money, Burnley manager Brian Miller offered me a chance to join his club on loan. Burnley had just won the third division championship and offered greater potential for improvement, or so it seemed. In fact, they were skint. So skint they couldn't afford to sign me. It was a shame because travelling to Lancashire from Liverpool for training every day was no hardship. Brian saw enough in me to suggest I would be an asset for his team and he tried to sign me. But Newport wanted £100,000. Reluctantly, Brian declined. He offered £40,000, a fee that would have put great strains on his club's finances. In reality, the Burnley manager's budget was nil. I went back to Somerton Park.

Eventually I signed a new contract with Newport. Committing myself to Colin Addison was no risk because he was such an inspiring manager. His ability to motivate could bring out the best in even the most average of players, so as we considered ourselves above average there was a feeling of optimism for the next campaign. Alas, the 1982–83 season was one of frustration.

In a Milk Cup second-round tie against Everton we lost 2–0 in the home leg and drew 2–2 at Goodison Park. We came close but, in reality, Everton were too good for us. Steve McMahon, their central midfielder, destroyed us at Somerton Park, scoring one of Everton's goals, and showing me what a class player he was. Years later, when he and I were team-mates at Liverpool, I considered him among the best players in Britain.

We gave Everton a tougher time in an FA Cup third-round tie in January 1983. Taking an early lead in the game at Somerton Park through David Gwyther, we fancied our chances of holding on for a famous victory. David, a reliable player with a Charles Atlas-like physique, had come on as a substitute. I'd only just passed a pre-match fitness test – there was no way I was going to miss that match – but I clearly wasn't functioning properly. With two minutes left of the match, Kevin Sheedy struck a speculative left-footed shot from twenty-five yards that crept under the body of our goalkeeper, Mark Kendall.

It was a sickener for us and my reaction was to go out and get drunk. It was round about the time Stella Artois was introduced to Britain so, of course, I gave the well-known lager a try. Six pints later, I was drunk. My mood and the alcohol conspired to turn me into a lunatic. At eleven o'clock, when I finally arrived home, I tried to destroy our front room. I dismantled the three-piece suite, turned the snooker table upside down and then pissed all over it. Joan, who had been at the game, came downstairs to see what all the fuss was about. She helped me to bed.

The draw meant a replay at Goodison Park. I scored with a memorable bicycle kick, which was one of the best goals I ever scored, but we lost 2–1. In four games against Everton we had acquitted ourselves well but failed to be ruthless when it mattered. Those failings affected us in the League, too.

But there are still some good memories. I recall the time we beat Bournemouth 1–0 on the south coast on 26 March. George Best, the former Manchester United superstar, was making his debut for Bournemouth and there were 9,121 people in the stadium, which was more than twice their average attendance that season. George wore the No. 7 shirt and, though a touch overweight and much slower than in his heyday, still showed the flashes of brilliance that set him apart. But what sticks out most for me was a girl who appeared to be there to watch him. She was sitting in the stand and she was beautiful. We spent so much time looking at her that it was a surprise we won. But thanks to Nigel Vaughan's first-half goal we were able to maintain our progress.

We went top of the table after beating South Wales rivals Cardiff City 1–0 on 4 April in front of more than 16,000 people. It was a typically tight game between teams whose supporters hated each other. Often, the acrimony on the terraces spilled over to the pitch, like at the Welsh Cup tie between the two teams one year. Phil Dwyer, the Cardiff defender who was also a Welsh international at the time, hurt me with a late tackle. Revenge was swift. Sensing the referee and linesmen were looking elsewhere, I went up to Phil and punched him in the face. I didn't like Phil at the time so I was pleased with myself. When I met him a few years later, he came across as a decent bloke. He said he had been told by his manager to tackle me unfairly. Phil also complimented me on getting away with hitting him. 'You were very shrewd,' he said, yet I was only doing what came naturally. Revenge is a powerful force. My life in football shows I am a slave to retribution.

Somehow, Newport failed to gain promotion in 1983. We lost five out of our last seven matches, missing out on a place in division two by four points. Our 1–0 defeat against Huddersfield on 7 May proved costly for that gave the Yorkshire club the points they needed to guarantee third place. They were promoted; we finished fourth and faced another season in division three.

Colin Addison has since gone on to achieve much in the game yet still refers to that débâcle as being among his worst moments. The deeper reason for Colin's reaction, of course, is that the club needed promotion for financial reasons. Newport was not run well as a club and, even though our crowds were good for a team of our standing (we averaged around 5,000 that season), money was tight. Somerton Park, an awkward but unique construction dominated by amber and black paint, was certainly not geared to second division football, and it is possible the money needed to bring it up to the standard required by the Safety of Sports Grounds Act would have proved elusive. We will never know.

I didn't know it then but Newport's glory days were behind them. Though they had purchased Somerton Park from the local council in 1980 for around £100,000, they were forced to sell it back to the authorities for £220,000 in 1986 in a bid to stay solvent. By that time, because the ground was out of date, the capacity had been slashed to a mere 8,000.

The club lost its Football League place after relegation to the GM Vauxhall Conference in 1988 and folded up soon afterwards. Too many people without feelings for the club had been making key decisions on the future. Somerton Park was flattened and now forms the foundations of a housing estate.

Thankfully, Newport re-formed almost immediately and now play non-league football. In some ways, they were dealt with badly and it is doubtful they will win back their Football League place in my lifetime. But good people became involved when they bounced back. Liverpool-born John Relish, a team-mate of mine during happier times, found it necessary to rejoin the club. The problem for Newport was that there were too few people like John. If there is any justice, Newport will regain their former status, but justice and football are not always compatible.

The failure to gain promotion was the beginning of the end for me at Somerton Park. While I wanted a higher level of football, Newport needed cash. That is why they couldn't wait to get rid of me. Bigger clubs had been showing interest in me for some time but only now was the club taking them seriously. Suddenly I was more than a goalscorer; I was an asset with which the club could guarantee their immediate survival. It was clearly in the club's interests to sell me before my contract ran out in May. Newport could not afford to risk the transfer fee going to a tribunal, as they had done with Steve Lownes, a striker, who joined Millwall for £55,000. 'We certainly were not happy with the £55,000 fixed by the tribunal for the young Welsh international Lownes,' said Richard Ford, the Newport chairman. 'We would expect far in excess of that fee for Aldridge.'

But while Newport were hoping I would make them a decent profit, my father was costing Hull City money. I was sent off in the first half of our dour 0–0 draw at Boothferry Park on 12 November 1983 for a clash with defender Dennis Booth. It was an unsavoury incident made worse by my father who, at full time, made his way to the match official's room under the stand and threw a punch at the referee. The referee couldn't get out of the way quickly enough and fell to the floor. So delighted was my father with his intervention that, had he been a cat, he would have been purring with enthusiasm.

I hadn't seen the punch but I had seen my father's expression as he entered the referee's room. That was all I needed to know something was going to go wrong. I immediately followed my father and told him to get out of Hull as soon as he could. Had Football League officials known the referee was attacked by a relative of John Aldridge, Newport would have been in trouble. Simultaneously, the police would surely have arrested my father.

In fact, to my delight, the referee suggested to police that the attack was made by an unknown Newport fan, by which time my father was on a train back to Liverpool. Hull City were fined £2,500 for failing to provide proper security in and around the dressing-room area. I am not usually one to accept injustice but this was one occasion when allowing the innocent to take the blame was necessary. While Newport could not have afforded the fine, Bill Aldridge would not have appreciated having charges pressed against him. Blood is thicker than water.

In March 1984, with twenty-nine goals for the season under my belt, I was ready to leave Somerton Park. Len Ashurst had taken over as manager of Sunderland, a first division club, the month before and I was convinced he would try to sign me. Richard Ford even invited Len to make an offer. 'We have asked Sunderland to put an offer in writing and they know the kind of fee we are talking about.' So I thought I knew what was coming when the chairman called me into his office a couple of days after our 2–2 draw at Orient.

'A club have made a £75,000 offer for you and we have accepted it,' he said.

'Is it Sunderland?'

'No, it's Oxford United.'

'Oxford! Where's that?' The chairman passed me the telephone.

'There's a man on the end of this line who wants to talk to you,' he said. The man in question was Robert Maxwell, the former Labour MP who owned a large publishing house and was said to be among the richest men in Britain. He was also the chairman of Oxford United, an unfashionable third division club with next to no footballing history but potential in abundance. The authority in Mr Maxwell's voice suggested he was used to people obeying his orders.

'Hello, John,' he said. 'Do you want to join me?'

'To be honest, I am not sure, Mr Maxwell.'

'Well, there's a good offer on the table. Maybe you would like to discuss it.'

It turned out Mr Maxwell was offering to more than double my wages. I whistled when he mentioned the figure.

'That's a lot of money,' I said. 'But I need time to talk about this with my wife.' Mr Maxwell allowed me twenty-four hours to make a decision, though deep down I knew I was heading to the Manor Ground. There was still doubt at the back of my mind, however. Oxford was famous for anything but football. They were not even in the Football League when I was born – they were called Headington United until the late 1950s – so they were hardly one of the game's giants. Joan was determined I should turn down the offer. Leaving Pinegrove Gardens, which we had grown to love, would have made sense if it was to join a big club, but not to join Oxford.

The money was a bonus, of course, as was the fact that the club were clearly moving forwards. Oxford seemed destined to land the third division championship and thus earn promotion to the second division, whereas Sunderland seemed destined to drop from the first division into the second. Unaware that Oxford had virtually secured my services, Sunderland offered Newport £50,000. They were too late.

The next lunchtime, I telephoned Jim Smith, the Oxford manager, and told him I would be accepting Mr Maxwell's offer.

— 3 —

MAXWELL HOUSE

ROBERT MAXWELL is said to have suffered great hardship as he made his way slowly from the former Czechoslovakia to Britain many years ago. Self-educated, self-confident, he turned himself into the classic multi-millionaire – the one who made it in spite of adversity. There was a time, before the Mirror Group pension fund was found to be mysteriously short, when everything Mr Maxwell touched turned to gold.

He lived in Oxford, so it was only natural that he should go on to own the city's football club. He invested wisely, brought in talented people, and helped turn the club into one that could compete both in the transfer market and on the soccer field. Though he had shortcomings as a football man, he was a unique businessman and a good chairman for the club.

When Oxford signed me in March 1984 – just before the transfer deadline – I found Mr Maxwell generous with his money. I got £10,000 from him for signing on, on top of a wage of £350 per week, plus appearance money and win bonuses. The three-year deal offered me security for the first time in my life. I even got £1,000 from Newport, though I asked for more. They had bought me for next to nothing and sold me for £75,000, a good profit for a club of their standing. My friends had suggested I push them for as much as possible, though at first Newport would only agree to pay off my outstanding phone bill at the club. The £1,000, when it came, was welcome. 'You wouldn't

41

have got it if you hadn't asked,' I remember a friend telling me. That taught me to open my mouth a bit more where cash was concerned.

But if money was a contributing factor in my decision to join Oxford, I soon realised they were a club going places. There was a sense of anticipation at the Manor Ground in 1984, and it wasn't just because the team was on the verge of securing the third division championship. With Mr Maxwell at the helm, and Jim Smith assuming control of team affairs, you knew the club's immediate future was in safe hands, which is why Oxford were ambitious. No longer happy just to plod along in the lower divisions, the club declared their desire for success, much to the delight of the long-suffering Manor Ground supporters.

Hindsight usually allows you to look clearly at things that were impossible to analyse at the time. But I knew I wouldn't be leaning on it this time; Oxford felt right from day one. I knew it was the right move for us.

Joan and I settled quickly. On the advice of club director John Delaney, we bought a house in Middle Barton, with reasonable mortgage repayments. The village had two pubs, one butcher and one shop. It was small, quiet and we loved it. The only miscalculation was that, in our desire to live near the northern run (for easier trips to Liverpool), I left myself with a forty-minute drive to work every morning. Geography wasn't my strong point in those days. Before checking a map, I thought Oxford to Liverpool was shorter than Newport to Liverpool. In fact, the difference is negligible.

As far as Jim Smith was concerned, my medical was a formality. I was fit, or so he thought. The truth was I had a hamstring injury which hindered me during my final days at Newport. I didn't tell anyone, of course. So when the injury became obvious, Jim flew into a rage.

'What are you trying to do to me? Get me the sack? I paid seventy-five grand for you, don't forget, and you're not even fit.'

That gave me an early insight into the workings of Jim Smith: you don't get on the wrong side of him. His infectious personality – he is among the most enthusiastic men I have met – conceals a fierce side, the side the general public doesn't see. When angry, his face and hairless head would turn purple. He is widely called the Bald Eagle, yet we called him Ribena Man. It was an affectionate nickname because we had so much respect for the man.

Oxford's first game after I signed was away at Burnley on 27 March 1984 and Jim agreed I could go to Liverpool the night after. The problem was I didn't even make the substitutes' bench, much to the disappointment of my father and brother-in-law, both of whom had come to see me play. When we drove back to Liverpool, my red Cortina kept overheating, turning a routine journey into a long one. I'd forgotten to put water in the engine.

Jim Smith wasn't the only person I upset in my first week at Oxford. Ray Graydon, the reserve-team manager, also found it necessary to have a go at me. I played in the Oxford reserve team against Norwich and Ray questioned my performance and commitment. His anger seemed without justification given that I had only joined the club that week and wasn't fully fit. It reminded me of my first reserve-team game for Newport when I'd also played poorly.

This time I had more confidence in myself and I played in eight of Oxford's final nine matches in that 1983–84 season, including the 3–2 win at home to Rotherham United when we celebrated winning the championship. I was actually on the substitutes' bench that day. Understandably, Jim had wanted to let the side who had played together for most of the season celebrate with the fans. I went on late in the match in place of Peter Rhoades-Brown.

In a sense, I felt a bit left out. While the rest of the players had earned their championship medals throughout a tough season, I had essentially jumped on the bandwagon. I felt like the nerd who goes to a party and knows nobody. I wasn't entitled to a medal – you needed fourteen appearances to qualify in those days – but Oxford had one struck for me. It wasn't the real thing but I appreciated the gesture and the tiny memento still sits nicely alongside the other medals I have won, carefully displayed in a top-floor room at home. Photographs adorn the walls and the match balls from the twenty-three career hat-tricks I've scored are packed tightly together on shelves. There are a lot of souvenirs from the Oxford days but I wonder how many of them I would have won had Billy Hamilton not joined the club in August 1984 for £85,000 after playing exactly 200 games for Burnley.

Billy was a target man of tremendous versatility. He had played for Northern Ireland in the 1982 World Cup, running hosts Spain ragged in one match, and scoring twice against Austria in another. He had shown his ability at the highest level so we knew he was a class player when he arrived at the Manor Ground that summer. What I didn't know at the time, however, was that he was my perfect partner. I've played with some of the best strikers in British football – Ian Rush and Peter Beardsley were world class when we were at Liverpool – but no forward has complemented me like Billy Hamilton. He made life easy for me. Second-division defenders can be tough yet Billy took most of the stick that was coming, deflecting attention away from me. He held the ball up well and was invariably first to a high ball into the penalty area. How Billy's legs coped with all the bruises is beyond me. I had the easier task of getting on the end of the chances being created by David Langan, full-back, Peter Rhoades-Brown, winger, and Kevin Brock, midfielder. Jim Smith's tactics were common knowledge: the emphasis was always on crosses into the penalty area. It was an attack-minded policy that made playing for Oxford such a pleasure.

In the 1984–85 season, Billy and I scored fifty-one goals between us, thirty-nine of them coming in the second division. Those goals went some way to ensuring a further season of success. From the moment we beat Huddersfield Town on the opening day of the season to the 4–0 victory against Barnsley on 11 May, we were virtually unstoppable. From March onwards there was little doubt we would secure the second-division championship. We could even afford the luxury of dropping seven points out of twelve in our last four matches.

I'd played my part by scoring thirty goals in the second division that season but I had my share of luck. Twice I scored a hat-trick, and on each occasion the 'Match of the Day' cameras were there to see me do it. We played Leeds United at the Manor Ground on 24 November 1984 and were trailing 2–1 at half-time. I'd hardly had a kick and ended up having a minor disagreement with Peter Lorimer, which ended with Leeds' former Scotland World Cup player being sent off. It all changed in the second half, however, after Jim Smith had given us a bollocking. Oxford piled forward, equalised through Gary Briggs, and seemed set for victory. I was buzzing from the moment I scored to give Oxford a 3–2 lead. Two more goals followed to give me the kind of exposure money cannot buy. I repeated the feat against Oldham Athletic on 20 April 1985. Again we won 5–2, and again I emerged with the match ball for a memorable trio of goals.

Don't ask me why it happened that way. For sure, knowing the television cameras were there was an extra incentive for all of us. The bigger stage clearly brought out the best in a talented Oxford team. But we were just as keyed-up for games that were not embellished by the presence of 'Match of the Day'. Perhaps it was simply good luck, the kind that comes at just the right time.

One thing I do know is this: my name was on the lips of people who hadn't previously heard of it. I was becoming well known outside the Oxford area. *Shoot* magazine did a special feature on my goalscoring exploits and the *Daily Mirror* made me their player of the month, which sounded good until I realised Robert Maxwell owned the newspaper. Most importantly, the sudden spurt of publicity meant bigger clubs were taking an interest in me. I still believe those two hat-tricks on 'Match of the Day' planted a seed in the minds of the top managers.

Winning the Adidas Golden Boot also helped my cause. All the divisions' leading scorers got the award for their achievement. Mine was especially pleasing because it came after a campaign in which I'd scored more league goals in one season than any player in Oxford United's history. I'd played in all forty-two league matches, being substituted only twice.

Oxford secured promotion to the top flight because they were the best team in the second division. I have already mentioned the effect of Billy Hamilton and the value of David Langan, Peter Rhoades-Brown and Kevin Brock. Then there was goalkeeper Steve Hardwick; defenders Bobby McDonald, Malcolm Shotton and Gary Briggs were reliable; midfielders Trevor Hebberd and John Trewick fitted neatly into Jim Smith's pattern. But there was more to Jim than a good pattern of play. His team talks were inspiring, often making us feel on top of the world. Before one game, against Grimsby at home on 30 March, he looked as though he was suffering from the effects of a drinking session the previous night so his advice was more simple than usual. He merely told us to go out and enjoy ourselves because we were a much better team than Grimsby. We won only 1–0, but our performance that day suggested Jim was correct.

So much seemed to happen around that time. A mystery punter placed an £8,000 bet at 16–1 on Oxford to land the second-division championship. When it came to picking up his winnings, the lucky man revealed himself as Robert Maxwell. He didn't need the money, of course, but as a publicity stunt it was brilliant. The *Oxford Mail* newspaper carried a headline which summed up our success: 'You've never had it so good'. They could not have been more correct.

When I look back on that first full season at Oxford I am drawn to one conclusion: I had gone from being a striker with potential to one with maturity; and to think I nearly joined Sunderland. That season they were relegated from the top flight, while Oxford were taking their place in the first division. Sunderland were always a bigger club than Oxford but, while the North Easterners were in temporary decline, Robert Maxwell was working wonders with our little club. My decision, one I considered a risk at the time, was being vindicated before my eyes.

I fancied our chances of doing well in the first division and was a contented figure when I took Joan and Paul on holiday that summer of 1985. Our daughter, Joanne, was born during the summer and, like Paul's birth before her, it was a thrilling moment.

I wasn't prepared for the telephone call that came the day I returned from the break. It was from Jim Smith.

'I want to thank you for what you have done for me. Things haven't worked out. I'm leaving.' It emerged he couldn't agree the terms of a new contract with the chairman. I asked Jim if he would reconsider – I understand all the players took the same course of action – but he was determined to stick to his decision, which came as a shock to players and fans alike. We all knew we were losing one of the best managers in the game. We could never understand why Mr Maxwell wouldn't pay that little bit extra to keep Jim. Queens Park Rangers agreed with us – they took Jim on as manager, paying him the salary Mr Maxwell thought was excessive.

Jim has since gone on to manage Newcastle United, Portsmouth and Derby County, which he has turned into a decent Premier League team. His departure from Oxford reminded me of a poster he had on his office wall. It said: 'Out of the gloom a voice said to me, smile and be happy, things could be worse, so I smiled and was happy and behold, things got worse.'

But things were getting better for Maurice Evans. A quiet, unassuming man, he had been on the coaching staff under Jim since the beginning of 1984. Maurice had tried to sign me when he was manager of Reading, a club to which he had given great service as a player. He seemed reluctant to take over from Jim and, initially, he was only caretaker manager. Two months later, however, in August 1985, he agreed to take the job on a permanent basis. Perhaps he was inspired by the prospect of top-flight football. I know I was. Suddenly we were in a division that boasted teams such as Liverpool, Manchester United, Arsenal and Everton.

It was an important period for me, and I soon had a new contract to match. One Sunday afternoon, I was in Liverpool having a pint with my brothers-in-law, John and Paul, when I received a message to telephone Robert Maxwell. On contacting the Oxford chairman, his sentiments were clear: I was to be down in Oxford within three hours to discuss a new deal. He invited me to meet him at his business headquarters, Pergamon Press.

I could hardly refuse, so I was down there within the specified time, and being ushered into a large boardroom. On the wall was a large picture of Prince Charles and at one end of a large table was Mr Maxwell himself. Whenever Mr Maxwell spoke he took you aback. He had authority and confidence and an amazing belief in his own ability. He was never patronising to me, however, and I felt I had a good working relationship with him – especially after this particular meeting. Mr Maxwell welcomed me and began praising my ability as a footballer.

'You're a great player, John, and I want to offer you £500 a week,' he said, knowing I was earning around £400 a week plus bonuses at the time. 'And I want you to have a long contract.'

'OK, that's . . .'

'No, you're far better than that. How about £550 a week?'

'But . . .'

'No, you're far better than that. How about £600 a week?'

'But . . .'

'No, you're far better than that. How about £650 a week?'

'But . . .'

'Tell you what – let's make it £750 a week. And on top of that, I'll give you a signing-on fee of £5,000 a year.'

'OK, that's . . .'

'No, I'll make it £6,000. Tell you what – let's make the signing-on fee £25,000 over three years.'

So on 1 July 1985, I tied myself to Oxford United for four years with a contract that exceeded my wildest expectations. Joan and I were settled in the area and our parents were coming down regularly. I was relishing the challenge that awaited us, as a family.

I think Maurice had the same optimism for his team. He knew he was different from Jim Smith, had different qualities, but a good manager is one who gets the best out of his players whatever his personality. Maurice was rarely given to outbursts of emotion. He was softer, quieter, but in his own way was equally as demanding as his predecessor. And so, even if the manager had changed, the emphasis had not. The aim was to continue playing neat football.

So I was confident about the forthcoming campaign. Though sure I could score goals at the highest level, I found it difficult to sleep the night before our opening match of the 1985–86 season, which was away at West Bromwich Albion on 17 August. I was nervous at the prospect of fulfilling yet another ambition: playing in the first division. It meant so much to me, yet I found it strange that I should do it with Oxford United and at such a relatively late stage in my life; I was approaching my twenty-seventh birthday. Billy Hamilton and I led the attack and defender Bobby McDonald who, along with Les Phillips, was a drinking colleague of mine, scored our goal in a creditable 1–1 draw. As I was forced to serve a suspension, I had to wait until our fourth match, away at Birmingham City, to score my first goal of the season. It was something of a rarity, too – a fierce shot twenty-five yards from goal. It did us no good; we lost 3–1. But there was a small consolation for me. Jim Pearson, the former Everton player, was at the match on behalf of Nike, the sportswear company for whom he worked. He obviously liked the goal and asked afterwards if his company could sign me on. After playing with Adidas boots for most of my career, I was being offered Nike boots and clothes for free. There was no money involved but I was still pleased to join up with a big company. It was a small sign of how things were progressing in my career.

The boots did me some good for I scored twenty-nine goals that season. We spent most of the campaign fighting against relegation, but it was one of intrigue and enjoyment for both Oxford United and myself. I was enjoying coming up against English football's biggest names, not to mention some of my former heroes. When Oxford played Tottenham Hotspur that season, I played against Ray Clemence, the former Liverpool goalkeeper, who provided me with much pleasure in my younger days.

In our 3–0 defeat against Manchester United at Old Trafford on 7 September I came up against Paul McGrath for the first time. He was a talented defender with the world at his feet and, inevitably, he gave me a tough time. He was fair – Paul has never been anything other than fair – but he was hard, too. I came off after that game with bumps all over the back of my head. Ten years later, by which time we were good friends and team-mates with the Republic of Ireland, I had no hesitation in saying Paul McGrath was among the best defenders of the modern age.

The week after, we played Liverpool at the Manor Ground. Liverpool were going through a tough time at that stage. The Heysel Stadium disaster – where thirty-nine football supporters died before the Reds' European Cup final with Juventus in Brussels – was still fresh in the memory. And Manchester United seemed to be running away with the first division. Kenny Dalglish had just taken over as player-manager but, initially at least, was adopting a *laissez faire* policy. I was still a Liverpool supporter so playing against them provided me with a magical experience. Members of my family, including my father and brothers-in-law, and friends wanted to be there which meant I had to get a wad of complimentary tickets to keep them happy. They probably had mixed feelings when I headed an early goal to give Oxford the lead but I was ecstatic. Liverpool scored twice in the second half and seemed set for victory – until I chased a loose ball late in the match. Alan Kennedy, their European Cup-winning left-back, was aware of my presence but seemed to lose his composure. I carried on running and watched Alan's intended back-pass beat the flailing arms of goalkeeper Bruce Grobbelaar to give Oxford a 2–2 draw. I had a great night afterwards with my family and friends.

Neither Alan Kennedy nor Phil Neal, a right-back, played for Liverpool again. Both had served Liverpool well over the years and will be remembered for their part in Liverpool's fine defensive performance when they conceded only sixteen goals in the 1978–79 season. That remains a record to this day. Whenever I see Alan, we joke about that match. He blames me for bringing his Liverpool career to a close.

Another player whose career was on the slide was Billy Hamilton. The striker with whom I had forged such a good partnership was told to give up playing or risk the possibility of permanent damage to his knees later in life. I was sad for him. His workrate and enthusiasm were admirable, and that was part of the problem in the end. He was forced to work so hard – too hard, I thought – that when he tried to make a comeback his knees were in even worse condition. If one player deserved a full season of top-flight football with Oxford it was Billy and I think we missed his influence up front. He played in four of the first five games of 1985–86 and four of the last six games, but was absent for everything in between.

Alas, Billy missed an amazing Milk Cup run that took us all the way to Wembley Stadium. We beat Northampton Town over two legs and easily disposed of Newcastle United at home, Norwich City at home, and Portsmouth at home, ensuring a two-legged semi-final with Aston Villa.

By that time, I had made it clear I was willing to play international football for the Republic of Ireland. David Langan, a Dubliner, was aware of my Irish background – my great-grandmother on my mother's side was from Athlone – and he contacted Eion Hand, who was the team's manager at that time. It wasn't long before the football authorities were able to confirm my eligibility which meant I could technically make my international debut against Wales in March 1986.

But before that, there was the Milk Cup semi-final – and what a memorable tie it turned out to be. I scored our goals in the 2–2 draw at Villa Park and played a part in our 2–1 win at the Manor Ground a month later which put Oxford into the final at Wembley. Villa marked me tightly that night but it served only to give more space to my team-mates. We had a great time in a nightclub after that win. The champagne flowed, though I stuck to lager. Better still, Jack Charlton, the new manager of Ireland, saw the Villa Park game and indicated to me I would be in his plans for the game against Wales later that month.

My hope at that stage was that Oxford would play Liverpool in the Milk Cup final, but it didn't work out that way. Scoring two own goals in the Anfield leg, Liverpool allowed QPR to draw 2–2 and thus win 3–2 on aggregate. It meant that Oxford would be coming face to face with Jim Smith at Wembley.

On 22 March, we went to Anfield to face Liverpool, who were

51

closing the gap on Manchester United at the top of the first division. I remember the BBC sending Tony Gubba to interview me the day before the match and my Liverpool connections were the main point of the story. The game itself is best forgotten at Oxford. We were thumped 6–0. The only consolation for me was that the Liverpool crowd sang my name throughout. 'John Aldridge is a Kopite' to Handel's Hallelujah Chorus was one song I remember. Walking off the Anfield pitch that day, I thought to myself how wonderful it would be to play for a Liverpool team.

Four days later, I played in Ireland's 1–0 defeat by Wales at Lansdowne Road, Dublin. It was the beginning of a remarkable relationship with Irish football, one that will be chronicled extensively in later chapters. Suddenly big games were coming up all the time. We were fighting against relegation which gave our matches a cup-tie feel. And then there was the Milk Cup final at Wembley on Sunday, 20 April. We travelled to a hotel just outside London on the Friday before the match and, after a hard training session, watched Tottenham Hotspur draw 0–0 with Manchester United at White Hart Lane the day after. The problem was I couldn't sleep on the Saturday night; I was too excited. It turned out that most of the Oxford players were nervous and excited and suffered the same bout of insomnia. Once at Wembley, we had a pre-match warm-up in the dressing-room. It was probably the worst warm-up of our lives – balls were constantly hitting the low ceiling and bouncing aimlessly around – but it was perfect in another sense. It took our minds off the match. So when we walked out to face QPR, we were confident and free of nerves.

It was strange seeing Jim Smith's balding head bobbing up and down as he led the QPR players out alongside us. But that head would be in his hands by the end of the match. We took the Londoners apart with a memorable display of attacking football, taking the trophy with a convincing 3–0 win. If there was one regret for me it was that I failed to score. I am never completely happy after a match unless I have put my name on the scoresheet and, despite the joy of landing a trophy at

Wembley, this was no different. Trevor Hebberd scored the first when I was nicely positioned at the far post. Ray Houghton scored an excellent second; again I was in a good position at the far post. I was becoming anxious. Late in the game, Les Phillips, my best friend at Oxford, gave me a great chance but I contrived to put it wide. Our third goal came after my twenty-yard shot had been saved and Jeremy Charles scored with the rebound.

Oxford were the biggest underdogs for a Wembley Cup final in years yet the side produced one of the most one-sided displays seen at the stadium. We had played to our full potential at a time when QPR were below par, making it a pleasurable experience, particularly for Robert Maxwell and Maurice Evans, two men who had made a mockery of their critics. The smile on Mr Maxwell's face summed up the greatest day in Oxford United's history.

That victory helped us in our fight against relegation. We now had more confidence in our own ability and by the time we faced Everton on 30 April, we needed two wins from our last three matches to be sure of survival. The Everton game came on a momentous night. The Blues needed to beat us and then West Ham the following week to secure the first-division championship. Liverpool had to beat Leicester but still needed Everton to drop points. We fought hard against Everton and you could see the determination in our performance. True, Gary Lineker missed a number of decent chances, and on another day Everton might have won, but when Les Phillips emerged to score late on we felt our efforts had been fully rewarded. To complete the night for me, Liverpool beat Leicester 2–0 and needed victory against Chelsea at Stamford Bridge to guarantee finishing in top place.

Oxford lost 2–1 to Nottingham Forest on 3 May after a fine display from Nigel Clough. On the same day a Kenny Dalglish goal gave Liverpool a 1–0 win over Chelsea. Survival was still in our own hands, however, as victory over Arsenal on 5 May would ensure another season in the first division. Arsenal were a good side but, as was the case in the Milk Cup final, we hit top form when it mattered. We won 3–0 thanks to goals by Ray Houghton, a penalty by myself, and Billy Hamilton. It was a dubious penalty and the then England defender Viv Anderson, who was adjudged to have fouled me, called me a cheat for my elaborate dive. I admit now I played for the penalty and I told Viv I couldn't give a damn what he thought. What mattered to me was that Oxford had managed to maintain their first-division status against all expectations.

Viv and I have got to know each other since then and he is a decent bloke; which is more than I could say for the person who sent me a death threat after Oxford's win against Everton. It was a wretched time for the poor guy, whom I assumed was an Everton supporter. The letter was so strong, I was asked to take it up to the police station. I left it with them and took Joan, Paul and Joanne on holiday. Well, it was a sort of a holiday. We went to Portugal by coach with Joan's mother and I found the twenty-four-hour journey from Liverpool about as relaxing as a wheel-barrow race up Mount Kenya.

Summer is always a time for footballers to reflect, and I was no different. I enjoyed the World Cup on television in Liverpool, caught up with family and old friends, and took stock of my life. Though Oxford had good players, and had ended the previous campaign remarkably well, I sensed we would again be fighting against relegation in the 1986–87 season.

And so it proved. We only picked up two points in our opening three matches and were already in the bottom three when we faced Everton at Goodison Park on 2 September. Trailing 2–1, we pushed strongly for an equaliser and had Everton on the run. That was when I challenged for a high ball with Everton defender Ian Marshall. Ian got there first but clearly handled the ball. I screamed for a penalty but the referee ignored my appeals. Within seconds, Everton scored a third goal, which was typical of our bad luck at that time. We should have had a penalty with a chance to make it 2–2; instead we lost 3–1. Maurice Evans was going berserk, kicking buckets of water around and swearing at the referee. I'd never seen him so upset before, which perhaps summed up the injustice of the result. Usually he was quiet and placid, yet now he was a man possessed. He was almost as angry when Oxford lost 6–1 at Sheffield Wednesday the following month. I was due to go to Liverpool for a few days after the match but, rightly, Maurice insisted we all go in for extra training on the Sunday morning.

It was round about that time that a striker called Billy Whitehurst strolled into the club. Apparently he had left Newcastle United on bad terms. We'd heard that, in his final match for Newcastle, he walked towards sections of the crowd who were booing him, and made gestures that were far from complimentary. There were supposed to be around 6,000 people waiting to lynch him after the match. So we knew we were getting a character – but even we were surprised with what we saw when Billy joined us for the first time. He was one of the strangest, most confident men I've come across. Signed essentially to replace Billy Hamilton as my forward partner, the quirky Billy Whitehurst more than made his mark at the Manor Ground. I liked him and got on well with him. It was he who nicknamed me Scully after a Scouse television character.

Our new signing made his debut in the game against Liverpool at Anfield on 18 October. We were all in the away team's dressing-room, waiting for Maurice to give us a pre-match team talk, when Billy chipped in.

'Maurice,' he said, 'I'd just like to say this. I had a dream last night. I had a dream that we were playing Liverpool at Anfield and that we ended up winning the game 2–1. What a dream it was – and that's exactly what we're going to do today.'

But things didn't go according to the dream. We were 2–0 down when Billy went up for a header, and that went wrong, too. I'd noticed he was starting to run like Max Wall. I asked him what the problem was.

'I've done my back in,' he said. 'But I am not going off at Anfield, I'm going to carry on.' He was so big and strong, Maurice was scared to bring him off. We lost the match 4–0 and, in the dressing-room afterwards, we waited for Maurice to speak. He was about to offer his reaction to the result when Billy chipped in again.

'Maurice,' he said. 'I've got to tell you this. That wasn't a dream I had – it was a sodding nightmare.' The effort to stop myself laughing caused pain. You could feel the tension in the air. Everyone wanted to laugh but we knew Maurice was in a bad mood. Billy missed five matches with his injury.

I was pleased when he returned to action, however, because I enjoyed playing with him. Whenever a big defender hit me hard in a match, Billy would threaten him. Big defenders were often going for me, especially early on. The logic was that a tough early tackle would affect a striker's performance for the rest of the match. Tony Adams, the Arsenal and England player, always did it to me. But I remember Billy approaching one defender who tackled me harshly. 'Do that again and I'll rip your head off,' he said. I had an easy match after that.

Billy did get me into trouble with Joan, however. Oxford had a Christmas party after a home match against QPR and all the players and their wives were there. At the end of it, Billy came up to me, grabbed me by the balls and said, 'See you, Scully.' Joan gave me a dirty look.

'Why did you let him do that?' she asked.

'You try stopping him!'

Without Billy, Oxford beat Manchester United 2–0 to move into the top ten of the first division on 8 November. But an incident the following week led to me falling out with Maurice and put my relationship with the club under pressure. We'd drawn 1–1 at QPR in London, which was a disappointment because we were a goal in front when John Byrne – a friend of mine – equalised with virtually the last kick of the match. Maurice, who wasn't happy about the result, told the players to be on the coach for half past five. Jeremy Charles, Peter Rhoades-Brown, Les Phillips and I went for a drink and headed back to the coach at the specified time. It wasn't there so we asked a few Oxford fans who were hanging around if Maurice had gone to pick up some fish and chips.

'No,' one supporter told us. 'The coach has left for Oxford. It's gone without you.' We couldn't believe it. It wasn't as if we were half-an-hour late; we were only three or four minutes late, if that. There were the four of us, standing around like lost children, angry with our manager for his lack of flexibility. I had been with Eric Hall, my business adviser, and he was equally surprised at Maurice's behaviour. After a few more drinks with my team-mates, I grabbed a lift with one of the Oxford fans and arrived home at around eleven o'clock in the evening.

My reaction was to ask the club for a transfer the following day. In my opinion the manager had acted in a petty manner, which was untypical of him. A number of journalists, sensing a story, contacted me at home that Sunday morning and I remember calling Maurice's decision a Mickey Mouse one, which I felt was true. Eric Hall and I discussed the issue. Rumours were rife that Arsenal wanted to sign me, and Liverpool were looking for a replacement for Ian Rush, who was due to sign for Italian giants Juventus at the end of the 1986–87 season. Eric told me the *Sun* newspaper were happy to run a story on my transfer request and the circumstances surrounding it. I also wrote out a formal transfer request for Maurice's perusal.

The following day, when I delivered my letter to the Oxford manager at training, my story was on the back page of the *Sun*. It was embarrassingly prominent and, worse still, was wrong in one key area. The article quoted me as calling Oxford a Mickey Mouse club. I'd not actually said that, of course, yet denying it was futile. When I handed my letter to Maurice he agreed to pass it on to Robert Maxwell.

To his credit, Maurice called all the players into a room and apologised for his behaviour following the QPR match. 'I was frustrated with the last-minute equaliser,' he said. 'Please accept my apology.'

Mr Maxwell contacted me later that day and, typically, his voice boomed down the telephone receiver. 'Why did you give your story to the *Sun*? You should know that if you need to do these things they must be done in the *Daily Mirror*.' He also criticised the manner of my transfer request, calling it 'rude and improper'. He even threatened to demote me to the reserve team unless I withdrew my request.

'No notice will be taken of Aldridge's transfer request,' Mr Maxwell told reporters. 'There will be no move now. John Aldridge is not for sale. He must realise his lack of professional conduct has diminished his chance of getting away. I have told Aldridge that I understand his desire to go to a top club and that, if he continues to perform for Oxford, I will give consideration to his wish – but not now.' On the same day, Ian Rush stepped up preparations for his move to Italy by hiring a minder. All I had to look forward to was my personal winter of discontent. Mr Maxwell and I eventually talked the issue over, shaking hands and exchanging smiles, but my desire to leave Oxford remained. The chairman knew that.

Billy Whitehurst was back in the side by the time we faced Luton Town on 6 December. The night before, however, I received a call from my father. He'd argued with my mother, travelled down to Oxford and wanted to see me. He asked me to pick him up from the station, which was nearly an hour's drive away (we had, by then, moved to a nice detached house in Bloxham). I picked him up. He wanted a pint and a chat about my mother. Though I didn't usually drink the night before a match, I reluctantly agreed. I had two pints of shandy and three pints of lager and got home at eleven o'clock.

The next day I scored a hat-trick in Oxford's 4–2 win against Luton, which made a mockery of the commonly held view that drinking the night before a game does more harm than good. I wouldn't recommend it on a regular basis but as a one-off it served me well. In fact, the drinking session relaxed me and helped me sleep. I was sober, which was perhaps the key. My life is littered with tales of drinking sessions but it would be wrong to suggest I am a drunkard. Footballers are no different from any other group. We like a drink and a laugh, providing it doesn't affect our performance, and as we are invariably under the media microscope, we need something to help relieve the pressure. That is where alcohol comes in handy. Throw in some good company and a string of funny jokes and you have got a winning combination.

A 3–1 victory over Southampton on New Year's Day 1987 kept

Oxford in a comfortable mid-table position. I didn't know it then but the goal I scored that day turned out to be my last for the club. Two days later, before our game away at Manchester City, I was confronted with the most sensational news of my life up to that point. I was asleep in the team hotel in Manchester when, at around ten o'clock in the morning, the ring of the telephone woke me up. Bobby McDonald, my room-mate, answered the call and I could hear him say: 'OK, I'll send him down, Boss.' Bobby put down the receiver and shouted to me: 'John, the Boss wants to see you in his room. You know what that means, don't you? That's your move to Liverpool.' I deliberately took my time because I knew transfers were never done on a Saturday. It was twenty minutes before I knocked on Maurice's door.

'Sit down, John,' he said, looking into my eyes, his face breaking into the strangest grin. 'I have some good news for you.'

'It's not Liverpool, surely?'

'Yes, it's Liverpool. We've been offered £750,000 for you and we can't afford to turn it down. Mr Maxwell wants you to go to his house tomorrow to discuss it.'

'When can I sign? Am I playing against Manchester City today? Are Liverpool in the hotel as we speak?'

Maurice tried to calm me down, which was difficult. He insisted, however, that I keep the news to myself. The story, he said, would be revealed exclusively in the *Daily Mirror* on the Monday. My first reaction was to telephone Joan. Our excitement was tangible. I didn't listen to Maurice's pre-match team talk and I played poorly in Oxford's 1–0 defeat at Maine Road. I wanted time to pass quickly but it never does in situations like that. Our coach broke down on the way back to Oxford and, during the ninety-minute delay, I lost £250 playing cards against Billy Whitehurst, Kevin Brock and Les Phillips.

I was nervous at the prospect of the meeting with Mr Maxwell. Although I had a lot of respect for his achievements, it didn't take me long to realise two things about him. Firstly, for a man with boyish enthusiasm for football, his knowledge of the game didn't stretch to much. Secondly, he was a powerful man; more powerful than anyone I'd known up to that point in my life, and as awe-inspiring a personality as there was in football at that time. Mr Maxwell wasn't just larger than life, he was larger than everything; or so it seemed. Even his house, tucked away in a leafy suburb of Oxfordshire, had the effect of unnerving visitors. It befitted a man of his wealth.

By the time I reached the house that Sunday morning in January 1987, I was a quivering wreck. Too alert to sleep, too tired to do anything constructive, I had stayed awake all of the previous night passing the time away wondering if my scheduled £750,000 transfer to Liverpool would really take place. I arrived early and was pleased to see that Maurice Evans and Jim Hunt, the Oxford secretary, were also there. Auguries were good; the presence of a secretary usually means transfer forms are waiting to be signed. We were led into Mr Maxwell's study and were greeted by the Oxford chairman himself. With little effort, he dominated the room and the conversation. His voice boomed, the emphasis on all the right words.

'I am pleased for you, John,' he said, turning his head to face me. 'I could have held out for more money but I didn't want to spoil it for you. I know how much this means.'

It was a pleasant introduction and it calmed my nerves, though I wondered why he'd considered holding out for more money. I was twenty-eight, and £750,000 already seemed excessive to acquire a player of my age. But who was I to argue? He had been doing deals all his life, building empires, launching newspapers, reviving the fortunes of ailing football clubs. After insisting the news of my impending move be exclusively revealed in the *Daily Mirror*, the Oxford chairman picked up the telephone and dialled a Merseyside number. He asked to speak to John Smith, the Liverpool chairman, and was put through.

'I want you to pay John really well because he deserves it,' Mr Maxwell told John Smith. 'He's a really good player, you know.'

Though eager to act in my best interests, Mr Maxwell was revealing his naivety, even going so far as to suggest Liverpool give me the same salary as Ian Rush. He continued on the telephone while I, becoming increasingly embarrassed, sank into my chair. John Smith didn't need a publishing tycoon to tell him how good I was at football. Liverpool didn't need a reference; they were paying £750,000 to hire me on the strength of what they already knew. But that was Mr Maxwell – the man who had my entire career in his hands. It was a thought which burdened me, and I was right to be concerned. My problems, after all, were only just beginning.

Oxford were desperate for a good run in the FA Cup and, according to Mr Maxwell, it was important I stayed at the club while we were still in the competition. That was where his innocence revealed itself. While I never planned to give Oxford anything less than one hundred per cent effort, the fear of injury was bound to be a factor in the quality of my performances. Mr Maxwell should have known I was of little use to him now. All I could think of was signing for Liverpool.

My instructions were to meet the Liverpool contingent at the Manchester Airport Hotel but Mr Maxwell, fearing people might decide to follow me, insisted I travel there alone. Anxious that the *Daily Mirror* publish the story first, he didn't want other tabloid newspapers knowing my movements. If I'd been a Russian spy, I might have understood Mr Maxwell's concern, but I was a footballer, that's all. A footballer. So I was a bag of nerves when I walked into a humble room to meet Peter Robinson, the Liverpool secretary, John Smith and Kenny Dalglish, their manager. The Liverpool chairman helped me relax with some useful small talk. He asked me where I was born. 'Sefton General Hospital, Liverpool,' I said, to which he responded by suggesting that his wife, who worked at the hospital as a midwife, could have brought me into the world all those years ago.

Liverpool's top trio were professional in their manner but they needn't have bothered with the protocol. I was happy to sign the contract whatever it said. As it happened, they offered me a deal which, including bonuses, was around the £80,000-a-year mark. It was another major wage rise yet money was ceasing to be important to me. I'd spent the previous quarter of a century dreaming of playing for Liverpool and, had the chance to play for them for nothing presented itself, I would have agreed. The only aspect of the discussions I questioned was the length of service. They were offering me a three-year deal; I wanted four years. I reckoned this would take me to the end of my playing career, by which time I would be thirty-two and probably looking for something else to do.

Liverpool agreed to my demands – in fact, they gave me a four-and-a-half-year deal – and Peter Robinson pulled the contract out of a briefcase and laid the paperwork on the table. Though he didn't know it, this was the worst thing he could have done. I was able to see the contract yet couldn't sign it. Oxford were still insisting I stayed with them until their interest in the FA Cup had subsided. Kenny Dalglish asked me to contact Mr Maxwell in the hope I could sign the contract there and then, but after ten minutes on the telephone to the Oxford chairman I'd made no headway. I was to stay an Oxford player for the time being. One exchange summed up his naivety in matters relating to football.

'You help us have a good run in the FA Cup, John, then you can join Liverpool, and then you can look towards playing for England,' Mr Maxwell told me.

'But Mr Maxwell, I am Irish.'

'That doesn't matter.'

Our third-round FA Cup tie was against Aldershot, and what a miserable affair it turned out to be. On a pitch you wouldn't let your dog loose on, we were trying to win an important football match. Worse still, we lost 3–0. Oxford performed atrociously, and I was the most ineffective player of all, fuelling suggestions I lacked interest and hadn't tried. So while the Oxford supporters accused me of apathy, everyone else it seemed questioned my ability. 'How can he expect to replace Ian Rush at Liverpool,' one newspaper asked, 'when he can't even score against Aldershot?'

Not for the first time that month, I was becoming worried my move to Liverpool might not materialise. This made me irritable and bad-tempered, putting me constantly on edge.

Maurice Evans and Mr Maxwell insisted on keeping me at Oxford until the end of January which, as it turned out, meant one final match, against Watford at the Manor Ground. I was presented with a silver salver prior to the game, in recognition of the eighty-nine goals I'd scored for the club in 132 matches. And so, though we lost 3–1 against Watford, I had a lump in my throat the size of a second head when the final whistle went.

I loved everything about Oxford; the fans, the club, the players, even the city itself. For sure, Maurice Evans and Robert Maxwell upset me towards the end of my stay there, but they were convinced they were acting in the best interests of the club. Alas, they failed to realise I had to act in the best interests of John Aldridge.

— 4 —

WHEN WE WERE KINGS

G ATHERING dust in newspaper archives is a picture of my first day as a professional at Anfield. In it I look pleased, but in trying to keep the photographer happy, the smile is hurting the muscles in my face. I am holding both the FA Cup and the League Championship trophy, the honours Liverpool had won the previous season. Take a closer look and you can see two plasters on my right hand. There is evidence of bruising. As my hand was not in a plaster cast, few people would have known it was broken.

Joan had arranged a party in the Hunts Cross Snooker Club. Touchingly, she had gone to great lengths to make sure all my family and friends were there to celebrate my move to Liverpool. The problem was we all ended up drunk and the night turned sour. I don't know how it started or how it finished, but somewhere in between I allowed my frustration to show by punching a window. If only I'd known there was a brick wall the other side of the glass! Liverpool don't like new players turning up with broken hands, so I reckoned suffering the pain was preferable to telling Kenny Dalglish the truth.

My first day at Anfield went well. I gave the obligatory interviews, posed for cameras, and nervously sipped water from a bottle. Then Ron Yeats showed up – Big Ron Yeats, the captain of the Liverpool team when they won the FA Cup in 1965.

'All right, John, how are you?' he said, grabbing my right hand and shaking it with enthusiasm. The pain shot through my body, ending up in my feet. On another day, a normal day, I might have fainted. But I had to keep up the façade so I grinned weakly at Big Ron, exchanging polite words with him. Screaming in agony could wait a little longer.

That opening day at Anfield summed up my first few months there. I found some players keen to take the mick out of me, which caused much irritation at the time. You couldn't do anything wrong without somebody taking the opportunity to laugh and belittle you; and, because I was so vulnerable and therefore inclined to bite back, it seemed as though the more I complained the worse it got. Mark Lawrenson and Alan Hansen, two defenders of class, were among the worst culprits. Perhaps it was the Liverpool way; who knows? But I had to tell the likes of Mark and Alan that I wasn't going to be mocked and made to look stupid just because I was a new player. What surprised me was that I had spent a lot of time with Mark on international duty with the Republic of Ireland and he was rarely like that. He was quieter, more accommodating, and certainly reluctant to make a newcomer feel unwelcome. Craig Johnstone tried to make me look stupid after training at Melwood one day and I had to put him straight, too. After that, I think the lads respected me a bit more and I got on well with everyone from then on.

It was to become a period of frustration which would, in turn, lead me to question the wisdom of signing for Liverpool. The problem was simple really. I couldn't get into the team. At the time of my arrival, Paul Walsh was hitting his best form up front, while Ian Rush was irreplaceable. Even Kenny Dalglish, the semi-retired player-manager, seemed ahead of me in the pecking order for a first-team place.

I made my Liverpool debut as a half-time substitute for Craig Johnstone in our game away at Aston Villa on 21 February 1987. We drew 2–2 and, though I didn't steal the show, I felt I'd done enough to warrant a place in the team. The following week, I received my chance, though it had more to do with Paul Walsh being sent off in a Littlewoods Cup semi-final tie against Southampton a few days before. I was handed the No. 7 shirt for the first-division game against Southampton at Anfield. I was so excited I couldn't keep still.

The day got better. In the sixty-first minute of the match, Jan Molby floated over an accurate cross from a free kick and I got on the end of it, heading the ball into the only place Southampton goalkeeper Peter Shilton couldn't reach it. To me, the roar of the crowd seemed deafening. We won 1–0 and remained on course to win the first-division championship. It was twenty years almost to the day since I first went to Anfield as a wide-eyed child and Liverpool beat Southampton 2–1.

I naturally thought scoring the winning goal in one match was enough to guarantee your place in the next. That wasn't the case on this occasion. Before Liverpool's match with Luton, Kenny told me I was a substitute. He said it was club policy to allow a suspended player back into the side, which meant Paul Walsh replaced me in the starting line-up. I felt like a hanger-on when, afterwards in the dressing-room, the rest of the players celebrated the 2–0 win that put Liverpool on top of the first division.

And that was how the rest of the season went. I was usually on the substitutes' bench, sometimes out of the side altogether. So I asked Kenny for a chat.

'I can't understand what's happening,' I said. 'I seem to be going backwards.'

'You have been signed for next season, John,' said Kenny. 'Don't worry, you'll be in the side then.' Kenny said he would be creating a new team with a slightly different style of play; a team with wingers, one tailor-made for the players at his disposal. 'You will be an integral part of my new team, John,' he added.

I was in the side for the final game of the season, a 3–3 draw at Chelsea. I scored, meaning I had found the net on each of my two full appearances for Liverpool. Ian Rush, in his last game for Liverpool before his departure for Juventus, also scored. It did us no good; Liverpool had faded towards the end of the season and finished runners-up to Everton in the first division.

So the last thing we needed was a trip to Israel for a friendly against their national side. Flying out from London straight after the Chelsea match, we got to Tel Aviv at six o'clock on a Sunday morning and decided against going to bed. Instead, we went straight for breakfast, washing down our food with large amounts of lager. In fact, we spent most of the day drinking and ended up in a square in the city centre. Drunk and tired due to lack of sleep, we could not have felt worse, which is why we didn't welcome the attentions of a photographer who insisted on taking pictures of us.

The following day, the morning of the match, we boarded a coach which would take us for a light training session. We all felt rough but the sight of Steve McMahon vomiting on the back seat lightened the atmosphere. He'd been drinking a local brew and it had obviously assaulted his digestive system. Ironically, in our 3–0 defeat, Steve was one of the best players. The same could not be said for me. I played up front with Kenny for the first time and did not impress.

We paid for our unprofessionalism. In the local newspaper on the Tuesday, the day we left the country, there was a picture of us looking worse for wear in that Tel Aviv square. The headline summed it up: 'Israel does not beat Liverpool 3–0 but it does beat eleven beer barrels 3–0'. John Smith and Peter Robinson, Liverpool's top officials, were less than happy. So was Kenny. He had spent most of the match moaning, probably because he felt we'd let him down by allowing our behaviour to be photographed.

When I went away for a family break that summer, I still didn't feel part of the Liverpool set-up. My feeling of isolation was worsened when I read one newspaper article suggesting I was a £750,000 misfit. Inevitably, speculation regarding my future increased. There was one story circulating Liverpool that I was supposed to have asked Kenny why he signed me. 'You'd better go and ask the chairman,' was the player-manager's alleged reply. In fact, no such conversation took place but it was a sign of how things had deteriorated. It all came to a head one summer evening when I returned from a fishing trip to a panicking and uncertain wife. Joan didn't speak, she simply showed me a copy of the *Sun* newspaper with a report suggesting Liverpool were planning to send me back to Oxford United and take my friend Ray Houghton in exchange. I was devastated. Even if it was speculation without foundation – and we all know the *Sun* have been accused of doing that in their time – it was enough to plant seeds of doubt in my mind. This move to Liverpool, the one I'd dreamed of since my childhood, was looking like the biggest mistake of my life.

I was too wound-up to do anything constructive and I spent most of the evening moping around. And that was when the telephone rang. It was Kenny.

'I've just seen the newspaper and I can't believe it,' he said. 'I know how you must be feeling because I know how much playing for Liverpool means to you. Don't worry, you'll be in the team at the start of the season.' I replaced the receiver and shared my relief with Joan. At that moment, Kenny Dalglish was the finest bloke in the world.

I already considered Kenny one of the best players of his generation, but sometimes you have to deal with people to realise how special they really are. He handled a difficult situation in a professional manner and worked wonders for my self-esteem. Looking at it logically – something I couldn't do at the time – I never really had cause to worry. Ian Rush was leaving and Kenny himself was near to retiring as a player, so I should have appreciated my importance to Liverpool. At a time when in my mind I was questioning their decision to sign me, I should have shown more foresight. Subjectivity can be a dangerous thing.

Kenny was true to his word that summer. After protracted negotiations, England winger John Barnes arrived from Watford for £900,000 in June. A month later, Peter Beardsley, another England player, arrived from Newcastle United for £1.9 million, which was a record deal between two British clubs. Suddenly, I could see where I was going to fit in. Kenny had wisely signed the players designed to create chances and bring out the best in me. After feeling so unsettled since my arrival from Oxford, I could look at the future with a bit more vehemence.

It was on the pre-season tour to Germany, Denmark, Sweden and Norway that I became Liverpool's penalty-taker. I wish I could say it was by design, but it wasn't. Before the Aalborg game in Denmark, I was relieving myself in the nearby toilet, oblivious to the fact that at that moment Kenny was telling Peter Beardsley to take our penalties. So when we did win a penalty, Peter picked up the ball ready to put it on the spot. 'OK, Peter, I'll take this,' I said to him. Bemused, but reluctant to cause a scene, the ever-tactful Peter handed me the ball. I scored and assumed Peter's role henceforth. To me, it was a natural reaction to take the penalty. I'd done it at all my previous clubs.

Afterwards, we went out for a drink and ran up a £170 champagne bill, even though most of the players were on lager. As the majority of the lads had already gone back to the hotel, it was left to Barry Venison to cover the bill with his credit card. He would have seen the joke had he not been drinking lager too.

I felt I was fitting in at last. I scored nine goals during the pre-season programme, including a hat-trick in Oslo, which gave me confidence entering the 1987–88 season. What followed was the fulfilment of all my footballing fantasies.

Outsiders searched for years to discover the secret of Liverpool's success, yet it took me only a matter of hours to realise there was no secret, just basic common sense – no fancy food, but lots of fish and chips after an away match; nothing excessive on the training field, but plenty of important stamina work and five-a-side matches. Simplicity was the key, whether it be team tactics on the field or the way business was conducted off it. The reasoning was if you do the simple things well you can't go too far wrong.

I was feeling fitter, too. The training at Melwood wasn't supposed to demand that much effort but I found it tough, tougher than I'd found it anywhere else. As I'd done at my previous clubs, I often stayed behind after training to improve my stamina and practise shooting and heading. That was where Kenny Dalglish was valuable. For all the constraints on his time, he would stay behind as often as was necessary to help the likes of myself with extra training.

I remember exactly what I was thinking when Liverpool ran out to face Arsenal at Highbury on 15 August 1987: 'If you can't produce the goods with this team you should give up now.' I was surrounded by some of the finest players in Britain and I felt then, on the opening day of the 1987–88 season, that I was set for a magical experience. Highbury was a cauldron and Liverpool were feeling the pressure, but it all slipped neatly into place inside the opening ten minutes. Peter Beardsley played the ball out wide to John Barnes who put in a fierce first-time cross. I could feel a great sense of anticipation as the ball came towards me. I outjumped Tony Adams, the England defender, to head a memorable goal. Even now it is one of my favourite moments in football.

Arsenal equalised soon after through Paul Davis and gave us a tough match, but Steve Nicol headed a goal from twenty yards to give Liverpool all three points. It was a good start. We followed it up with a 4–1 win away at Coventry City, the FA Cup holders. Liverpool were devastating that day. There were goals for Steve Nicol (2) and Peter Beardsley. Steve might have completed a hat-trick. After his second goal, we won a penalty. I agreed to let Steve take it but Alan Hansen intervened. 'No, Aldo, you're taking it. If he misses and Coventry score there is a chance we could lose our lead.' I duly scored from the penalty spot.

John Sillett, the Coventry manager, said afterwards: 'Before it was balls into channels for Rush. Now it's balls into channels, balls to feet, balls every-bloody-where.' Somewhere hidden in that statement is a compliment.

The performance at Coventry was so good we replayed the video of it when we travelled to West Ham the following week. But, though we played well and dominated proceedings, we allowed West Ham a point in a 1–1 draw when Alan Hansen made an uncharacteristic mistake late on. I was just as guilty for our failure to win. I'd scored our goal but should have had a hat-trick.

Seven points from three opening away games was something we would have settled for, however, and when we were allowed to return to Anfield – we had to wait a few weeks until they fixed the drains under the Kop – it was to face Oxford United on 12 September. That was the day the majority of Liverpool fans saw John Barnes in action for the first time and he didn't let them down. He was superb. After I'd given Liverpool the lead, John scored with a free kick to secure the three points. I'd enjoyed a tough battle with my old team-mate, Gary Briggs, while the visiting supporters kept chanting 'Oxford reject' whenever I went near the ball. They hadn't forgotten me.

Those early months of the season remain like a photograph in my mind. While Liverpool strolled to the top of the first division, I scored in every one of our opening ten league games which, I understand, is a record for the Anfield club. The run had to end, of course, and so it proved at Luton Town in late October when a Gary Gillespie goal gave us a 1–0 win.

By that time, we'd signed right midfielder Ray Houghton from Oxford United. Ray was (and still is) a good friend of mine and, having played with him at Oxford and with the Republic of Ireland, was someone I rated highly. It was an irony that Ray was signed at a time when Craig Johnstone was playing superbly for Liverpool on the right flank. Ray was always noted for his hard work. I can see him now, running at speed, his legs pumping with energy. For the Republic of Ireland and Liverpool he covered more ground than most of his contemporaries. Off the field, he is a lovely man and admirably modest. Indeed, I'd like to think I played a part in the Ray Houghton signing. Late in the previous season, Kenny Dalglish had told me of his intention to sign Ray and the manager asked me if I could drop a few hints to Ray without getting Liverpool into trouble for illegal poaching. So I telephoned Ray and told him how highly Kenny rated him as a player. Without revealing the Liverpool manager's intentions – that was, after all, against the rules – I wanted Ray to assume Kenny would be ready to make a formal bid.

Ray was the final piece of the jigsaw, even though his arrival coincided with the end of our unbeaten start to the season when we lost to Everton in the Littlewoods Cup at Anfield. A Gary Stevens goal separated the sides in the most electric of atmospheres, though the match has since gone down in history for the racial abuse John Barnes received from Everton fans. Patrick Barclay of the *Independent* newspaper noted: 'The sheer volume of bananas, which are not cheap in a city taking longer than most to get out of the recession, showed how much Everton supporters wanted to make their point.' According to author Dave Hill in his book *Out of his Skin*, 'Barnes took corner kicks in a hail of spit.' Not that Liverpool played well and, indeed, Kenny Dalglish said in the dressing-room afterwards: 'Everton wanted to win more than you did.' It might have looked that way but at no point did I give Liverpool less than one hundred per cent effort.

Joan had gone to the match with her mother and my father, but it would have been better if she hadn't. After a quick drink in the players' bar after the match, we were stopped from leaving Anfield by a group of abusive Everton fans. I could take the derogatory chants – that has never bothered me – but it was the fact that they swore in front of Joan and her mother that wound me up. I was stopped from retaliating by my father of all people, and that probably saved me from trouble. At this point, I have to say Everton fans are generally among the best in football. Indeed, some of my friends are avid Evertonians.

I ended up in real trouble a few weeks later, after our 0–0 draw with Norwich City at Anfield. Joan and I went for a drink with Ray Houghton, his wife and a few friends. It was pleasant for a time, until I suggested we go to a nightclub to end the evening. When I tried to get a round of drinks, the woman behind the bar refused to serve me, saying I'd been swearing. It turned into an argument and, before I knew it, two bouncers approached me and asked what the problem was.

'The woman behind the bar said I was swearing,' I replied, 'but if you can't swear in a dive like this, where can you swear?'

One of the bouncers started prodding my chest with his finger.

I pushed him away and, in the confrontation, a bottle of Britvic orange smashed on the floor. The bouncers grabbed me, frog-marched me to the door, and threw me down a flight of stairs. That should have been the end of the trouble. In fact, it was only the beginning.

Outside, I was telling a group of policemen how badly I'd been treated when one of the bouncers emerged. With my pride in tatters, I immediately went for him. The policemen probably couldn't believe their luck. They grabbed me, threw me into their van, and drove me off to the nearest police station. It emerged that I was supposed to have called the woman behind the bar a slut and thrown a bottle at her, neither of which was true. The policemen didn't want my side of the story. They put me in a cell and locked the door.

Joan had arrived at the police station by then and she was, understandably, going berserk. I was released from the cell two hours later and driven home by a policeman. He seemed sympathetic but said the matter could go all the way to court (it did go to court, but I was quite rightly found not guilty).

First thing the following morning I telephoned Kenny Dalglish to break the news to him before he read about it in the news-papers. He was disappointed in my behaviour but said he appreciated me telling him. 'Forget it but whatever you do, don't fight it,' Kenny said.

On the Monday, I received a telephone call at home. 'Mr Aldridge, this is Liverpool CID.' Sensing it was a wind-up, I sniggered. 'What are you laughing about, Mr Aldridge? This is a very serious matter.' Ian Rush might have been a great goalscorer but master of practical jokes he certainly was not. I welcomed his call from Italy, however. We spoke for nearly an hour, which cheered me up. He told me of a time he had a few drinks during a night out in Turin and was subsequently called an English slob by an Italian newspaper. The Juventus president responded by sending Ian a crate of lager, telling him to drink at home in future.

The two-hour spell in jail, and the subsequent publicity, didn't affect my form on the field. I scored in Liverpool's 4–0 win against Watford the Tuesday after the incident and the Kop spent most of the night chanting my name. By the turn of the year there was little doubt that Liverpool would win the first-division championship. In John Barnes and Peter Beardsley we had two of the best players in the country, while Steve McMahon was orchestrating things superbly at the heart of the midfield. In defence, we had the class of Alan Hansen and Gary Gillespie, with quality full-backs like Steve Nicol (when he wasn't in midfield), Barry Venison and, later in the season, Gary Ablett. Throw in midfielders Ray Houghton, Ronnie Whelan and Nigel Spackman and you can see why we won twenty-two and drew six of our opening twenty-eight games.

We equalled Leeds United's twenty-nine-game unbeaten start to a season when we drew 1–1 at Derby County on 16 March 1988 and needed only to avoid defeat against Everton at Goodison Park four days later to take the record. But I'd had a bad feeling about that Everton match long before it arrived. They had played so well against us early in the season and would relish the chance to end our hopes of going down in history as the first side in the twentieth century to go a whole season unbeaten. So I was not surprised by our 1–0 defeat. In a sense, it was a relief. The unbeaten start to the season was like a millstone around our collective neck. In a poor game, Wayne Clarke took advantage of a mistake by our goalkeeper, Bruce Grobbelaar, to score. It was a rare mistake by Bruce and it gave Everton their second victory of the season over us.

That was as close as Liverpool came to a bad run that season. And whenever Liverpool had a tough time of things – which was rare – it meant one thing: a night out. The tradition stemmed back to the Bill Shankly days: the captain would take the rest of the players out for a meal and a few lagers in a bid to foster team spirit. You only have to glance at Liverpool's list of honours to know the ritual has worked well over the years. It was, and still is, called a Dog Day and is something I have tried to introduce at Tranmere.

I actually watched the Everton match from the sidelines. I'd picked up a hamstring injury in Sammy Lee's testimonial in Spain earlier that month and missed four matches. It was a miserable time for me as I'd convinced myself that once you go out of the Liverpool team you never get back in. I was therefore delighted to return to the side for our home clash with Wimbledon, a game in which I scored.

As a team, we were marching towards something special. It all came to a head when we faced Nottingham Forest in the first division on 13 April at Anfield. We won 5–0, it could have been twice as many, and England legend Tom Finney said afterwards it was the greatest exhibition of football he'd seen. It was no exaggeration. Almost from start to finish – I say almost because we were poor in the opening ten minutes! – we ripped Forest to pieces, pulverising them in front of the BBC Television cameras. Ray Houghton gave us the lead in the eighteenth minute and I scored the second in the thirty-seventh, taking advantage of Peter Beardsley's pass to chip the ball over advancing goalkeeper Steve Sutton. In the second half, Gary Gillespie, Peter himself and I completed the rout.

It wasn't just the skill of players like John Barnes and Nigel Spackman that impressed, it was the pace of our passing and the intelligence of our movement. The Anfield crowd loved it; but if it was good to watch, imagine what it was like to play in. There was a buzz in the dressing-room afterwards yet wisely, Kenny Dalglish didn't go overboard in praising us. He wanted to leave that until after we'd clinched the first-division championship.

Ten days later, we did just that. An anti-climactic 1–0 victory over Tottenham Hotspur at Anfield was enough to give Liverpool their seventeenth Football League title. It made me think of how far I'd come. Promoted from the fourth division with Newport County, from the third and second divisions with Oxford United, and then a first-division championship medal with Liverpool; it is a record of which I am proud.

Alas, Newport were going down like a one-legged man doing the moon walk. Rock bottom of the fourth division, they were destined for non-league football at the end of that 1987–88 season. I bumped into a few of my former team-mates in a hotel before Liverpool's match against Tottenham. Newport were playing Bolton and stopped off for a pre-match lunch.

It was then I found out for the first time how badly run the club had been. Their demise, and the haunted look of manager Dai Williams, who gave me the bad news, took the shine off my title celebrations.

By the end of the season, I'd scored twenty-six league goals, which was enough to give me the first division's Adidas Golden Boot. I'd been chasing it all season and made that particular ambition clear – that was until Kenny Dalglish told me my only concern should have been that Liverpool won trophies.

With one trophy already in the bag, we could concentrate on trying to win the FA Cup. After a tough start against Stoke City in the third round, we beat Aston Villa, Everton, and Manchester City to reach the semi-final. There we faced Nottingham Forest at Hillsborough and won 2–1. I knew we would win. Before the match, one of the Forest players, Steve Chettle, claimed in a newspaper interview that he would get the better of John Barnes. The headline was 'Barnes on toast', which was the ideal preparation for Liverpool. John was fouled early on and I scored with the resulting penalty. In the second half, he linked up well with Peter Beardsley on the left flank to give me the opportunity to volley our second goal. Roger Hunt, my childhood hero, later voted it the BBC Goal of the Season, which was a big thrill for me. It was, however, a typical Liverpool goal, one where a number of players were involved. Again the passing was swift; again the movement off the ball was intelligent.

We were the hottest FA Cup final favourites for years when we walked out to face Wimbledon at Wembley Stadium on 14 May 1988. Defeat was unthinkable. Liverpool were in such good form that few teams in Europe would have lived with us. Wimbledon, therefore, should not have provided too many problems. The match was characterised as rich versus poor, beauty versus beast. So why didn't we win? Who knows. Perhaps, as some reporters suggested, it was one match too many for us. For sure, we didn't even come close to performing as we knew we could; and Wimbledon played to their strengths, made virtues of their vices, and rose to the occasion. That combination brought about one of the most surprising FA Cup final results in history. Liverpool 0, Wimbledon 1 – even today I can't say it without enduring feelings of frustration.

The pre-match build-up was enjoyable. I slept well the night before and relished the prospect of meeting Princess Diana before the kick-off. But from the moment the final began I felt as if my legs had gone. The first time I tried to run, I felt weak. It was the feeling you get if you have spent too long in a sauna. Perhaps the tension had, after all, got to me. I certainly felt it had got to Brian Hill, the referee. He made a host of mistakes that proved crucial. There was a bad early tackle by Vinnie Jones on Steve McMahon which went unpunished. Then the referee should have allowed Peter Beardsley to run on and score after being fouled by Andy Thorn, instead of giving Liverpool a free kick. He missed a clear foul by Eric Young on myself in the penalty area; and then he gave a penalty for a foul on the hour mark when Clive Goodyear tackled me fairly.

Lawrie Sanchez had already given Wimbledon the lead so it was vital I equalised with the penalty. As I put the ball on the spot, Dennis Wise, the Wimbledon midfielder, hurled a host of swear words in my direction. But that didn't put me off. I missed the penalty because David Beasant, the Wimbledon goalkeeper, did his homework. He knew I generally put my penalties to the goalkeeper's left. He moved slightly forward to narrow the angle and dived to push my right-footed shot away for a corner. At first I couldn't believe it. But it started to sink in when a group of Wimbledon players gathered around David to congratulate him. It was the first time a player had missed a penalty in an FA Cup final at Wembley.

There isn't anything anyone can say that will comfort you at a time like that. I felt humiliated. I had the chance to put Liverpool level in the FA Cup final and fluffed it. As I went down on my knees following David's save, Dennis shouted more abuse at me. I wanted to melt into the surroundings. Worse still, Kenny Dalglish substituted me straightaway. He was apparently going to replace me in any case, but knowing that was no consolation. Had I stayed on the field I would at least have had the chance of making amends. Frustrated and depressed, I watched the rest of the match from the bench, just behind the manager, and felt helpless. When the final whistle went to herald Wimbledon's success, I wanted to be anywhere but Wembley.

At the post-match banquet, I drank as many pints of lager as my body would take. I was hoping the alcohol would ease the pain, take away the bad memories, but I got more depressed as the night wore on. Joan had the best solution. 'Let's go on holiday,' she said. So we did. We arranged to leave England for two weeks straight after Alan Hansen's testimonial at Anfield on the Monday. Alan, who I had grown to like, jokingly blamed me for costing him £50,000. 'If you'd scored that penalty and we'd won the FA Cup, I'd have had a full house for my testimonial,' he said.

It was five days before I was able to accept what had happened, though I was constantly aware that I had invented a new football quiz question: who was the first player to miss a penalty in a Wembley FA Cup final? At least I would never get that one wrong.

In some ways, I was lucky. The Republic of Ireland had qualified for the European Championships in West Germany later that summer so at least I had that to look forward to. I met up with the Irish players in Dublin soon after but, in a warm-up match against a team from Cork, I missed another penalty. Ray Houghton and Ronnie Whelan, who were also in the Ireland squad bound for West Germany, spent the next few days taking the mick out of me.

The 1987–88 football season is one of my favourite subjects. If you catch me in a bad mood, turn the conversation to the events of that period of my life and you can guarantee I'll cheer up. Being part of that Liverpool team, with the likes of John Barnes, Peter Beardsley and Steve McMahon at their peak, was an amazing experience. I do not have the superlatives to describe how I really felt playing alongside players of such quality.

But that campaign did not show me at my best. I performed

better when Oxford United won the second-division championship in 1984–85. I think I was overawed by my surroundings in my first full season at Liverpool. I was probably the only player who felt proud just to sit in the dressing-rooms and get changed with the rest of the lads. Somehow it all seemed so unreal. For sure, I scored the goals I was signed to score, yet I should have finished the season with a far superior tally. I had mixed feelings.

I had my fair share of criticism, too. After our 1–1 draw against Manchester United at Old Trafford in November, Gary Lineker, the Barcelona striker, criticised my goal which had given us the lead. Offering analysis on television, he said someone like Peter Shilton, the England goalkeeper at the time, would have saved my header. In one fell swoop, he degraded a good goal and brought into question the ability of goalkeeper Gary Walsh.

I also fell foul of former England internationals Alan Mullery and Malcolm Macdonald. Alan said I wasn't worth £250,000 never mind £750,000, while Malcolm suggested I wasn't a good player, even if I was adept at scoring goals. I could never work out why former professionals jumped on the bandwagon of criticising the players in the spotlight. Alan and Malcolm did their reputations no good with their cheap insults. Though hurt, I welcomed the chance to prove them wrong.

But that was nothing compared with what happened with Bob Paisley. Over Easter, Kenny Dalglish called me into the office and asked me to study an article by Bob in the *Sunday Express*. Bob, the most successful manager in English football history, seemed to be taking pleasure in criticising me, saying I was not fit to lace Ian Rush's boots, and that I didn't do much apart from score two goals in the FA Cup semi-final against Nottingham Forest. He did, however, say I was a good penalty-taker. The surprising thing was that Bob was an esteemed director of Liverpool at the time and was rarely one to shout his mouth off to the press. Earlier in the season he had suggested the first division was the weakest it had been in some time, a statement which caused offence at a number of clubs, not least Liverpool.

Kenny told me to rise above it but I made the mistake of

ignoring his advice. Allowing my response to be published in the *Sun*, I was quoted as saying Bob was eaten up with jealousy because we were heading towards another successful season. The *Sun*, to my disappointment, turned the story into something much bigger than it should have been.

With the benefit of hindsight, I now believe Bob was showing the first signs of the illness that would dog him for the rest of his days. I don't believe he would voluntarily have said those things about me and I am inclined to the view that he was prompted in key areas. Perhaps he even had the words put into his mouth. Bob and I ended up shaking hands and, having agreed to put our differences behind us, posed for a *Liverpool Echo* photographer. When we spoke, Bob insisted he never said half the things which were attributed to him. I was sad when he died in 1996. He was a great manager for Liverpool and I like to think of the happier times he gave me. Watching his sides in the 1970s gave me so much pleasure.

So did watching John Barnes in 1987–88. He rightly won the Professional Footballers Association Player of the Year award. In reality, he was the only candidate. On the field, he would dribble past players with little effort and demanded so much attention from the opposition that the rest of us enjoyed the freedom and space his ability provided. He could pass the ball well and, of course, his ratio of goals per game was high for a winger. Under difficult circumstances, especially early in the season, he confounded his critics with a brand of football that had rarely been displayed by a Liverpool player. Bobby Robson, the manager of England at the time, said John was as good as George Best, which was a valid point. How many right-backs dreaded playing against John Barnes that season? So many goals stemmed from his fluent skills down the left flank that the outcome was becoming predictable towards the end of the season. Predictable? Yes, like a nuclear missile – you know what's coming but you can do nothing about it, if you are a defender, that is. The rest of us would marvel and assume our positions in accordance with his movements. When John found space on the left, I always sensed I would get a goal.

He is a good bloke, too. I remember there was a lot of discussion about him being the first black player to appear regularly for Liverpool. The day before a game against Tottenham Hotspur at White Hart Lane, Kenny Dalglish gave a team talk. He had eleven little figures on a board, indicating the Liverpool players. Ten of the figures were red, one was black. 'This one is you, Barnesy,' said Kenny, pointing to the black figure. John saw the joke. At the Liverpool Christmas party, the players traditionally go in fancy dress. In 1987, John went as a member of the Ku Klux Klan and stole the show.

When he went to pick up his PFA award at the Grosvenor Hotel, London, a few of the Liverpool players joined him at the function. You always know when you are in London; the price of lager is frightening. On this occasion, I was charged £4.60 for a half. The PFA put us on a table right by the door, behind the top table, which was surprising given that John was the evening's VIP and that five Liverpool players were in the PFA's team of the year. We were not happy and threatened to leave. Gordon Taylor, the PFA chief executive, came over towards our table to apologise.

'No,' said Alan Hansen, pushing back his chair, 'we're leaving now.'

'You can't go,' Gordon replied, as we all stood up and made our way towards the exit door. 'Listen, Alan, what would it take to make you all stay?'

'We want all our drinks on the house and we want the PFA to cover the price of our tickets.' Gordon went to consult a colleague and returned a minute later.

'OK, that's fine,' he said. 'Order whatever you want. We'll pay.'

We took full advantage. Alan ordered twenty bottles of Bollinger champagne, which tasted wonderful, and we drank the lot. I dread to think how much it cost the PFA to foot the bill. Three days later, we thrashed Nottingham Forest 5–0 in that Anfield thriller.

A snappy dresser, John would nevertheless have looked good in a boiler suit. Some of his clothes were shocking, though, as was his haircut when we beat Everton in the FA Cup fifth round. 'I fancied a change,' he said, showing us his shaven head.

Another character in the Liverpool side was Steve Nicol. Possibly the most versatile of all our players at the time, Steve was one bloke with whom you avoided sharing a room. I made the mistake of rooming with him once and regretted it. It was in Haydock, the day before a game against Watford, and he spent virtually the whole of his time in the hotel eating. He was regularly in touch with room service (he didn't believe me when I said they were ex-directory) and on at least three occasions he ordered a club sandwich. I thought he might have spoiled his appetite for dinner, but no; when we were called down for our customary feast, Steve tucked it away with obvious glee. Later on, he fell asleep while I watched television, but he woke up shouting, 'Any crisps, any crisps?' Worse was to come. At around five o'clock in the morning, I was awakened by Steve rocking my bed to and fro. Not content with this, he tried to push me on to the floor. I shouted at him to stop the fooling and get back into his own bed, but this was clearly futile; he was still asleep. When I told him the story in the morning he knew nothing about it. He didn't even believe me.

Steve McMahon was another player to have a brilliant season. Though the victim of some tough tackles (particularly by Vinnie Jones in the FA Cup final and by Norman Whiteside when we drew 3–3 with Manchester United in an Anfield thriller), Steve was dominant at the heart of our midfield. It was no surprise to me when he was called up to the England squad, though he might not have lived to see the day. On the golf course with the rest of the Liverpool players, Steve was struck by lightning. Apparently his hair stood on end for some time, which aroused much mirth, even if it could have proved tragic.

Also memorable from that season was Kenny Dalglish's often-repeated response to Alex Ferguson's criticism of the Anfield atmosphere. The Manchester United manager was incensed after the 3–3 draw on Easter Monday and happened to be telling a reporter this when Kenny walked by with his new-born baby girl.

Alex (to reporter): 'I can understand why clubs go away from here biting their tongues and choking on their own vomit, knowing they have been done by referees. In this intimidating atmosphere, you need a miracle to win.'

Kenny (shouting to same reporter): 'You might as well talk to my daughter. You'll get more sense out of her.'

It was typical Kenny. Those who don't know him think he is dull and uncommunicative. In fact, he is the opposite. He has a great sense of humour and has that natural, street-wise intelligence to match. Kenny commanded respect for a number of reasons. Firstly, his ability as a player meant you couldn't help but listen to him when he spoke. Secondly, as manager, the speed with which he mastered the job impressed people far beyond Anfield. Thirdly, he was so fair. He didn't criticise his players in public. He kept his dirty washing hidden.

That was the season a youngster called Paul Gascoigne emerged as a player with the potential to be world class. He played against Liverpool for Newcastle United at Anfield in December, a match we won 4–0. Sadly for him, a lot of his team-mates accused him of being selfish on the field and only playing for himself. Afterwards I heard he'd been punched by one of his own players and was getting the train back home. 'I am not going back on the coach,' he said, checking his Rolex watch. Except it wasn't a Rolex watch; it was one of the fakes that were going around at the time. We all had them. Now, of course, Gazza could afford six real ones on each arm. I've spoken to him many times since and he is among the most likeable men I've met. It is such a shame the press seem hell-bent on plotting his downfall.

A few players left Liverpool that season. Mark Lawrenson, my Republic of Ireland team-mate, was forced to retire when doctors told him his Achilles tendon was weakening. If it had snapped it would have left him crippled. He took the sensible option. At his peak, he was one of the best defenders in Europe so it was a shame when he left. The consolation for him was that he took over from Maurice Evans as manager of Oxford United in March 1988.

John Wark returned to Ipswich Town after nearly four success-ful seasons at Anfield. I've always liked John, always rated him as a player, and I even tried to take him to Tranmere Rovers as my assistant when I became manager in 1996. Like Steve Nicol, John scored an abundance of goals from midfield, something which served Liverpool well in their pursuit of success. John could also hold his ale remarkably well. He had consumed at least a dozen pints of lager on one occasion – far more than I'd had – yet the following day in training he was among the liveliest players, running as if on air. By contrast, I was feeling the effects of the previous night.

Craig Johnstone, the right-sided midfielder, left the club fol-lowing the FA Cup final defeat against Wimbledon. We were surprised, especially when he revealed he was going to live in Australia and give up playing football altogether. I know there were family issues which helped Craig decide it was time to move on but I found it odd he should call it a day with Liverpool at a time when we were among the best club sides in the world. I would never have quit Liverpool voluntarily. Only circumstances beyond my control would have forced me away from Anfield. It is nice to see Craig doing well, travelling around the world and making a name for himself by marketing various products. His creative imagination will take him far. You only had to hear the 'Anfield Rap' song, which he wrote and produced in 1988, to confirm that.

I was playing snooker in our new Calderstones home in south Liverpool when I heard the news on the radio. Ian Rush was leaving Juventus and coming back to Liverpool for £2.7 million. It was a hot August day and I felt cold. Though defiant and anxious to prove I was better suited to Liverpool's new system under Kenny Dalglish, I knew deep down Ian's return would hasten my departure from Anfield. Footballers might occasion-ally be paranoid and insecure, but they can smell a threat to their place in the team in a gale-force wind.

I found out later that Ian had been snapped up while Liverpool were on a pre-season tour in Spain. We had lost 5–1 to Atletico Madrid and followed it up with a 4–0 win against Real Sociedad. There was a lot of talk among the players that Ian was coming back to Liverpool but we dismissed it as rumour. After the win over Real Sociedad, a few of the Liverpool officials were drunk and looking happy with life. I thought nothing of it, but it later emerged that Ian had been signed that day. The officials were not celebrating the victory over Real Sociedad, they were celebrating the return to Anfield of a genuine striking legend.

For sure, it was good news for Liverpool and I know the majority of supporters were pleased with the deal. If Liverpool could be so dominant without Ian Rush, the theory went, imagine what they would be like with him back in the team. He was, in the mid 1980s, one of the best players in the world and was still a striker all clubs craved. But I had to look upon it in terms of how it would affect me. I was a John Aldridge fan far more than I was a Liverpool fan. So was I disappointed at Ian Rush's return? Too damn right I was!

It might have meant that Kenny wanted Ian and me to forge a striking partnership. We had certainly played well together during the 1986–87 season and had enough differences in our play to complement each other and play to each other's strengths. We were good friends, too. On the other hand, I had to be realistic. Just as I had been signed to replace Ian, so he had been signed to replace me. I knew that. And subsequent events have provided me with nothing to suggest I was wrong. I asked to speak to Kenny the following day and he assured me I had a big part to play in the future at Anfield. He even hinted Ian and I could be used as a partnership (Kenny reminded me that we had both scored in our last appearance together, away at Chelsea in May 1987), though I still had doubts when I left the manager's office.

Inevitably, the newspapers drew their own conclusions. The story was always the same, with few reporters taking the trouble to suggest my efforts in Ian's absence might actually stand me in good stead for the games ahead. Little wonder I developed feelings of insecurity.

embley woe – missing a penalty in the 1988 FA Cup final

embley joy – scoring for Liverpool against Everton in the 1989 FA Cup final

When everything seemed possible –
circa 1969

Success at fishing – on holiday, circa 197[?]

Young hopefuls – Banks Road School
Under 11s of 1968–69 (I am on the
extreme left)

BANKS RD
C P
FOOTBALL
1968-9

Tying the knot – my marriage to Joan, June 1980

With my mother and father at my wedding, June 1980

Tommy Tynan (*left*) and Len Ashurst –
Newport giants

In action for Oxford – circa 1985

Robert Maxwell – maverick chairman
who helped take me on to Oxford

ger Hunt – my boyhood hero

ly Hamilton – striking partner at
xford

ere I am scoring one of two goals in
alta – putting Ireland into Italia '90

Magical moment – my first goal for Liverpool, against Southampton, February 1987

Nostalgia – my final game for Liverpool, against Crystal Palace, at Anfield, September 198

artache – with Gary Ablett after the 1988
Cup final defeat against Wimbledon

John Wark – team-mate at Liverpool

ree wise men? – with Peter Beardsley (*centre*) and John Barnes, summer 1987

Hillsborough – the view from the touchline as the disaster unfolds – 15 April 1989

Kenny Dalglish – Liverpool manager at the time of the tragedy

I knew I had to improve on my form of the previous season to keep my place in the team. I'd scored twenty-nine goals in all competitions in 1987–88, a tally of which I was proud, but one I clearly needed to improve upon in 1988–89. A slump in performance and I was out; simple as that. In a sense, it was the first time I had been under this kind of pressure since my early days at Newport County. Whereas then everything seemed new and I had little to lose, now I was possessive over my first-team place and I had a lot more to lose. It was a natural reaction, one Ian Rush fully understood.

Ian was not fit when he arrived, which meant I was virtually guaranteed a place in the starting line-up for the FA Charity Shield match at Wembley against Wimbledon. The traditional curtain-raiser to the football season between the league champions and the FA Cup winners from the previous season is always a strange affair. Some years it is a serious fixture with a competitive edge, some years it is a glorified friendly. It depends on which teams are involved. But on 20 August 1988, I was fired up for it as if on trial, as if my whole future depended on it. It was the beginning of a new challenge for me at Liverpool.

For a side supposedly in turmoil after a difficult summer, Wimbledon competed remarkably well. On a wet day, they took the lead through John Fashanu and threatened another surprise against Liverpool. But the day was a triumph for me. I scored our goals in the 2–1 victory and enjoyed the experience. The second goal gave me particular pleasure. John Barnes crossed the ball from the left, allowing me the opportunity to hook the ball from over my shoulder and comfortably into the net. If Ian Rush's return posed questions, I was happy to provide the answers.

The following week, on the opening day of the first-division campaign, I scored a hat-trick in Liverpool's potentially tricky game at Charlton Athletic in London. We won 3–0 but, though the team played well, I couldn't help but personalise it. Five goals in the opening two games was a dream start.

It was during the 1–0 victory over Manchester United at Anfield on 3 September that I felt we would again finish the season with the championship firmly in our grasp. We outclassed Alex Ferguson's team, with John Barnes in tremendous form. He gave Viv Anderson, the United right-back, a particularly torrid time. Indeed, some of John's turns that day defied logic and it was among the best games he ever played for Liverpool. Danish international midfielder Jan Molby scored the only goal, from the penalty spot. I didn't even consider taking the kick, not after my miss at Wembley the previous May. No, I still wasn't over the worst of it, though it did feel strange seeing another player slam the ball into the goal from the spot. It was eighteen months since a player other than me had taken a penalty in the first division for Liverpool.

That was during Ian Rush's first period at Liverpool but now, in his second spell, he wasn't having the best of times. Struggling with injury and loss of form, the early stages of the 1988–89 season were not his most pleasurable. Returning from Italy was never going to be easy and, of course, much had changed at Anfield since he was last there. New players had arrived and the system of play, though essentially the same, was more fluid, with a greater emphasis on work down the flanks. It didn't give me any pleasure to see Ian take time to settle. I was actually looking forward to seeing how we would play together on a regular basis.

But for a time I stopped fearing for the immediate future. In the twenty-one games I played from the beginning of the season to the end of the calendar year, I scored ten goals. I felt this record more than justified my place in the team and, much to my delight, Kenny Dalglish usually selected me as first-choice striker, often alongside Ian Rush, but sometimes alongside Peter Beardsley.

The problem was Liverpool had slipped behind in the race for the first-division championship. Arsenal were runaway leaders and, on New Year's Day 1989, we lost 3–1 against Manchester United at Old Trafford. John Barnes gave us the lead with a right-footed shot in the seventieth minute, and then we crumbled like an undercooked apple pie. We were living precariously. We drew 2–2 against Sheffield Wednesday at Hillsborough after going two goals down, and we came from behind to draw by the same score against Newcastle United at St James' Park in driving rain. I hit goals in each match to maintain a reasonable personal scoring average, while the team hung on wearily to hopes of further success.

Though we didn't know it at the time, it all began clicking into place when we beat Charlton Athletic 2–0 at Anfield on 1 March. We were not at our best that night but the result kick-started a return to form. It was the start of a nine-match-winning league sequence which put us back on the heels of leaders Arsenal. Suddenly, after a baffling period of underachievement, we were looking like a team capable of retaining the first-division championship. Ian Rush was absent through injury for each of those nine games.

For me, it is no coincidence that our best form of 1988–89 came with a similar team and system to the one which dominated the 1987–88 season. That is why I believe Kenny Dalglish was wrong to replace me with Ian. One of the greatest strikers of all time, Ian was a joy to watch. But the facts prove this: I was a more appropriate option for the system.

I scored my second hat-trick of the season when Liverpool beat Luton Town 5–0 at Anfield on 14 March and completed a run of scoring in ten successive matches when we beat Tottenham Hotspur two weeks later. It was beginning to feel like 1988 again. We made progress in the FA Cup, too. Victories against Carlisle United at Brunton Park (3–0), Millwall at The Den (2–0), Hull City at Boothferry Park (3–2) and Brentford at Anfield (4–0) put us comfortably into the semi-final. The Hull game gave me a chance to renew acquaintance with Billy Whitehurst. My former Oxford United team-mate was, you may recall, a unique character and still, as he proved, a decent player. Hull and Billy gave us a tough time, belying their lower-league status.

The draw for the FA Cup semi-final paired Liverpool with Nottingham Forest for the second season running. The date set for the tie was 15 April 1989; the venue, Hillsborough.

— 5 —

'THEY ONLY CAME TO WATCH FOOTBALL'

I F I hadn't become a footballer it is almost certain I would have been in the middle of the Leppings Lane terrace at Hillsborough on Saturday, 15 April 1989. In the days when I was a fan I would never have considered missing an FA Cup semi-final involving Liverpool so I have to assume I would have travelled with everyone else to Sheffield for the game against Nottingham Forest. But fate decreed that John Aldridge be elsewhere that day. I was not on the Leppings Lane terrace, I was on the Hillsborough playing field, oblivious to what was going on among the Liverpool contingent.

When the full extent of the disaster that eventually claimed the lives of ninety-six people unfolded, my emotions were of great sadness for the victims whose only mistake was choosing the wrong day to watch a football match; a football match in which I was playing. Yes, time does heal, but if I am still alive on 15 April 2039, the fiftieth anniversary of Hillsborough, I will shed tears. That is because I shed tears every year on 15 April. Not out of ritual. Not out of obligation. Not out of duty. But out of a deep sense of grief for the lost and a genuine feeling for the loved ones they left behind.

Hillsborough was a real tragedy on a real day involving real people. We often talk of nightmares in our lives, of disasters, of tragedies, but most of us don't really know what we're talking about. I was injured playing for Liverpool the season before

Hillsborough and I called it a personal disaster. Disaster? When you know people have died in your vicinity you realise missing a football match or two through injury is irrelevant. Most things are irrelevant. The death of the innocent – the suffering, the injustice – is a real disaster. A real tragedy.

In the ten years since, more eloquent wordsmiths than I have offered their assessments of the day and its aftermath. But as it remains one of the most significant events in my life, I have to write about it. I don't want to, but I have to. Thinking about it hurts, so talking about it and putting it down on paper serves only to bring back the horror of it all.

So much about Hillsborough is still disputed but there is one inescapable fact. Too many people were allowed into a small pen behind the goal at the Leppings Lane end, causing a major crush which eventually claimed ninety-six victims. It is not my place to comment on who was responsible for the deaths; that is a matter for the experts and the families of the ninety-six. I do hope, however, that those who made mistakes that day, whoever they are, are brought to justice and are forced to answer for their misjudgements.

I was the Liverpool player furthest away from the Leppings Lane terrace when a fan decked out in Liverpool red approached Ray Houghton and shouted something at him. I assumed it was some kind of pitch invasion. The last action I could remember was Peter Beardsley hitting the crossbar with a fierce shot. But soon a policeman with a look of concern approached referee Ray Lewis and began talking to him. The game was brought to a halt. I remember Steve Nicol saying something to the referee, though I was too far away to hear anything. I didn't have a clue what was going on. At six minutes past three, the players were ushered off the field and into the dressing-rooms. A lot of people suspected crowd trouble but, even then, even before the full facts had emerged, there was a kind of eerie atmosphere that suggested something far worse had taken place. On our way into the dressing-rooms we had the first inkling that, far from crowd trouble being the reason for the delay, there had in fact been a tragedy. I overheard people talking of serious injuries to Liverpool fans and, worse still, deaths. Deaths? At a football match? I could not comprehend it. I was still convinced a barrier had collapsed and we'd only been taken off for fifteen minutes or so. If only that was true. I could not have been more wrong. This was fast developing into the worst disaster in English football history.

In the dressing-room, Kenny Dalglish told us to keep warm as the match was bound to re-start. But Kenny was walking round nervously, refusing to sit down. Most of us were seated, though some were standing, doing stretches and simple exercises. Some were reading the programme. I don't remember what I was doing. But I do remember seeing fans walking past the dressing-room door with tears in their eyes. That was when I began to realise this was something serious. Yet Ray Lewis came into our dressing-room at around half-past three and told us to be ready to go back on the playing field. The match, he said, would re-start as soon as possible.

That was the last communication for thirty minutes. We were still trying to psych ourselves up for the match. Looking back on it, I am sure the Liverpool staff knew what was going on but chose to keep the full facts from us. I think Kenny must have known, too. I didn't know it at the time, but his face told the story. It was only when we heard screaming outside the dressing-room that we finally understood something wasn't right. Kenny went out into a corridor and I heard one fan shouting at him, 'People are dying, Kenny.' Or words to that effect.

At four o'clock, Ray Lewis came back to say the match had been abandoned. The confirmation that Liverpool fans had died reached us while we were getting changed. Some of us were showering, though some had already put their clothes back on. Again, I don't remember exactly what I did. I cast my eyes over to John Barnes and could see he had tears in his eyes. He was sitting there quietly, not wanting to be disturbed. A few of the other players looked stunned. I couldn't talk. Nobody could. There was a strange sort of silence. Usually there is much conversation and banter when the lads are all together in the dressing-room. Not now. Too many thoughts were flashing through our minds. The sense of logic was disappearing.

I knew of people, fun-loving Liverpool supporters, who had tickets for the Leppings Lane terrace. My friends. Naturally, I had to find out whether or not they were safe. But how? Kenny was determined to keep us all together in the dressing-room, out of the way. When we were all dressed, the Liverpool manager told us to go quietly to the players' lounge upstairs. Minute by minute we could feel the situation getting worse. Even before we got into the lounge we could see the girls working there were sobbing. They obviously knew more than us. At the other side of the lounge there was a television screen showing live pictures of Hillsborough. The reporter spoke of deaths, the figure rising minute by minute. Struggling to take it all in, I became edgy. I couldn't stand still. The picture was becoming clearer in my mind and I didn't like it one bit.

There was too much to take in at Hillsborough and it was a relief to get away from the place. It was only when I got home that night that it all began to sink in. I was watching television with Joan and, inevitably, it was the main story on the news. That was when we broke down as one, bursting into tears and hugging each other. We cried for most of the night and slept little.

Kenny telephoned me the following morning. He said he wanted me to join the rest of the players at Anfield for a meeting. In the immediate aftermath of Hillsborough, Kenny showed tremendous leadership qualities a lot of people didn't think he possessed. He told us to be dignified and insisted we set an example. In the afternoon, I took my daughter, Joanne, to Anfield to lay some red roses by the Shankly Gates. There were already a lot of scarves tied to the railings – not all of them were Liverpool scarves – and there was an overwhelming scent of flowers in the air. I didn't want to be seen but a group of reporters spotted me. That spoiled what should have been a private moment. I was, after all, a Liverpool fan. I wanted the same anonymity as any other person. I deserved it.

We had a special mass at the Catholic Cathedral that night.

Again, the enormity of what had happened hit me hard. We were beginning to see how it was affecting the city. People were breaking down, not really knowing what to do. All the players were at the Cathedral that night to hear Bruce Grobbelaar read the lesson. Each player dealt with the tragedy in his own way. My first tangible response was to pull out of the Republic of Ireland's World Cup qualifying match against Spain in Dublin on 26 April. Playing football was the last thing I wanted to do. I remember giving an interview to the *Liverpool Echo* in which I said I didn't care if I never played again. I meant every word. For the two weeks following the disaster I was in a state of shock, helpless to do anything. I feel no shame in admitting Hillsborough affected me mentally for a time, a long time. I couldn't cope. It weakened me physically, emotionally and mentally.

The thought of training never entered my head. I remember trying to go jogging but I couldn't run. There was a time when I wondered if I would ever muster the strength to play. I seriously considered retirement. I was learning about what was relevant in life. I didn't really see the point in football. Reading about the parents who lost sons or daughters at Hillsborough made me think of my own children. My son, Paul, was only seven at the time. I was only a little older when I went to my first football match in the 1960s. Paul and Joanne have never been less than the most important things in my life, yet after Hillsborough they became even more precious, if that was possible. We all became closer as a family.

The Liverpool players spent much of their time talking to people affected by the tragedy. It meant going into hospitals to see the injured. In some cases, it meant trying to talk people out of comas. We spoke to people who had lost loved ones. The immediate aftermath became a succession of funerals. I don't know how many funerals I went to but they were becoming more difficult to deal with. Alan Hansen said much the same thing. He thought he'd get used to the funerals after the first few but by the twelfth he felt worse. I'd only been to one before Hillsborough, which was when my grandmother died.

Within days, Anfield had become a shrine. It began when

a Liverpool director agreed to let one fan lay flowers on the Kop. Two weeks later, the whole of the goalmouth at the Kop end was covered with flowers. It was one of the most beautiful sights I have ever seen. Anfield was an open house. If anyone needed advice on how to deal with the effects of the tragedy, they were welcomed. Players and their wives were on hand to offer words of comfort and support. Joan and I found this particularly difficult. We were not trained in these skills and sometimes it was difficult to know what to say. We had experienced bereavement in our own family but nothing on this scale. We were being asked to console people at a time when we needed it ourselves.

I think people sometimes forget about how Hillsborough affected the players. Ray Houghton said the experience of visiting so many hospitals and attending so many funerals made him more upset than he'd ever been before. Ray's way of dealing with the tragedy was to play football as soon as he could. That is why he played for Ireland against Spain in that World Cup qualifier. Ronnie Whelan played, too. I couldn't. I didn't have the physical or mental energy. Alan Hansen, the Liverpool captain, was said to be visibly shaking at times. Bruce Grobbelaar had, like myself, considered retirement. Steve McMahon claimed the Hillsborough tragedy was a watershed in his life. 'I grew up almost overnight,' he said. Players openly wept in front of each other, which was incredible. There had never been such a display of emotion among the Liverpool players before. Usually we spent most of our time taking the mick out of each other, but Hillsborough pulled down the façade and showed us up for what we were: vulnerable human beings.

What it was all doing to Kenny Dalglish would become apparent when he resigned as Liverpool manager in 1991, but at the time he did a remarkable job. He became an unofficial spokesman for the players and was particularly eloquent. This was a man who many thought uncommunicative. This was a man who many thought had no interests outside of football. These myths were shattered. Kenny was dignified throughout and worked tirelessly. I think he realised, for perhaps the first time, how much Liverpool Football Club meant to the ordinary person in the street. This, of course, carried with it certain responsibilities but Kenny was up to the challenge. He proved himself to be a good listener to those who had something to get off their chests.

The entire country was sympathetic and I know bridges were built between the cities of Liverpool, Sheffield and Nottingham. Football would never be the same again. Decaying football grounds were at last considered inadequate and Lord Justice Taylor, whose report on the Hillsborough tragedy did so much to reveal the truth, set a plan that would destroy terracing once and for all. All grounds would, in time, become all-seated, making them safer.

The *Sun* chose not to enter into the spirit of things. Their allegations about so-called loutish behaviour by Liverpool fans were distasteful. They have yet to provide evidence to support such claims and, rightly, people on Merseyside shunned the newspaper after that. Even today I will not speak directly to a reporter from the *Sun*.

Something else I regretted was a disagreement I had with Kenny's wife, Marina. It was in Glasgow when Liverpool played Celtic in a Hillsborough Memorial Match on 30 April. It was a game in which I didn't really want to play. After it – I scored twice in Liverpool's 4–0 win – the players and their wives went to a hotel for a meal where Joan and I had a bit of a row. We were both feeling the pressure of Hillsborough and, unwisely, took it out on each other in public. It was nothing really, but it probably looked worse than it was, which was why Marina intervened.

'Leave Joan alone, John,' she said. 'Go easy on her. We're all suffering, not just you.'

'Fuck off, Marina. It's none of your fucking business,' I replied. 'Leave me alone.'

The next day, when we were leaving on the coach to go back to Liverpool, Kenny came up to me.

'My wife isn't happy with you, Aldo,' Kenny said. 'She said you told her to fuck off.'

'Yes, I did, Kenny. She involved herself in something that had nothing to do with her. But, fair enough, maybe I used words which were too harsh. I'll apologise.'

So when I saw Marina I told her I was sorry for what happened.

'I shouldn't have used language like that to a woman,' I said. 'But really you should have minded your own business. The row between Joan and me was nothing. It was under control.'

'You're all right, John. There's no problem,' she replied.

I was no longer able to keep my emotions to myself. The tensions of Hillsborough, already overwhelming, were beginning to affect my behaviour in public. Depression, not to mention the guilt, was starting to show in all the wrong ways and, for a short time, I struggled to handle myself in an appropriate manner. That feeling – when you think your head is going to explode – makes you react in strange ways and I had a temporary loss of control.

It is inevitable, I suppose, that grievance on such a large scale should take its toll on people. Joan and I knew it only too well, and yet, even today, a decade or so on, we cannot comprehend what other people, particularly those who lost loved ones, really went through. Under the circumstances, the tensions were handled admirably – but that doesn't even begin to tell the story of how people felt deep down.

Though I didn't want to play against Celtic, I had already received a number of letters from Liverpool fans urging me not to retire. Most of the correspondence amounted to the same thing: get your boots back on in the name of Liverpool FC. It gave me a new surge of enthusiasm for football and I suddenly felt able to train. The tragedy was still at the forefront of my mind but I was at least acquiring the strength to deal with it.

Hillsborough was nevertheless the worst thing to happen to me. It was probably the worst thing to happen to the city of Liverpool. True, the city was bombed constantly during the Second World War and many people suffered, but when there is war you acquire a war mentality. It helps you deal with the problem even if it doesn't ease the pain. There was no such war mentality at Hillsborough or during its aftermath. People had gone to a football match to enjoy themselves and nearly a hundred of them died. How can you begin to cope with that? I wondered how a young lad called Ian coped when he went home to say the brother in his care was lost in the crowd at Hillsborough. Consider for a moment how Ian felt when it was discovered his fifteen-year-old brother was among the ninety-six who died. What do you say to your parents when that happens? Liverpool was wounded. The hundreds of memorials published in the *Liverpool Echo* at the time summed up the mood. There was a black cloud hanging over the city.

Whenever I think of Hillsborough I am drawn to the story of young Lee Nicol from Bootle. Lee was fourteen but looked about ten. He reminded me of my son, Paul. Lee was in the middle of the crush at Leppings Lane but was still alive when he was pulled out. I went to see him in hospital. He looked a lovely kid. As he lay there in a coma, I whispered words into his ears. I asked the doctor about his chances of recovery. 'He's clinically dead, John,' he said. I hadn't realised how badly he was injured. That news ripped into me. My heart went out to Lee's family, decent people who didn't deserve to be victims of such a tragedy.

As I have said, I hope those responsible for Hillsborough will be brought to justice and made to answer for their misjudgements. Perhaps then people like Lee Nicol can rest in peace.

Liverpool returned to action on 3 May, fittingly against neighbours Everton. The truth is, however, we were all shattered; not so much physically shattered as mentally fatigued, and there is nothing worse than that when you're playing football. A few of the players, myself included, were still having trouble getting to sleep so really we were in no fit state to play six first-division matches plus the possibility of two more in the FA Cup.

The goalless draw with Everton wasn't a bad result, even though we saw it as two points dropped. Really, we were glad to get it over and done with. The intensity of the occasion, the fact that the entire country was watching us, made for a claustrophobic atmosphere inside Goodison Park. Don't get me wrong, both sets of supporters showed great character and the minute's silence before the match was touchingly observed. Yet there was something strange about it all. Perhaps there were too many different types of emotion going round in people's heads. I know that was the case where I was concerned.

I was substituted towards the end of the match, a decision I did not like. I had lost all composure when I walked through the tunnel and into the dressing-rooms while the match was still going on. I smashed a door after kicking it, and damaged other items in the dressing-room. Perhaps it was Kenny's way of getting my mind back on football, but I was angry and upset. Everton eventually sent me a bill for the damage to the door.

Battling to retain the first-division title meant every match was a big one. And, of course, there was the FA Cup semi-final against Nottingham Forest to play. It was rescheduled for 7 May at Old Trafford and, for Liverpool at least, it became a memorable affair. After finding out I was in the side, I don't think I was ever so pumped up for a game. Victory wasn't just important, it was essential. This was, after all, the tie in which people had died. In a sense, that made it more important than the final itself.

And that is why our 3–1 victory was special. I still smile when I see video footage of the final whistle. The camera zooms in on me and I can be seen punching the air in delight. That was how much it meant. In fact, there was never a time during that match when I thought we would lose. We wanted victory so badly I think Nottingham Forest were always swimming against the tide.

I scored twice, both of them headers, but it was Liverpool's third goal which will remain most associated with me. Brian Laws, the Forest defender, somehow contrived to miskick the ball into his own goal effectively to confirm our victory. In the heat of the moment, without thinking of how my actions would be interpreted, I ran towards him and rubbed the top of his head. It was a stupid thing to do and, quite rightly, Brian was far from happy about it. My only defence is that I was so determined to win the game I lost the ability to think straight. It was so unlike me and I regretted the incident immediately. Three days later, Liverpool played Forest at Anfield in a first-division fixture. Before the game, I approached Brian as he came off the coach and offered an apology. His reaction was short and firm and totally unexpected.

'Damn you,' he said, not even looking at me.

'Fine, if that's the way you want it.'

During the game, Brian and I chased the ball as it rolled towards the corner flag. I got there first and, though he tried to kick me, I managed to jump out of the way. He was on the floor so I ran up to him and rubbed his head for the second time in less than a week. This time I was pleased with my intervention. I meant to be patronising and, for his failure to accept my apology, Brian deserved it. I am happy to say Brian and I get on well these days. We met up in Spain once and regularly swap information about players. But for a time I thought he'd never forgive me.

Despite Forest's desire to keep men behind the ball, we won a crucial and difficult game 1–0. David Burrows, our left-back, was brought down inside the penalty area in the eighty-first minute and I converted the penalty to secure the three points. I also scored in our 2–1 win against Wimbledon away and in our 2–0 win against QPR at Anfield. And while Liverpool were hitting top form, Arsenal were dropping points. We even went to the top of the first division for a brief period, which was remarkable given that we trailed leaders Arsenal by nineteen points at one stage.

So we were in a good frame of mind for the FA Cup final at Wembley against Everton on 20 May. As FA Cup finals go, it must rank as the most emotional in history. The 80,000 supporters created a special atmosphere. The prevailing view was that no people deserved to die at a football match. There was also a sense of injustice; as if Hillsborough was no accident, more an act of negligence. Wembley captured that feeling. As most of the tickets had gone to Liverpool and Everton fans, it was a truly Merseyside occasion. The noise was amazing when we made our way on to the pitch for the National Anthem. But, in a sense, the minute's silence which preceded the match carried with it a more unique sound. It was beautifully observed – like the ones at Goodison Park and Old Trafford earlier in the month – and in a strange way the silence was deafening.

Liverpool began the match well. After four minutes, Steve Nicol played a fine long pass into the path of Steve McMahon who immediately squared the ball to me. With Everton defender Kevin Ratcliffe out of position, I found myself with a clear run on goal. I had two options. Do I control the ball and use space in front of me to make the chance easier? Or do I hit the ball first time? I went for the latter option, which took Everton goalkeeper Neville Southall by surprise. As soon as the ball beat him and flew into the top corner of the goal I was running towards the Liverpool fans with my arms up in the air. It was a glorious moment. It wasn't just Neville I took by surprise; I think most people were shocked I hit the ball first time. But I knew what I was doing. I wanted to put the ball exactly where I should have put the penalty against Wimbledon the year before. Amazingly, that penalty was my last touch in the 1988 FA Cup final, while the goal against Everton was my first touch in the 1989 FA Cup final.

But though the final against Everton was a great occasion, it wasn't a great football match. There seemed too much at stake and the remaining eighty-six minutes lacked real excitement, especially for the rest of the country watching on television at home. But when Everton equalised through Stuart McCall in the ninetieth minute to take the game into extra time, Liverpool suddenly had a fight on their hands.

I was off the field by then, replaced by Ian Rush, who repaid the faith shown in him by Kenny Dalglish. Ian scored twice in extra time to ensure Liverpool won the FA Cup with a 3–2 scoreline (Stuart McCall scored Everton's second goal). Ronnie Whelan, Liverpool's captain in place of Alan Hansen, received the trophy and the fans spilled on to the pitch, denying us the chance to do a lap of honour. I suppose it didn't matter, really. A lot of those fans had suffered. This was their day of glory, too.

With the FA Cup safely in the Anfield trophy room we set

about adding the first-division championship to it. We had two games, both at Anfield, against West Ham United and Arsenal, and Liverpool were in control of the situation. A victory and a draw would be enough to secure the league and FA Cup double. If we beat West Ham by a high margin, we could even afford to lose against Arsenal. In the event, we did beat West Ham by a high margin. I scored our first in the 5–1 victory which meant Arsenal had to beat us by at least two clear goals to win the championship. Anything else and the title was ours for the second successive season.

So we were all set for the decider at Anfield on 26 May, and what an anti-climax it proved for me. Arsenal arrived with everything to play for while Liverpool didn't really know how to handle it. I think we were too defensive, which has never been Liverpool's game. By doing that, we simply handed the initiative to Arsenal.

Kenny decided to play Ian Rush and me up front in a line-up which, on paper at least, seemed attack-minded. But it never worked out. Ian went off injured at half-time and was replaced by Peter Beardsley and once Arsenal scored at the beginning of the second half through Alan Smith, we seemed nervous. The last few minutes of the match seemed to take forever and even when it was obvious the ninety minutes were up and there was only stoppage time left, we were still on edge, fearing Arsenal would score a second goal. And score it they did: John Barnes won the ball in midfield and started to run at the Arsenal defence. Usually we would have urged him on but on this occasion it might have been better had he moved with the ball towards the corner flag to waste more time. Alas, he lost possession and the ball was played back to Arsenal goalkeeper John Lukic. Usually when a goalkeeper is about to throw the ball out and I am nearby, I raise my hands in an effort to stop him. For some reason – and I don't know why – I didn't do it on this occasion, and it proved costly. John threw the ball out to right-back Lee Dixon who in turn played the ball long to striker Alan Smith. Alan turned quickly and played the ball inside to midfielder Michael Thomas. Running at speed, Michael seemed to lose control of the ball, but Steve Nicol's attempted clearance bounced straight into the path of the Arsenal player. He was now through on goal with only Bruce Grobbelaar to beat. I could see Ray Houghton was close enough to foul Michael but, in what seemed like an instant, the Arsenal player dispatched the ball into the goal with the outside of his right foot. Two-nil.

As the small number of Arsenal fans at the Anfield Road end cheered with delight I crouched to the ground, unable to believe it. I could see other Liverpool players looking equally disillusioned. There could not have been more than a few seconds remaining so there was no way we would bounce back. And so it was. We restarted the game but before we were able to attempt a worthwhile effort on goal, the referee blew for full time. By the smallest of margins, Arsenal were the new first-division champions.

At times like that you don't really know how to handle it. My immediate reaction was to slump to the ground in genuine shock. David O'Leary, my Republic of Ireland team-mate, tried to console me but I ushered him away. I was far too upset to talk to anyone. My dream of winning the league and FA Cup double with Liverpool was in tatters. Tony Adams, the Arsenal captain, is supposed to have rubbed the top of my head, though I don't remember it. Apparently he did it because he was annoyed when I did the same thing to Brian Laws at Old Trafford.

At the time, it was of little consolation to me that I finished the season by scoring more goals per game than in the previous campaign.

Arsenal were presented with their trophy and the Liverpool fans sportingly gave them a standing ovation. It reminded me of the time Leeds United won the first-division title at Anfield in 1969. The Leeds players were enjoying a well-deserved lap of honour when the Kop began to chant 'champions, champions'. Twenty years on, the Liverpool fans were still as fair-minded. I was proud to be part of them.

It is irrelevant, of course, but I do believe we would have won the first-division championship under normal circumstances. Hillsborough took a two-week chunk out of our season at a crucial time, which meant we had to play eight big games in twenty-four days. Emotion had carried us forward but in the end we snapped. I suppose it was inevitable. It was an almost super-human effort from the Liverpool players, but in the end, asking us to win the league and FA Cup double in such trying times was too much. But our sense of loss was nothing, not when you compare it with the loss suffered by the families and friends of the ninety-six victims of Hillsborough. Everything was firmly in perspective after that.

From the moment Ian Rush returned to Liverpool in August 1988, I sensed I would not see out my four-and-a-half-year contract at Anfield. I felt from that day on that he had been purchased by Kenny Dalglish to replace me, so I was never surprised when newspapers printed speculative articles linking me with other clubs. By the summer of 1989, however, I suspected Kenny wanted to get rid of me. You have to appreciate how big a name Ian Rush was at the time. He was a mega-star. They say no player is bigger than the club but Ian came close to disproving that in his time at Liverpool. I suppose the club had to accommodate him in some way, and that meant my days at Anfield were numbered. It took me back to a conversation I had with Dennis Roach, an agent, in the summer of 1988.

'Ian Rush is going back to Liverpool, John,' he said, 'and PSV Eindhoven want to sign you. Go and tell Kenny Dalglish you want a move.'

'I'm not telling anyone anything,' I replied. 'I don't want to move.' But Dennis kept giving me these figures which, he said, was how much PSV were prepared to pay me. 'I don't want the money,' I said. 'I'd much rather play for Liverpool Football Club.' PSV, the famous Dutch team, did come in for me after I scored a hat-trick against Charlton Athletic in August 1988 and offered around £1 million, which at that time was a lot of money for a thirty-year-old player. Kenny called me into his office and my immediate thought was: 'I am leaving Liverpool.' But Kenny had different ideas.

'Keep playing like that, Aldo, and you're staying at Liverpool.'

'That's fine, Kenny. I just want to play for Liverpool.'

By July 1989, however, Kenny was less benevolent. We were in Scandinavia on a pre-season tour when I finally gave Liverpool an excuse to dispense with my services. I scored in our first match in Norway, while in the second game I was up front with Peter Beardsley against a local side in Stockholm, who went a goal in front. The Swedish defenders were giving me a particularly tough time and one of them took the liberty of striking me in the face. Typically, I sought retribution. I waited for the ball to go into the other half of the field, checked to see if the referee and linesmen were looking elsewhere, and walked towards the defender. To make sure he didn't suspect I was after revenge, I avoided eye contact and walked past him. Then I turned and elbowed him full in the face. The defender dropped to the ground and didn't move. 'Oh, God!' I said to myself. 'This guy is not going to get up.' To make matters worse, there was a deep cut in my elbow and blood was pouring all over my arm. It was the tell-tale sign that I was the culprit. The Swedish players in the vicinity ran towards me with facial expressions that suggested they wanted to kill me. They might have done had the referee not intervened. Luckily, neither he nor his linesmen had seen me hit the defender, which meant I could not be sent off.

I stayed on the field and even managed to score Liverpool's equalising goal. With the rest of the Swedish defenders anxious to hurt me, I had somehow survived in one piece until the referee blew the half-time whistle. In the dressing-room, Kenny Dalglish walked up to where I was seated.

'Aldo, off,' he said sharply.

'What?'

'You're being substituted, Aldo. Off.'

'I'm not coming off.'

'If you don't come off now, you'll come off on a stretcher, because they are going to kill you.' Kenny turned to Ian Rush and shouted: 'Ian, on you go.' Then Kenny called for a doctor. 'We need stitches in Aldo's elbow,' the Liverpool manager added. The doctor put three stitches in my injury. The game, meanwhile, finished at 1–1 and I managed to avoid further confrontation.

The next morning I woke up in agony. There seemed to be something stuck to my elbow. I pulled my arm out of the bed covers and saw that the elbow was swollen to the size of a balloon. I showed it to Nigel Spackman, my room-mate, and he couldn't believe the extent of the infection. We trained that afternoon but I could hardly move my arm. I showed Kenny who, clearly unhappy, immediately called for the doctor.

'How did Aldo's arm get like that?' he fumed.

The following day, we had another match against a Swedish team and Kenny put Ian Rush up front with Peter Beardsley. I don't know whether I was being taught a lesson for my behaviour in the previous match or whether Kenny wanted to try something different, but I never would get back into the Liverpool team.

I didn't know that at the time, of course, so I still had high hopes of being involved in Liverpool's Charity Shield match against Arsenal at Wembley in August. It is Liverpool's custom three days before a Charity Shield game to have a behind-closed-doors friendly between the first team and the reserves. The first team was usually the one that would start the Charity Shield. So when I found myself in the reserve team, I knew I wouldn't be in the starting line-up at Wembley. I was disappointed, especially as I had scored more goals in the pre-season matches than any other player. But I was a professional and I had to accept it. I worked hard and scored in the reserves' 4–1 defeat. After the match, as I dried myself following a shower, Roy Evans came to sit next to me.

'You're playing for the reserves at Stafford Rangers tonight, Aldo,' Roy said casually.

'I'm what? Playing where? I'm thirty-one in September. You expect me to play two matches in a day? Bugger off.' I'd lost my head by this stage. 'And by the way, Roy, tell Kenny Dalglish to come and tell me himself.'

Roy was anxious to calm me down.

'Don't do anything rash, Aldo,' Roy said. 'Just get on with it.'

I collected my belongings and dashed out of the dressing-room. I played up front with Mike Marsh at Stafford and we scored a goal apiece in a 2–1 victory, but I was still unhappy. When I got home that evening I went straight to bed. Even the kids were still up. My mind was too active, however, and I couldn't sleep. I was already hoping the club would give me an improved contract but now I had something else to sort out. I was first outside Kenny's office the following morning. Out of respect I knocked twice on the door.

'What do you want?' Kenny asked.

'I want you.' There was an awkward pause of a few seconds, a pause I was happy to break. 'Thank you very much, Kenny,' I said sarcastically. 'Thank you for shitting on me.'

'I've shit on you? More like you've shit on Liverpool, Aldo.'

'Oh, sorry, Kenny. I was locked up for doing something silly a couple of years ago. But I was provoked and I was pushed down a flight of stairs. OK, I put Liverpool's name in the dirt for that, but I apologised for it. The truth is, Kenny, I've never shit on anyone in my life. But you've shit on me from a skyscraper. I came to Liverpool when you had nobody to score your goals. But I came and scored goals for you. I did the business on the pitch for you and this is how you treat me.' I stormed out of the door. Later that day, at training, Kenny arrived late. He called me over and said Peter Robinson wanted to talk to me.

'There are forms to be filled in at Peter's office,' Kenny said. 'An addition to your contract.' It turned out that Liverpool were offering to give me an extra £20,000 that day as a loyalty payment. They assumed it would keep me sweet. They could not have been more wrong. I knew they didn't want me for the full term of my contract. When I signed for Liverpool it was for four-and-a-half years, yet I suspected they really only wanted me for three years.

So when the 1989–90 season began, I was not surprised to find out Peter Beardsley and Ian Rush were the preferred strikers. My first appearance of the season was as a substitute away at Luton Town in Liverpool's third match, which ended in a drab goalless draw. I came closest to scoring when I hit the crossbar.

After that we were due to fly out to Spain for a prestige friendly against Real Madrid, but there was another twist to come. Dennis Roach telephoned me before our flight and said officials from Real Sociedad were in Madrid waiting to talk to officials from Liverpool about a possible deal involving me. Apparently, Real Sociedad were trying to buy me for around £1 million.

After Liverpool's 3–0 defeat against Madrid, I saw officials from Real Sociedad and Liverpool together. I wondered what they were talking about. Spanish journalists were constantly asking me about my future and I didn't know what to say to them. I knew absolutely nothing. After shrugging my shoulders to yet another journalist, my curiosity got the better of me. I walked straight into the room where Peter Robinson and John Smith were sitting with their Real Sociedad counterparts.

'Will somebody please tell me what's going on with me and my football?' I said. The room went quiet. I muttered an apology and walked back out. The next day I asked Kenny for his version of the discussions.

'Look, Aldo,' he said. 'Liverpool are talking to Real Sociedad. All I will say is this: don't undersell yourself.'

'Kenny, I don't want to leave Liverpool. You put me in the team and I'll stay.'

'I can't do that.'

I knew then I had no future at Liverpool. I never wanted to leave Anfield but I had to be objective about it. The Republic of Ireland looked set to qualify for the World Cup and if I was to stand a chance of representing them at Italia '90, I had to be playing regular first-team football, preferably in a top league.

A week or so later, by which time there was talk of Glasgow Celtic trying to sign me, Liverpool asked me if I wanted to meet with the Real Sociedad officials. I agreed and heard what the Spaniards had to say. It was incredible. They were offering the kind of money I only dreamed about. By the standards of top-flight professionals in the late 1990s, I was never brilliantly paid at Anfield. None of the players were. I think the average was around £100,000 a year. But then it was never about money with me because playing for Liverpool was enough. If, however,

I was going to leave Liverpool, that was a different matter. You have to take as much as you can get to make sure your family is secure. It's the way of the world. So when Real Sociedad offered me a substantial salary, my eyes nearly popped out of my head. This was big money.

The way the Real Sociedad officials handled the situation impressed me. They were professional, efficient and likeable people who sold their club well. The Sociedad president ended the meeting by telling me to expect a telephone call from Liverpool the following day. The call duly came. Could I go to Anfield to meet with the chairman, John Smith? I was happy to. Apparently the deal between Liverpool and Real Sociedad was only awaiting my signature. Dennis Roach, the agent who was mediating between the clubs, said there were few problems and that I would soon be going to San Sebastian to play for Sociedad. So when I arrived at Anfield, and was ushered into a room where Peter Robinson and John Smith were seated, I expected to see Tony Ensor, the club's solicitor, but he wasn't there. I later found out he had walked out because he objected to the way Liverpool were treating me. Mr Ensor, so it was said, wanted me to remain a Liverpool player, but that is another story.

The Liverpool chairman welcomed me and asked me to sit down. He seemed happy and probably regarded me as a soft touch. But, unlike my first meeting with John Smith, when I would have signed anything, I now had my business head on.

'A club has come in for you, John,' the chairman said.

'Who is it?' I asked, knowing full well who it was.

'Real Sociedad of Spain.'

'How much are they paying Liverpool for me?'

'£1.15 million . . .'

'That much?'

'. . . and we've accepted it. It's a tremendous opportunity for you and your family to go to Spain and earn some good money . . .'

'Hold on,' I said, cutting the chairman short. 'What are you giving me to go?' John Smith turned to face Peter Robinson.

'We'll give you the money you would have got from Oxford

United had you finished your contract with them,' Peter said. That amounted to £15,000, a figure I was not prepared to accept.

'Piss off,' I said.

'Pardon?' replied Peter.

'Let's get this straight,' I said, my voice rising. 'You got me two-and-a-half years ago for £750,000, yes?'

'Yes.'

'You're selling me for £1.15 million, yes?'

'Yes.'

'So you've got sixty-three goals out of me and now nearly £400,000 profit. And you're giving me £15,000.'

'But John, you could have come here and had a nightmare.'

'Yes, but I came here and didn't have a nightmare. I scored sixty-three goals for you.'

I felt as if I'd put Peter Robinson in his place and even today he will barely speak to me. I couldn't believe his attitude. I thought he was cleverer than that. Even allowing for my wages, the club were expecting to come out of the deal with £150,000 profit. To offer me £15,000 was unacceptable to the point of being derogatory. There was a silence. John Smith broke it.

'OK, John, what exactly are you looking for?'

'£250,000,' I said, taking pleasure in seeing the chairman and Peter look stunned.

'We can't give you that,' the chairman said. 'We don't do that kind of thing.'

'OK, don't do it. I'll get the agent to come up.' I left the room and Dennis Roach went to speak with John Smith and Peter Robinson in my place. Afterwards, he came looking for me.

'Dear me, John,' Dennis said. 'You've thrown the cat among the pigeons there.'

'I don't care, Dennis. They are not going to make money out of me. There is a principle at stake here.'

I went back into the room and John Smith made me an offer. It wasn't the figure I was looking for but it was acceptable under the circumstances. As I was getting a signing-on fee from Real Sociedad I felt I was getting a reasonable sum of money. But it wasn't about money – it was about principles. I am a proud man. Liverpool FC is a business and the attitude of their chairman and secretary sickened me. Beating them at their own game gave me as much pleasure as scoring a hat-trick. That meeting soured my feelings for Liverpool. I'd always been a fan of the club and always will be, but I felt as though the club treated me as a butcher would treat a piece of meat. I was being sold for profit. That hurt. I'd given Liverpool my all. For sure, I'd made mistakes. But I never gave less than one hundred per cent on the playing field. My enthusiasm and workrate, not to mention those sixty-three goals, warranted better treatment.

The fans, whom I always loved and felt a part of, treated me rather better. When Liverpool played Crystal Palace at Anfield on 12 September 1989, everyone on Merseyside knew it was my last game for the club. Inevitably, I was named as a substitute, but by the time Liverpool had gone into a five-goal lead, I knew I would mark my departure from the club with an appearance. It came in fairytale circumstances. Liverpool won a penalty at the Kop end and Kenny asked me if I wanted to take the kick.

'Of course,' I said. Peter Beardsley was brought off and I was sent on to replace him. I walked to the penalty spot, picked the ball up before replacing it on the spot, and then fired it to the goalkeeper's left. When the ball went into the goal, nestling at the back of the net, it was one of the sweetest moments of my life. The Kop surged forward and I could feel the mutual affection. We won the game 9–0 – a record for Liverpool in the top flight – but that barely mattered to me. When the game ended, and I realised my days at Liverpool were over, my emotions got the better of me. I took off my shirt and threw it into the Kop. My socks and my boots went the same way. All I had left was my shorts, and some fans even wanted those! In the dressing-room afterwards I was overcome with emotion.

I will always believe Liverpool sold me two or three seasons too early. I remained an international striker until I was thirty-six and proved, by scoring in the World Cup for Ireland five years after leaving Anfield, that I could maintain a high level of performance at a top level. I also believe Kenny regretted selling me when he did, though he might not admit it. When he was manager of Blackburn Rovers and I was playing for Tranmere Rovers, Kenny tried to sign me. That was a sign he rated me.

The facts suggest I was good for Liverpool. In the 1988–89 campaign, we played our best football when we reverted to the system that had served us so well in 1987–88, with Peter Beardsley and me up front. That is no criticism of Ian Rush, but I felt I was a more appropriate option for the system which Kenny had lovingly created. Why mess about with it just to accommodate Ian? Yes, I accept Liverpool won the first-division championship in 1990 but it wasn't with the same fluency that made our 1988 triumph so memorable. And apart from the FA Cup in 1992, what have Liverpool won since? The Coca-Cola Cup in 1995, that's all. I am still friends with Ian and I still believe he was the greatest striker in the world in the mid 1980s. It must be noted that on only two occasions when we played together for Liverpool did we both fail to score. Crucially, the second of the two was the match with Arsenal at Anfield that cost us the first-division championship.

My feelings for Liverpool are now mixed. I have nothing but compliments for the fans and I am still friends with some of the players. But while Peter Robinson is there, I don't think I will fully love the club in the way I did. Perhaps, once Peter has left and I am not involved in another club, I will get a season ticket for Anfield and support the team like I did as a child. But at the moment I am a victim of reality; the reality that saw Liverpool, the club I loved, treat me like dirt at a time when I was prepared to do almost anything to play for them. Liverpool FC is the fans and players, not people like Peter Robinson. Clubs have to be run by officials, but those officials never inspire feelings of affection, not in the way players and fans do. Liverpool had changed since the days of Bill Shankly. In those days, a player was never sold too early. If a striker was still scoring goals he was encouraged to stay at the club.

Just before I flew out to Bilbao on my way to meeting up with Real Sociedad for the first time, I received a letter from an older Liverpool fan. The writer claimed to have supported the Reds for more than fifty years and went to all of their matches. 'I am giving up my season ticket,' he wrote. 'The way they have treated you is an absolute disgrace. Liverpool never thought of you having to uproot your family after you thought you'd settled in Liverpool.'

I could not have agreed with him more.

— 6 —

BRAVE NEW WORLD

THE Royal Society Club of Spain, based in beautiful San Sebastian in the north of the country, was always a bastion of Basque pride. Outsiders were so mistrusted that their football team, Real Sociedad, had only employed ten foreign players in all their history. It hardly mattered if you were Spanish. You had to be Basque to be fully accepted. So when I signed for Real Sociedad, I knew I was walking into a politically sensitive climate. I was their eleventh foreigner but, crucially, the first for nearly thirty years. This, and the fact that I was leaving Liverpool against my will, ensured my Spanish mission was more than just a career move. This was a whole new life.

I felt apprehensive, but this move did not scare me like the one to Newport a decade earlier. Then I was a boy hardly used to the ways of the world outside Garston. Now I was older, I'd travelled, and I had the support of a marvellous family alongside me. I was aware things could go badly wrong, but I could only fail professionally. From a financial point of view, the contract I signed with Real Sociedad made us secure for the rest of our lives. I have stressed elsewhere that football for me was more about glory than money, but if you can get both at the same time, so much the better.

Liverpool's 9–0 win over Crystal Palace set the entire English football community talking. Every football writer was discussing our triumph, comparing it with all the great nights at Anfield, and generally whipping up the hype in the way newspapers often do. Some newspapers, sensing the irony of my goal, even managed to pay tribute to the success of my thirty months at Liverpool. It was nice to know I wasn't forgotten but the day after the match, I was far from happy. I somehow felt cheated; as if the thing I craved most – a career at Liverpool – had been ruthlessly denied me by people who didn't care that I was at my peak. And so, as I sat at home reflecting on my misfortune, feelings of anti-climax threatened to overwhelm me. Not that Joan allowed me to wallow in my self-pity. We had much to sort out. We were going to Spain the following day and this was one move we had to get right.

Having decided to leave the kids in Liverpool for a few days, it took Joan and me the best part of a day to get to San Sebastian. So much for the speed of modern transport. We had to drive to Manchester, then fly from Manchester to London, and from London to Bilbao. We were met at Bilbao airport by two Real Sociedad officials and Dennis Roach. We were extremely weary when we arrived at the airport, but that soon changed. A number of cameramen gathered around, sending the adrenalin pumping through my veins, putting Joan and me on edge. We didn't have time to settle, however, because there was important documentation to be signed in Bilbao. To live in Spain in those days necessitated official clearance. It meant a few hours waiting in the consulate, a boring situation that for a time turned us into caged animals. When you are about to live in a new country, you immediately want to see the town; you want to see the accommodation on offer; you want to meet the people. But we were spending so much time with men in suits, twisting our faces into false smiles of diplomacy, that we began to feel irritated. I wanted to fall asleep during the car journey back to San Sebastian, but this was impossible; everyone wanted to talk.

Back in San Sebastian, we were taken to the hotel that would be our home for the next three days. It was luxurious but that hardly mattered at the time; we didn't want to be stuck inside while the sun was shining outside. Our hosts suggested we go to the beach and our spirits rose. It was one of the most impressive sights I've seen. As the six o'clock sun gleamed on the water, the glorious sand provided the perfect setting for the myriad people relaxing after work. As if that wasn't enough, the promenade near the beach was magnificent. I turned to Joan and said, 'I didn't expect it to be this good.' Her smile made me realise there were many good times ahead of us. San Sebastian is stunning, particularly in summer. Close to the French border, it has two impressive beaches. La Concha is the most accessible but Ondaretta is just as beautiful. Away from the coast, San Sebastian has an old quarter where people gather in the evenings to make use of the bars or stalls selling fresh seafood. The town, which can attract richer Spaniards in high season, was never cheap but I had to be positive. It could have been a lot worse.

On that first tour around San Sebastian we were followed by a group of reporters from England. The *Daily Mirror* journalist was there with a photographer, as Dennis Roach had sold them the exclusive rights to our story. A *Sun* journalist introduced himself to me.

'On your way,' I said to him, remembering how much damage his newspaper did to the city of Liverpool in the days following the Hillsborough tragedy. 'I don't speak to the *Sun*. Nothing against you as a person but I will not speak to you directly.' In the end, the *Sun* reporter picked up a few quotes from other sources and turned it into a story about John Aldridge. I couldn't stop them from doing that, but I was determined never to co-operate with the *Sun*, a principle I have maintained to this day.

The following morning, I was met by John Toshack, the former Liverpool striker who was manager of Real Madrid and who had recommended me to Sociedad. We spent an hour or so talking through the pitfalls that were likely to confront me in Spain. His advice was welcome. He told me how to handle the press, how to handle living in the town from a political perspective, and how to get the best out of my move. I then went to the hospital for my medical. I considered myself reasonably fit so I didn't expect any problems, but this medical was like nothing I'd had before. The attention to detail was amazing. I had a blood test, X-rays on all my joints, and heart tests. They measured my fat content, put sucker pads on my shaven chest, covered my face with an oxygen mask – everything. Worse still, they insisted on giving me a tough work-out on an exercise bike. Sweat was pouring out of me by the end. Fortunately, my medical results were good. When they told me my heart was in great shape, I felt a sense of relief. Why, I don't know. I suppose I feared they might find a defect undetected in all my years playing football in England. But as Real Sociedad had paid £1.15 million for a player nearing thirty-one, they had to make sure I was up to acceptable physical standards.

After a welcome meal with two club officials and a translator, we were driven to a hotel near Real Sociedad's Estadio Atocha to meet the Spanish media. We were directed to a press room which resembled the inside of a church. There were two rows of what looked like pews separated by an aisle down the middle. I was given a seat on the pulpit-like stage at the front, alongside my employers. There seemed to be journalists and cameramen everywhere. I knew there would be some kind of response to my arrival, but nothing on this scale. In a sense, it was new to me. Press conferences at Liverpool were never like this, while journalists at international matches usually only wanted to speak to managers. For the largest press conference I'd seen, I was the centre of attention. Facing a predominantly foreign press can be daunting but I'd already been told what to say. It was contrived and I was therefore prepared for the tricky questions that came up about the political implications of my arrival. 'I am not a politician,' I said. 'I am a footballer. I am here to score goals and pay back the money Real Sociedad have spent on me. If anyone holds anything political against me, there is nothing I can do about it. Goals are the same in any language.' The words might have been put into my mouth but I meant what I said. I really did respect the club for risking a large sum of money on a player the wrong side of thirty.

When I reached the training ground to join the rest of the Sociedad players later in the day, I realised for the first time how difficult my move was going to be. For a start, there was a lot of graffiti daubed on the training ground wall. When I asked my interpreter what one particular sentence meant he told me to ignore it. I later found out that one slogan said: 'No outsiders welcome here'. It was a clear response to my arrival. Worse still, the Sociedad supporters' club president was quoted as saying: 'I'd rather see Real in the third division than see a foreigner wear a club shirt.' It was disheartening, for sure, but not as bad as it could have been.

Meeting the players for the first time made things easier for me, as did meeting the manager, Marco Boronat. I remember renewing acquaintance with Gorriz, a defender with whom I'd fallen out during a Real Sociedad–Liverpool friendly a year or so before. We had a laugh about an incident where he and I exchanged punches, and there was a feeling of mutual respect when we shook hands. It was inevitable that I should be the victim of the players' jokes, however. I knew they were laughing at me but as I couldn't speak Spanish, I had no way of dealing with it. It is probably like that at every club throughout the world. I had to grin and bear it.

A few thousand supporters were there to watch us train, which gave me an insight into the intensity of Spanish football. The fans stayed on to see a friendly match among the players. I managed to score and the majority of the supporters seemed to react well to that. A few barriers were broken that day. Afterwards, I signed autographs and did some essential public relations work. With simple acts of diplomacy, I had the feeling I was winning over the majority of people. People could see I was keen to make my mark.

There seemed so much to do that we found it hard to fit in the time to view properties in the area. Our hotel was not a place to stay for more than a few days. We needed a permanent residence. High in the hills of San Sebastian there were some beautiful apartments. We looked at apartments of all shapes and sizes but never seriously considered them. They were unacceptable to a family used to its independence. We wanted a house, the kind that had served us so well in places like Newport, Oxford and Liverpool; but it would have to wait.

On the Saturday – 16 September 1989 – Joan and I returned to Liverpool to make the final preparations for our big move. We'd enjoyed our brief acclimatisation but now we were set for the real thing. The kids would be coming with us and how they handled the change would be the most important thing. So we didn't want to rush things. We wanted to make sure our new house was the right one and that the kids' school would be the best in the area. My career was not the most important aspect of the move, neither was Joan's happiness. The most important consideration was the kids' education and their ability to settle. If they could not be successfully integrated into Spanish society, the move was doomed.

I left Joan with the kids in Liverpool and returned to Spain on the Tuesday. I faced a hard week of training as I prepared to make my debut for Sociedad against CA Osasuna at Estadio Atocha on the Sunday. The night before the match we were taken to a hotel which seemed to be in the middle of nowhere. I really thought we'd left earth as the coach slogged towards its destination. But the hotel was old and grand, serving some of the best food I've tasted. There was pasta, salad, rice, and red wine in abundance. I was surprised we were allowed wine before an important game but Marco Boronat seemed to know what he was doing. Even the desserts seemed excessive but, again, I was happy to join in. I remember eating what looked like mini cakes with strawberries. They were only the size of a ten-pence piece but they had a sweetness which reminded me of my childhood. And, as I found out later, these cakes were essential forms of carbohydrate. Food was almost an obsession with Spanish clubs and the need for carbohydrates cannot be overstated. There was, however, a price to pay for the luxurious food. Come the evening, I was spending more time on the toilet than in my bed. I had what Liverpudlians call 'the shits', though this was diarrhoea on a higher level. It destroyed any hopes I had of a good night's sleep, weakening me for my debut. It was plain cornflakes for breakfast the following morning, a generous helping of fresh hake for the pre-match meal just after noon, and rest before the five o'clock kick-off against Osasuna. It wasn't my first game against Osasuna. In 1988, I had played against them for Liverpool in Sammy Lee's testimonial. I don't look upon that match with much affection, however; I sustained an injury that kept me out of four crucial Liverpool matches.

There were around 15,000 people in the Estadio Atocha for my debut and I felt a sense of anticipation when I walked out to the roar of the crowd. I enjoyed a reasonably successful game. I threw myself about and made life difficult for the opponents, without coming close to a goal. We did win 1–0, however, and this was bound to overshadow my opening game. Encouragingly, the daily sports newspapers the following day suggested my debut was of an acceptable standard. Every player is marked out of ten in each of several papers and my average was a creditable seven. It wasn't the fairytale way to begin my career with Sociedad – with my stomach still very delicate, it was never going to be that – but I felt I had taken a step in the right direction.

Our next match, away at Real Oviedo on 1 October, could hardly have been more different. We flew there, as we did to a lot of away matches, but it might have been better if we'd stayed at home and had a fancy-dress party. We lost 5–0 and, in modern footballing parlance, were lucky to get nil. I didn't play well but that was hardly surprising: I never had a chance all night and felt no more part of the team than the lady who cleaned the kit. The newspapers took it out on me. The mentality over there is to blame the forwards when your team doesn't score, so my average mark was a mere one out of ten. The fact that my inactivity had more to do with our overall team performance seemed irrelevant to the Spanish journalists. In truth, their criticism hurt. I met John Toshack in the week after that defeat and he reassured me that newspapers tended to exaggerate when a team has conceded five goals. Thrashings of that magnitude didn't happen often in Spain, John said. Teams were usually too well organised at the back. But I'd learned a vital lesson: the defence can have a nightmare but still the strikers get the blame. I didn't take much notice of player markings in English newspapers, but over in Spain the fans took them seriously.

Games seemed to be coming thick and fast. We were expected to do better against Real Madrileno in Madrid's Estadio Calderon in the Spanish Cup. One of the nursery teams of giants Atletico Madrid, Madrileno proved to be a difficult side to break down. But I took great delight in scoring our goals in a 2–2 draw. I was relieved when the first goal went in but by the end of the match, such was my greed, I was disappointed not to score a hat-trick.

I was living alone in the Landres Hotel. Joan was tying up the loose ends at home and popping over to Spain for brief periods to look for a house. My acclimatisation was helped by a relationship I struck up with one of the experienced Sociedad players, Alaba. A clever, gregarious man, he would often come to my hotel for coffee and, as his English was fluent, we enjoyed many memorable conversations. It was the ever-reliable Alaba who drove me to training in the days before I had a car. I valued his friendship. For sure, I felt the isolation, but Alaba helped ease the loneliness. We would often go to the beach to sunbathe and then go for pleasant strolls through the town. There was no sense of urgency, which made for a healthy, relaxing atmosphere. My Spanish lessons were going well, too. I had a teacher coming to see me for an hour three times a week and I learned the language quicker than I expected. It wasn't long before I could conduct television interviews in Spanish, though it is still a source of personal mirth that my accent remained Scouse throughout my time in San Sebastian.

Joan and I eventually found a suitable house. Joan had come over to Spain with her mother and the kids and we were shown a property which would have looked nice had a large guard dog not stood menacingly in front of it. As we approached the front door, the dog, which was tied to a lead, went berserk and tried to attack us. Joan understandably seemed to go off the house, solely because of the dog. After we'd seen the inside of the property, we were impressed. It was nicely furnished and spacious, offering us the independence we needed.

'We'll take the house,' said Joan, 'but the dog has got to go.'

'Don't worry,' said the man showing us the house, 'the dog will be fine once he gets to know you.'

The man was right. The dog, a German Shepherd called Keme, proved to be an important part of the family. The kids loved him and, of course, he was a deterrent to any would-be burglar. Even Joan grew to like him in the end. I felt a bit sorry for the animal. Most of his fur was missing and he didn't seem to have been shown much affection. That is one thing I noticed in Spain. The locals generally didn't seem to treat their animals well, which was obviously the case with Keme. He had insects living in his skin so we took him to the vet for treatment. The house, built in its own grounds, was an appropriate setting. I suppose you could call the property a luxury villa but Joan felt it was too remote. The kids ended up going to an English school but they were the only two English pupils there. Every day they would run home from school to watch 'The Simpsons' on Sky television. Satellite TV was vital in those first few weeks and added to the initial feeling of contentment.

But one incident reminded me that not everyone in San Sebastian was on my side. I was walking through the town centre one day when a man stopped me in the streets.

'Ald-rigger,' he said, mispronouncing my name. I waited for him to complete the sentence but he simply spat on the ground after he called my name. I was momentarily stunned, but things were too politically delicate for me to risk a response. Suspecting he could have been a Basque separatist looking for trouble, I ignored him and walked on.

Fortunately, my football was going well. The turning point for me was when we played Barcelona at home on 21 October. The match was to be televised live and, prior to the kick-off, there was a special feature on my progress in Spain. It could not have come at a better time. Though Barcelona took a two-goal lead – their first came through a brilliant thirty-yard shot from Ronald Koeman – I managed to pull one back. Late in the game, I found myself with a clear run on goal and only goalkeeper Zubizarreta to beat. I took the ball past Zubizarreta and stumbled as he backed off. Incredibly, though there was no foul, the referee gave a penalty. A few Barcelona players called me a cheat because Zubizarreta clearly hadn't touched me. But I regained my composure and scored to make it 2–2. That was my first goal from the penalty spot for Sociedad. After signing from Liverpool, Marco Boronat told me I was the designated penalty-taker. 'We've seen you take them for Liverpool and you will take them for us,' he said.

I followed that up with a winning goal against Real Madrileno in the return leg of the Spanish Cup tie. With the scores at 2–2 and the game well into extra time, we won a penalty. I confidently struck the ball into the goal but, as the net wasn't fixed properly to the ground, the ball went right through to the advertising boards. It looked to most people as though I'd missed. The referee allowed the goal but we had strong words with the groundsman afterwards.

Drawing against Barcelona was a good result but nothing like the victory over Real Madrid at home on 4 November. It had been pouring with rain for two days prior to the kick-off but as the game was live on television it had to go ahead. The television company were, after all, paying £200,000 for the privilege of showing the game so a postponement was out of the question. The players stood to gain financially. Sociedad paid the players an extra bonus – twice as much as usual – on three games per season if we won. We chose one of the games – an easy one – while the officials chose the other two. Inevitably, the Real Madrid game was one of the games selected by the club. There was actually a double bonus at stake because Real Madrid was the central government team and all Basques loved to beat them. 'We must win this game, Aldo,' one of the players told me. 'It's a doubler – and we don't like Madrid.' It turned out to be a bit of a farce, however. There were puddles of water all over the pitch and it ruined the match as a spectacle. Not that it mattered much to the Sociedad supporters. I scored in our 2–1 win and they went home happy enough. With our bonuses – around £3,000 per player – we went out to celebrate, but there was no-one around to join us. As it was still pouring with rain, most people in San Sebastian decided to stay at home.

That goal against Real Madrid was my sixth for Sociedad but my last until the end of the month. I failed to score in the following four matches, which was frustrating. I was playing quite well but, in Spain, strikers have to score. Failure to do so is neither acceptable nor understood. The system employed by Marco Boronat meant I was up front alone. As a result, goal opportunities were as common as a blue moon in daylight. The favoured outlet was Goicoechea, a winger, who was adept at crossing the ball. A chirpy character with personality to spare, he later earned a big-money move to Barcelona. For the system to work we had to get Goicoechea into the game as often as possible, which meant we needed three good defenders who were comfortable on the ball. My friend Alaba was usually one of the three. Larranaga was the player who sat in the midfield, while Villabona – my room-mate on occasions – was in a slightly more advanced midfield role. The system was a good one, though there were times when I would go through an entire match without a goalscoring chance. I remember coming off after some games wondering if I had been playing football or chess. Even on good days, chances were few, so I had to be ruthless in front of goal. Often I was marked by two defenders, not the usual one. And if that wasn't bad enough, players tended to perform for themselves, a selfish attitude which meant opportunities for me to shine were rare.

Ironically, though I failed to score in four successive matches, we secured some useful results. We beat CE Sabadell 1–0 in the Spanish Cup, CD Tenerife 1–0, drew 0–0 with RC Celta Vigo, and beat CD Logrones 1–0. When I did return to the scoresheet, it was to help Sociedad complete an aggregate victory over Sabadell in the Spanish Cup. I was relieved – I always am when I break a run of games without scoring a goal – but I was also sent off for elbowing a player. I deserved to be dismissed, even though the defender exaggerated the extent of his pain. The Sociedad fans took retribution by throwing rotten fruit and vegetables at the referee, making for marvellous entertainment, even if the club were fined for it. It showed the supporters were on my side.

After defeats against Sporting Gijon and Valencia CF, Joan

and I took the kids back to Liverpool for Christmas. The Spanish football season always closes for a fortnight so the players can spend time with their families. It meant I was able to have my first Christmas Day party as a married man. I enjoyed the stress-free feeling of being back home in Calderstones. I trained during the two-week period away from Spain and went out with friends I hadn't seen for months.

The break seemed to do me good. I scored in Sociedad's 2–0 win at home to Cadiz CF on 30 December and in the 2–0 win away in CD Malaga on 7 January. I remember taking a stroll in Malaga before the match and enjoying the sunshine. In Britain it would have been cold, while San Sebastian, where it could rain heavily for days on end, was not much warmer. But Malaga, in the south of Spain, has warm weather throughout the year. The town is nice and the hot sun made everything look beautiful. I had to pinch myself sometimes to realise this was work, not play. There were times when I felt as though I was on holiday, so impressive were the surroundings. Joan felt the same way but she wasn't seeing as much of me as she would have liked; neither were the kids. They had settled in reasonably well without the suggestion that Spain could be a permanent residence.

We returned to face Barcelona in the Spanish Cup quarter-final and lost 1–0 at home but followed it up with a 2–1 win against Sevilla which kept Sociedad in the hunt for a UEFA Cup spot. The goalless draw against Athletic Bilbao on 21 January was tedious. There was a lot of local rivalry between Bilbao and Sociedad and I likened the fixture to a Liverpool–Everton game in England. Alas, there was too much at stake. I was marked tightly and don't recall even touching the ball. The lack of goals was inevitable.

The next match, however, could not have been more different. Battling to maintain our interest in the Spanish Cup, we went to Estadio Nou Camp in Barcelona for the second leg of our quarter-final tie. The Nou Camp is an awe-inspiring place. The size of it takes your breath away, even if closer inspection suggests it is an older and more traditional stadium than it at first appears. When we walked through the entrance we noticed there was a club chapel. Our surroundings had a tremendous effect; we outplayed Barcelona for long periods. I scored twice and we took a 3–1 lead. Agonisingly, Barca then scored in the last minute of normal time to make it level on aggregate. When the goal went in I noticed on the stadium clock it was quarter past ten at night. In extra time, Barca scored again and we lost 4–3 on aggregate. It was still a good result, however, because Barca were one of the best teams in Europe at that time – they would win the European Cup in 1992 – and scoring twice in their stadium was one of the most memorable moments of my career. And of course, that made it four goals in two matches against the Spanish giants.

I could hardly have been more confident for our trip to Real Zaragoza's Estadio Romareda. So when I pulled a calf muscle in the pre-match warm-up I was genuinely disillusioned. I had to watch the match from the manager's bench, which is never much fun. In fact, it was depressing for the most part, but a Paraguayan goalkeeper called Chilavert cheered me up when he decided to take a penalty for Zaragoza in the last minute. Our opponents were already a goal up when Chilavert ran the full length of the field and scored to make it 2–0. He was being congratulated by his team-mates when the referee gave Sociedad the all-clear to restart the game. Chilavert was still waving to the ecstatic supporters in the stadium when Goicoechea, seeing the goalkeeper way out of position, scored directly from the centre spot. I found it hard to stop laughing when I saw the ball nestling in the goal after it had flown past the goalkeeper. Chilavert, who remains one of the best goalkeepers in South America and has always been a great character, cut a comical figure as he looked to the heavens in embarrassment.

I missed two matches with the injury but followed it up by creating a Sociedad record. My goal in the 1–1 draw against Osasuna on 4 February began a run of form in which I scored in six successive matches. No Sociedad player had done that before. I was rewarded by one local tradesman who gave me twenty vintage bottles of wine and a generous supply of food. I'd actually scored eight goals in those six matches – including two more against Barcelona in Estadio Nou Camp – so by the time we beat AD Rayo Vallecano 4–1 at home, I had registered twenty for Sociedad. The two against Barcelona had taken my tally to six against them in four matches. On this occasion we drew 2–2 and deserved the point. Equally pleasing was the fact that a coach-load of supporters had travelled from Liverpool to watch me. Around seventy people took advantage of a *Liverpool Echo*-sponsored trip to Lloret, which included a day-trip to the Barcelona game. The stadium was only a quarter full and as Barcelona were not performing well, for a lot of the game all you could hear was 'You'll Never Walk Alone' sung by the tourists from Merseyside. They gave me a great response afterwards.

I enjoyed playing against the giants of Spanish football, even if the results were not always to our liking. Against Real Madrid, for example, we played in the Estadio Santiago Bernabeu, which was as grand as the Nou Camp. Real had one of the world's top strikers at that time, Mexico's Hugo Sanchez. He was in excellent form when Real Madrid beat Sociedad 3–0. Hugo always gave the wrong impression to people who didn't know him. Some thought he was lazy but I found him to be among the most hard-working footballers I've come across. When he was man-marked, as was usually the case, he would run to the touchline, taking the defender with him. With the defender out of position, Hugo would run back into the penalty area and would revel in the space his intelligence had created. It took an amazing amount of fitness to do that successfully. His finishing was good, too. He knew it. People would say he was big-headed and arrogant but when you're that talented you can get away with it. I had a lot of admiration for him and was especially pleased when he exchanged shirts with me after the Republic of Ireland–Mexico World Cup match in Orlando in 1994.

After Sociedad's defeat in Madrid, I was particularly low on the eight-hour coach journey from the capital back to San Sebastian. There had been few opportunities to impress in the game and I grew more and more frustrated as it went on. I really needed a few pints of lager after the final whistle but such open displays of having fun were frowned upon. I was so bored by the time we reached San Sebastian I could feel rigor mortis setting in.

That was why I decided to take Joan and the kids to Tenerife for a three-day holiday. Sociedad had a game against the Canary Island team and we felt it was right to make the best of the time; at least, that was the plan. In a training match prior to the flight, however, I dislocated my shoulder in a freak collision with our reserve-team goalkeeper. It was the last minute of the session when the goalkeeper sent me flying about five feet into the air. Landing awkwardly, I could hear a ripping sound as my shoulder came out of its socket. The pain was so intense I was surprised I didn't pass out. Alaba, who was injured himself at the time, drove me to the hospital. 'You've got to be brave now,' the doctor told me as he cut strips of plaster and stuck them to a table. 'This will hurt,' he added, taking the plasters and using them one by one to help thrust the shoulder back into place. The pain caused me to break into a sweat.

That put me out of action for three weeks. So instead of taking Joan and the kids to Tenerife, we decided to go back to Liverpool for four days. Liverpool had a game on the Tuesday and I went to Anfield to watch it. It was great meeting the lads in the dressing-room afterwards, though I found it strange going back. I hadn't forgotten the circumstances surrounding my departure, so though I welcomed conversation with my former team-mates, I didn't feel as comfortable as I should have done. At that time, Liverpool were well on the way to securing their eighteenth first-division championship, though this time without the finesse of 1988.

I returned to the Sociedad team in time for the season's conclusion. It turned out that we needed to beat Sevilla at Estadio Atocha on 6 May to secure an important UEFA Cup spot. Sevilla had Tony Polster, the Austrian striker, in their team and he was one of the top players in the Spanish League that season. The locals made much of his presence but we kept him quiet for the most part. With the game entering the final five minutes, Sociedad won a penalty. As I picked up the ball and placed it casually on the penalty spot, I realised we were close to confirming our place in European competition for the following season. In goal was Desayev, the USSR keeper who was one of the best in the world. I could feel the tension but taking penalties rarely made me nervous. My kick sent Desayev the wrong way and it was enough to give us a 1–0 victory and confirm our place in the top six of the Spanish League.

It was a big goal in Sociedad's recent history. The club hadn't had much success over the years yet now they were in the UEFA Cup. There was also much personal relief. I always wanted to help pay back the £1.15 million Sociedad paid Liverpool for my services and I felt my twenty-two goals that season helped justify the fee and the generous wages. I finished the campaign among the top six scorers in the Spanish League, not far short of leader Emilio Butragueño of Real Madrid, a feat which made me proud. It also put me in good spirits for the World Cup in Italy. The Republic of Ireland had qualified with ease and were, intriguingly, placed in England's first-round group.

After Sociedad's victory over Sevilla, we showed our collective face at a party for Tony Polster, before Marco Boronat took us to a restaurant for our own celebration. There were dancing girls everywhere at Marco's favourite eating place and this made for a happy, relaxed atmosphere. At last I was able to enjoy some serious lager. Marco, a lovely man for whom I had a lot of respect, paid for everything and was anxious to make sure we had a good time. Back in San Sebastian, people were out in the streets dancing with delight. I could relate to that. It was the perfect end to an interesting season for me.

After a highly successful World Cup for Ireland, in which we reached the quarter-finals and were unfortunate not to progress further, I went home to Liverpool for two weeks to see Joan and the kids. I was tired but happy. I felt I was making a success of playing abroad and there was a pleasurable sense of anticipation as I considered the prospects for the 1990–91 season. I returned to San Sebastian alone. When I arrived I was pleased to see the club had signed Kevin Richardson, the former Everton midfielder. I had played against Kevin before and his presence was bound to be to my benefit. I was reasonably fit so missing some of the pre-season programme was no hardship. In any case, Sociedad played few friendlies. As they had no reserve team, they mainly played against each other, which was probably a mistake. It was a chance for the fringe players to show the manager what they could do but that only encouraged them to tackle the more established players with too much enthusiasm. Fouls were commonplace, as were injuries.

After losing 3–1 at Anfield against Liverpool in Kenny Dalglish's testimonial, we flew to Japan to face Brazilian giants Flamenco in a prestige friendly. I'd never been to Tokyo, so I was looking forward to the trip, but it was something of a disappointment. I didn't really think much of the city and while the Tokyo Dome stadium was impressive, the pitch was awful. It was supposed to be astro-turf but in reality it was some kind of carpet that gave you friction burns every time you fell over. Not that we made the pitch an excuse for our performance. We were well and truly hammered. The 7–1 defeat tells only part of the story. I don't recall playing in a match so one-sided. By way of consolation, the programme for the match had two pictures on the cover: one of Flamenco's top players, and one of me. I took it as a big compliment.

I emerged from the Tokyo excursion with the reputation for being a deep sleeper. When we first arrived after a tedious twelve-hour flight, I was so tired and so jetlagged I went straight to bed. The following morning, everyone was in deep conversation. The players looked as though they were arranging something and, feeling left out, I moved towards the group.

'What's up?' I asked one player in my improving Spanish.

'Don't you know?' he replied.

'Know? Know what?'

'There was an earthquake last night.'

'An earthquake?'

'Well, a kind of a tremor. The whole of Tokyo, including the hotel, was shaking. We all thought we were going to die. Why didn't you know about it?'

'I was asleep.'

'Asleep? You mean you slept through the earthquake, while the hotel shook?'

None of the lads could believe it. Just to make sure it wasn't a joke, I asked the Sociedad officials whether there had been a tremor. They said there had. My first earthquake and I missed it! But then, perhaps it would have been better if I'd slept for the whole three-day trip. I thought it was a waste of time, really. It was a long way to go for one match and I can only assume Sociedad were being handsomely paid for sending a team over to Japan. It was hot and humid when we trained and sticky even when we walked through the city centre at night. Though we acquired some top-of-the-range electrical items at cheap prices, I was glad to leave the country and get back to the simpler lifestyle on offer in Spain.

When Joan and the kids came back to join me in San Sebastian I realised all was not well. The kids had enjoyed the summer in Liverpool and were not keen on another two years away from England. I could see it on their faces. I was determined to complete my three-year contract but I was also anxious to make sure my family were happy and if something had to give, it would have to be Sociedad. The family always has to come first but under the circumstances, we agreed on a compromise. 'We'll stick it out for another season and see how it goes,' I told Joan. 'If things don't improve, we'll leave.'

We began the Spanish League season with a home game against Real Zaragoza. I scored in our 1–0 victory but didn't enjoy the match. I was man-marked by a defender who seemed to take delight in trying to hurt me. I am not even sure if trying to win the ball was his intention because every time I had possession he kicked me with relish. He hit me once too often, however, and when the ball went for a corner I turned and hit him in the face with my left elbow. Covering my elbow, which was bleeding, was an inspired move and I managed to get away with the foul. Later on, I played to win a penalty and that was how we won the game. As soon as the full-time whistle was heard, the Zaragoza players ran towards me and began making threats. Verbal threats, of course; Spanish players are usually braver with their mouths than their fists.

'We'll get you when we play the return match at our place,' one of them said, running his finger across his throat.

'Why not now, in the tunnel?' I said. 'Come on, let's sort it out now if you want.'

There were no takers. But when we played the return game at the Estadio Romareda on 27 January 1991, I found the Zaragoza players had long memories. The Sociedad defender Lumbreras used to play for Zaragoza and one day he came up to me with a message.

'If I was you, Aldo, I wouldn't go to Zaragoza,' he told me. 'They are going to have you. They want revenge.'

'OK,' I said. 'You telephone your friends and tell them the first one who gets me must kill me. Tell him to make sure I don't get up. Because if he doesn't kill me, he'll regret it. And if I don't get him back on the pitch, I'll get my revenge in the tunnel afterwards. You tell them that.'

Lumbreras was laughing but when I repeated my words he knew I was being serious. Sure enough, the defender who was on the receiving end of my elbow in the first match was man-marking me in the second. Early on, we chased a ball. I got there first and was surprised that he allowed me space to turn. I laid the ball off to a team-mate, stumbling to the floor in the process. Amazingly, this guy picked me up and started to dust me down with his hands. He even offered to shake my hand. Lumbreras had obviously relayed my message to the Zaragoza players and, more to the point, they were clearly taking my threats seriously. The episode illustrates my point about how a lot of Spanish players are good at talking but not so good when it comes to carrying out threats. I didn't score in that match but we were pleased with the 1–1 draw.

By that stage, we knew the 1990–91 season would not be as smooth as the previous one. Our UEFA Cup campaign began well enough. We were drawn to face Lausanne Sports of Switzerland and were booked into a plush hotel in a beautiful part of the country. We were 2–1 ahead when Marco brought me off and sent on a substitute. I was surprised, but that gave way to frustration when we lost the game 3–2. I had my first argument with Marco after that. I found his decision strange, as did many Spanish journalists, some of whom criticised Marco.

Dalian Atkinson, another English player, had been signed from Sheffield Wednesday by then. Basques love English football and they appreciate the unique talents of English players. They watched English first-division matches as often as they could on television and thrilled to the pace of the game. I would often go to Robinson's bar on a Monday and have a drink with friends while we watched the previous Saturday's English soccer programme. Indeed, the Basque love of the Football League is probably why Sociedad were so keen to sign me, and why Athletic Bilbao were so keen to have Howard Kendall as their manager in the late 1980s.

But Dalian Atkinson, a striker, was different in one key respect – he is black. He was certainly the first black English player at Sociedad, and probably the first black player of any kind to join the club. It didn't go down well in some quarters but Dalian had the advantage of being an exciting footballer. So whereas in the 1989–90 season I was the only Englishman at Sociedad, now there were three of us. Dalian would become my striking partner with Kevin Richardson, a former Everton player, occupying the key sitting role at the heart of the midfield.

I bounced back from the Lausanne disappointment by scoring both goals in our 2–0 league win against Logrones at home. But we followed that up with a 2–1 defeat at Oviedo. With the scores at 1–1, and half-an-hour remaining, we found ourselves in the middle of a snowstorm. I'd never seen anything like it in England. The snow was so thick you could hardly see more than a few yards in front of you. Inevitably, the referee ordered us off the field. While we were in the dressing-rooms, the fans amused themselves by throwing snowballs at each other. We emerged from a half-hour break and conceded a late goal. Interestingly, had the game been abandoned, only the remaining half-hour would have been played. Unlike the Football League in England where matches are replayed in full, Spanish League rules demand you replay only the minutes you have lost. So even if the game is abandoned after eighty-nine minutes, a team might have to return later in the season to replay the remaining minute. It doesn't matter if a thousand miles separate the teams involved, the away team has to make the journey. Fortunately, it never happened while I was in Spain. The Oviedo game was the nearest I came to it.

I managed to score our only goal in the 1–0 win against Lausanne in the return leg of our UEFA Cup tie. Though it meant the aggregate score was 3–3, we went through to the second round having scored more away goals. It was a boost and it meant the club made more money, both from ticket sales and television exposure. We were drawn at home to Partizan Belgrade, then of Yugoslavia, who gave us a difficult time. As expected, I was man-marked by a tough defender. This particular one had an evil face and a horrible manner. He spent much of the game spitting in my face and didn't seem to care how much I objected. Still, a Larranga goal gave us a 1–0 victory and hope for the second leg. We lost the return game 1–0 in Belgrade and, with the scores level on aggregate, the tie moved into a penalty shoot-out. Both Bengoechea and I missed our kicks and Sociedad lost the tie 5–4 in the shoot-out. It was a blow because we played well and deserved a place in the third round. We consoled ourselves in the duty-free shop by purchasing large bottles of quality vodka at ridiculously cheap prices.

The Belgrade defeat wasn't the only thing playing on my mind. I was also in the middle of a goal drought, the worst since my days at Newport County. I am never good company when I am not scoring goals, so Marco suggested I go home to Liverpool for a few days. In any event, I was due to join up with the Republic of Ireland squad, so I flew back to England with Kevin Richardson. The break didn't have the desired effect because in Sociedad's next match we lost 1–0 at home at neighbours Athletic Bilbao. Our supporters found that result particularly hard to take, while I was feeling the pressure of going a sixth game without a goal.

I ended the run with a goal against Osasuna but we still lost 3–1, a result that kept the pressure on the manager. Our subsequent 1–0 win against Gijon should have lightened the atmosphere at Sociedad, but Kevin Richardson, Dalian Atkinson and I saw to it that the club's problems mounted.

Joan and I had a friend called Amaia, a sixteen-year-old girl who was a great help to us in the early days. She would often babysit the kids and help ease Joan's workload. We grew close to her father, Carlos, and her mother, Lucia, and they provided much support at a time when we needed it most. Carlos was involved in a society which met every Thursday night. No women were allowed. Carlos, whose friends would bring food and beer, invited us one Thursday night. Joan was in Liverpool with the kids, while Kevin's wife was also away, so we decided to accept Carlos' well-timed invitation. There was an abundance of food and alcohol, and we were happy to take advantage. Full of good cheer, we later went into the town centre to end the evening with another intake of alcohol. I still don't know how we got home that night.

At training the next day I felt terrible. My tongue felt like Gandhi's flip-flop, while my mouth tasted worse. I tried hard to train, but couldn't. Realising I was devoid of all energy, Marco called me over and ordered me into the changing rooms.

'No, no, Marco, I don't want to let you down,' I said. 'I want to train.' But Marco knew what I knew: I was still drunk. He also knew that if word got out, the club would suffer days of unwelcome bad publicity. When journalists questioned Marco, he told them that suggestions we'd been out drinking were way off the mark. But after our 4–0 defeat against Atletico Madrid the following Sunday, the Spanish press had a field day. A lot of locals had seen us drunk and some of them contacted the newspapers. Ironically, Kevin, Dalian and I were our best players against Atletico. I saw the funny side of the whole affair, however, when a newspaper cartoon took pleasure in mocking the three of us. The downside was that Sociedad fined us £1,000 each for our misdemeanours.

The last thing I needed this time around was the two-week

Christmas break. When you are having a difficult spell, as I was at the time, you want the next match to come quickly. Going back to Liverpool for a week's holiday would have been great under normal circumstances. But these were not normal circumstances. I was feeling guilty for letting Marco down and I was anxious to bounce back, to show him how worried I was. When I did get back into action I started to score goals regularly. We drew 1–1 against Barcelona when we should have won, and drew 1–1 against Castellon. I scored against Castellon to give Sociedad a one-goal lead and had a chance virtually to secure the points with a penalty. My kick struck the crossbar before Castellon equalised in the last minute.

We were becoming unpredictable. We could perform badly against the likes of Sporting Gijon, as we did when we lost against them in the Spanish Cup, yet we could go to Real Madrid and produce superlative football to win 3–2. Nobody – not our fans, nor the press, nor our manager – knew what was coming next.

Dalian and I really hit it off against Real Madrid and scored a goal apiece. The Estadio Santiago Bernabeu is a great place to play, especially if you have managed to beat the home side. Alas, that victory wasn't enough for Marco. After our 2–1 defeat at the Estadio San Mames in Bilbao on 20 April 1991, he was relieved of his duties. I was sad to see him go. Marco took a big risk in signing me and showed great loyalty in the times I was failing to find the net. When he left the Estadio Atocha for the last time, I realised how much I respected him, and the debt I owed him. In a sense, Marco was a victim of his own success. Sociedad had done so well the season before that expectations were high. He knew this. Somebody was bound to pay if things didn't improve and Marco didn't seem surprised when the club's top brass called him in for the valedictory chat. The newspapers had been predicting his departure for some time.

Marco wasn't the only one to suffer after the Bilbao defeat. Dalian and I went to Robinson's bar in San Sebastian and found ourselves being insulted by a group of Sociedad fans. The abuse was tame but I found it significant because it was the first time any fans of the club had been negative in my presence. It hurt. But people had rightly been anticipating much from Sociedad's three English players. We had to expect a reaction when things didn't go according to plan.

It could have been different, however. Dalian began the season so well that Atletico Madrid were keen to sign him. Atletico were a big club who would pay big money. The problem was Dalian didn't have anyone to represent him or sort out his affairs.

'I don't want to use Dennis Roach because we didn't get on before,' Dalian told me. 'Will you represent me, Aldo?'

'I'll talk to them for you, Dalian,' I said, knowing full well the practice was about as acceptable as opening a brothel in a convent. We met with two officials from Atletico Madrid, who were top of the Spanish League at the time. Though my Spanish was now quite good, I insisted on an interpreter, just to make sure the Atletico officials knew exactly what Dalian was looking for.

'So what does Dalian want?' an Atletico official asked me. He looked shocked when I mentioned a figure. 'Futre's not earning that,' he said. Paolo Futre, the Portuguese international, was one of the best players in the Spanish League at that time and was reputed to be earning big money.

'Dalian is playing well with an average team and scoring goals,' I said. 'With a good team such as yourselves he will be even better. He will score more goals. I think Dalian should be on the same money as Futre.'

'No, no, you must come down a bit.'

Atletico mentioned a figure and I turned to Dalian for his response. He raised his eyebrows, which suggested he was happy for me to proceed. When Dalian realised Atletico were interested in paying him a decent wage, and were offering a house, he tried to push the issue further.

'Tell them I want a car,' he told me. 'And tell them I want the car bought in Spain but driven home to my house in England.' I turned to the Atletico officials.

'Dalian would like a car.'

'What kind of car?' I turned to Dalian.

'What kind of car, Dalian?'

'A Testarossa.' I turned to the Atletico officials.

'Dalian wants a Testarossa.'

It turned out that the cheapest Testarossa would cost Atletico around £75,000. I couldn't believe Dalian had the nerve to ask for it, but he was such a unique character that he was capable of anything. Atletico agreed to think about Dalian's demands. They said they would contact us for another meeting but they never did. Dalian hit a poor run of form soon after and the Madrid club must have gone off the idea. But for a time it looked as though Dalian was about to sign the deal of his life. At times that season, Dalian's manner and humour kept me sane. I enjoyed his company immensely.

His failure to maintain his early season form hardly helped Sociedad's cause. Marco's replacement was John Toshack, though not immediately. Spanish League rules don't allow a club to change its manager mid-season, so though John was in charge of team affairs along with Javier Hasposa, it was on a strictly unofficial basis. John's arrival must have been the change we needed because we remained undefeated in our final six matches.

Our hopes of finishing high enough for another UEFA Cup place had died long before that, but we did have a small say in where the Spanish championship went. We faced Atletico Madrid at home on 12 May knowing a victory would make Barcelona champions. With the scores at 1–1, I secured the points for Sociedad with a header in the seventy-fifth minute, thus denying Atletico the title. In years to come, I can tell my grandchildren that I scored the goal that clinched the Spanish title for Barcelona.

Luckily for me, we played Barcelona at the Nou Camp the following week. When we arrived, Barca fans were approaching me with smiling faces, thanking me for helping them win the championship. Barca received their trophy in front of 120,000 delirious fans before the kick-off. The atmosphere was electrifying and just to our liking. We had no intention of allowing Barca to celebrate in style. We won 3–1, with Dalian and me again forging a fine partnership. I created one goal for Dalian, he created two for me. In six games against Barcelona I had scored eight goals, six of them in the Nou Camp. It meant I had scored forty goals in two seasons for Sociedad. We went out with some of the Barca players in the city centre that night and lapped up the glory as if we had won the championship.

But even before that, I knew I would not be seeing out the rest of my contract at Real Sociedad. I was due to stay until the end of the 1991–92 season but there was little hope of that. My family were too unsettled. The final confirmation came in the spring of 1991 when I dropped my daughter, Joanne, off at school. As I didn't take her to school very often I decided to hang around and make sure she was all right. I was on the other side of the school railings when I saw a group of girls circle her and start singing: 'Joanne is stupid, Joanne is stupid'. It was a red rag to a bull. I ran into the school and complained to the head teacher. When I got to training later that morning, I asked to speak with John Toshack.

'Tosh,' I said, 'I am not having my daughter upset like that again. We're too unsettled as a family. It's not going to work. I want to leave Spain. You can't stop me. I've got to go for the sake of my kids.'

John wasn't happy. He had already been told Kevin Richardson and Dalian Atkinson were leaving, though Dalian's impending departure was to be expected. He never really liked John Toshack and the feeling was mutual. I once had to stop Dalian and John having a go at each other. It was a shame because when John came to Sociedad – he was relieved of his duties by Real Madrid early in 1991 – he took Kevin, Dalian and me out for a meal and had the best of intentions. It was sad things didn't work out. The manager was keen to do a good job and get on with all his players. With that in mind, he changed training for a time. Concerned at Sociedad's lack of movement off the ball in matches, he once got us to train as if we were a rugby team. In rugby it is essential your movement off the ball is good. Our six-game unbeaten end to the season suggested John's tactics had worked.

But I wasn't staying around for another season to find out if the improvement would work over a longer period. John informed Luis Arconada, the man who was now presiding over Real Sociedad, of my desire to leave the club. Luis had been a long-serving goalkeeper for Spain but I found him less impressive as a club official. He and I had a big argument when I told him I wanted to leave Sociedad. Only the fact that we were responsible adults stopped us from coming to blows. Though I found Luis narrow-minded, I suppose I had to see his side of the story. I was second leading scorer for the second successive season in Spain and I sensed the crowd were in favour of keeping me at all costs. But Sociedad had to see it from my side. The family is a priority and the moment I realised my kids were unsettled, there was no contest. I was leaving – end of story.

Three days after that argument, Luis took me for lunch in a bid to change my mind. The food was nice and Luis was better company than expected, but as we shook hands to bring the afternoon to a conclusion, he realised I would not be staying on for another season.

Our final game of the campaign was at home to RDC Mallorca and a victory for Sociedad would ensure Español avoided relegation. A couple of days before the game, one of my team-mates told me we would be offered money to win the match. 'Never,' I said. But sure enough, somebody claiming to be from Español contacted a Sociedad player and said there would be a considerable sum of money available for the rest of us if we won the match. The money was around £4,000 per man, tax free. We drew the game 0–0 but twice when I was fouled the referee refused to give Sociedad a penalty. It led to rumours that the referee had been paid by Mallorca. The draw meant Español were relegated; Mallorca survived.

Tranmere Rovers chairman Peter Johnson and his manager, John King, were at the Estadio Atocha to watch me that day. They had heard I was unsettled in Spain and were keen to bring me back to Merseyside. Graham Beacroft, the soccer commentator for Radio City in Liverpool, had been in touch with me, as had the Liverpool *Daily Post* and *Echo*. They were keen to relay the story of my growing disillusionment. Once the story had been revealed, Tranmere stepped in. Leeds United manager Howard Wilkinson was also believed to be interested. He had even seen me score the two goals in Barcelona, which should have been in my favour. But for reasons best known to himself, Howard did not pursue the matter. John Toshack was hoping Leeds would sign me because they would have paid Sociedad £400,000. Tranmere, then on the verge of promotion to the second division, had already made it clear they would pay only £250,000, which was an enormous amount of money for them.

Looking back, I am glad Leeds backed out of a possible deal. For sure, it would have been nice to have gone back to the top flight in England, and Leeds have always been a big club with good support. But I'd put my family through too much by moving to Spain. They deserved the chance to go back home to Merseyside. Tranmere seemed attractive for that reason. It meant we could go back to our home in Calderstones without the need to look for alternative accommodation.

My last game for Sociedad was a charity match against Real Madrid and I knew afterwards I would be seeing most of my team-mates for the last time. They could see it in my face. I was becoming emotional as the lads, one by one, approached me to say goodbye. I told some of the players that I was keen to see out my three-year contract but that family matters were far more important. The players I think respected me for that. Football's importance only goes so far. Having kids taught me that, and events at Hillsborough in 1989 confirmed it.

When Tranmere did make an official bid for me, Sociedad seemed determined to make life difficult for the tiny Merseyside club. I was back in Liverpool by then but John Toshack was anxious to make sure I returned for the start of the 1991–92 season. When a Tranmere official went to San Sebastian to push the deal through, he came back to say he had been treated badly. That surprised me because the Sociedad officials were efficient and fair in their previous dealings with me. To his credit, John

Toshack said he appreciated my dilemma. I heard later that he even tried to resign in response to Sociedad's refusal to sell me.

When John King's £250,000 bid for me was accepted, John Toshack told me to sign for Tranmere. The problem was the Sociedad secretary telephoned me to say: 'If you sign for Tranmere we want you to pay us compensation. If you don't see your contract through, you must pay us.' Sociedad wanted £25,000.

'No way,' I said. 'You've had your money's worth out of me.'

The secretary continued to demand money so I decided to add a new twist to the plot. Contractually, Sociedad were due to pay me £75,000 the following September so I used that as my trump card.

'OK, I'll stay at Sociedad,' I said. 'But I want my £75,000 in September. I will stay in Spain but I won't score for you. I'll go through the motions in training. I'll stay throughout the season and potter around.' I was bluffing him, of course. My pride would not have let me give anything less than a hundred per cent effort. But I reckoned this was the best way to handle the situation. Again, John Toshack telephoned me.

'Just sign for Tranmere and I'll sort things out this end,' he said. 'Don't worry about anything, Aldo.'

The whole affair soured my relations with Sociedad but increased my respect for John Toshack. I didn't want to fall out with anyone in San Sebastian, but I felt I'd been badly treated. The club seemed to be playing games with my career and John was reluctantly caught in the middle of it.

But if I was upset with the club, the opposite was the case where the people of San Sebastian were concerned. They were great to me. I didn't meet many bad people there. I made a host of friends, some of whom I still see. I miss the players, too, which is a testimony to how well things went for me. I was particularly sad when I said goodbye to Alaba, who had done much to make life easier for me. Without him, I might have left San Sebastian earlier than I did.

I scored forty goals in seventy-five matches for Real Sociedad, something which made my career in Spain a successful one. I believe I more than repaid the £1.15 million the club shelled out for my services, and that gives me more pleasure than I can express.

Alas, I haven't been back to San Sebastian since I left in 1991. My schedule since then has given me little time to contemplate a holiday there. But I will go back to meet up with my old Spanish friends, shake their hands, buy them all a drink and talk about the good old days. I am reliably told that, after eight years away, football fans in San Sebastian still remember me. Compliments don't come much higher than that.

— 7 —

THE TEAM THAT
JACK BUILT

A MONG my proudest possessions is a small book which is of little monetary value. Worn out due to overuse, its very existence has enabled me to fulfil a number of lifetime ambitions. It is my Republic of Ireland passport and it means everything to me. Having spent the last twelve years defending my right to represent Ireland at football, I have become immune to criticism. My family and closest friends know how much Ireland and the Irish people are in my affections. That is the real truth. I have no time for those people who say I only played for Ireland for the money. When I was first asked to play for Ireland in 1986, money was the last thing on my mind. It was a welcome bonus, nothing more. But my connections with Ireland begin way before 1986.

My great-grandmother, Mary Mills, was born in Athlone in the last century. Like a lot of Irish folk, Mary moved to England and put down roots in Liverpool, starting a family and becoming an integral part of the community. With the docks providing much work for a growing population, Liverpool was a pleasant place to live between the wars. Mary gave birth to Sally, my grandmother, who in turn gave birth to Elizabeth, my mother. Better known as Betty, my mother was born in Liverpool in 1930 and grew up in a family which enjoyed the Irish culture. The McNamaras would often have parties that ended with Irish sing-alongs. The parties were still going on when I was old enough to enjoy them. It was entertaining stuff. And whenever

Ireland played football, we always wanted them to win, even if they did underachieve badly at international level.

So when it was suggested I might like to play football for Ireland, I was naturally pleased. I was an Oxford United player at the time and Dublin-born David Langan, my team-mate at the Manor Ground, thought it might be an idea if I investigated football's ancestry rules. It was always at the back of my mind that I might be eligible but you don't push these things too hard. Deep down, however, I hoped things would work out in my favour. Much to my delight, the rules clearly stated that a player could inherit the nationality of his great-grandparents, which meant I could play for Ireland.

It is one thing being eligible and another being selected. Fortunately, David Langan was an Irish international at that time and particularly friendly with the manager, Eoin Hand. In late 1985, Eoin contacted me through Dave to say he wanted to integrate me into his squad. I would have won my first international cap under Eion had he not left his post with the Football Association of Ireland. Eion's departure could have been a blow to my hopes, but fortunately Jack Charlton had much the same opinion of me when he took over as manager six months later. Jack came to watch me play for Oxford against Aston Villa in the Milk Cup semi-final at Villa Park early in 1986. Both Ray Houghton and I had impressive games for Oxford which helped secure a good result. Happy with what he saw, Jack approached me in the players' lounge after the match.

'How do you fancy playing for Ireland?' Jack asked me.

'I'd love to, Jack,' I said. 'By the way, you know about Ray Houghton, don't you?'

'No.'

'He's more Irish than I am. His parents are from Donegal.'

'Is that right?'

In one memorable evening, Jack Charlton acquired the services of us both. In later years, Jack was quoted as saying: 'That night, getting Aldo and Ray, was the best bit of business I've done.'

Prior to the friendly against Wales at Lansdowne Road on 26 March 1986, I flew from Birmingham to Dublin to meet up with the Irish players. I wasn't prepared for the prospect of snow on the ground in Dublin; neither was I prepared for the prospect of getting lost. I was told to go to a large hotel outside the airport. Though there was nobody there to meet me, I didn't expect it to be a problem finding the hotel. I didn't even ask one of the multitude of taxi drivers who had congregated outside the airport. I saw a giant grey building which looked like a hotel and made my way towards it. As I got closer, I realised it was not a hotel but the Aer Lingus offices. There was another building half a mile away and this thankfully was the right place.

On entering the hotel, I met Mick Byrne, the Ireland physiotherapist, who was most welcoming. Kevin Moran sought me out and put his long right arm around me. 'Welcome to Dublin, John,' he said, proving to me how nice a guy he really is. I felt most at home when Ray Houghton arrived, but I was back on edge when I discovered the identity of my room-mate. Liam Brady was the finest player in Ireland's history at the time and a charismatic figure. He was the star; I was the new boy. The thought of sharing a room with him unnerved me a little. As he was playing in Italy at that time, Liam was not due to arrive in Dublin until later that evening. The wait increased my anxiety, though in reality Liam was good company. We spent a lot of the night talking about our contrasting fortunes in football.

The following day, we had a training session on a pitch just across the road from the airport. In truth, the facilities were appalling and perhaps summed up the financial plight of the FAI at that time. Lansdowne Road was hardly better – a grey, dreary stadium with a leaky roof.

'This is international football?' Ray Houghton said to me as we surveyed the depressing scene. Worse still, the pitch was terrible. Lansdowne Road was home to the Irish rugby union team and the surface was hardly better than a ploughed field.

The pre-match preparations were relaxed enough and even Jack looked as though he was enjoying himself. He pulled us all to one side and told us how he wanted Irish teams of the future to play. The emphasis was on playing only in the final third of the field. Playing the ball across the back four or across the midfield was frowned upon. There would be a runner up front to take advantage of the fact that most international teams lacked width at the back. The reasoning was that most teams were better than Ireland. Our only hope was to stick to a defined system. The running man in attack was to be a key position in Jack's team; it was the position to which I was assigned.

Though we outplayed Wales, we lost 1–0. It was a freak result, really. Our system allowed the Welsh few opportunities yet they scored a goal through Ian Rush. We failed to convert any of our chances. Jack wasn't too displeased, however. 'We'll get it right once we play together more,' he said. We knew he was right.

Significantly, the Lansdowne Road pitch came in for criticism when Neville Southall, the Wales and Everton goalkeeper, challenged me for a corner and fell awkwardly. He broke his ankle and missed the rest of the season. In his absence, Everton lost both the first-division championship and the FA Cup to Liverpool, while Jack used the incident as an excuse to complain about the state of the pitch.

Our next game was in Dublin against Uruguay, who were bound for the World Cup in Mexico that summer. With more or less the same team and the same tactics, we showed improvement to draw 1–1. Our goal, a Gerry Daly penalty, came after I was punched in the face by a defender inside the penalty area. The Uruguayan should have been sent off. Like many of his team-mates, he spent a lot of his time spitting at us and nudging us off the ball. It was an education, however, and the result had shown we were heading in the right direction. Ray and I earned rave reviews for our performances and one Irish journalist suggested the two of us were 'here to stay', a statement I found pleasing.

I was enjoying my early tastes of international football. Ray and I were away training with Oxford United in Orlando when we were called up to the squad for a three-team international tournament in Iceland. Robert Maxwell, the Oxford chairman, had arranged for the players and their wives to go to the USA for an end-of-season break. Neither Joan nor Brenda, Ray's wife, were happy when we left them in Orlando and flew to Reykjavic via London and Glasgow. But we had no intention of missing the games against Iceland and Czechoslovakia, which endeared us to Jack. The same could not be said of David O'Leary and Kevin Sheedy. Neither player turned up and Jack went berserk. He had agreed to take part in the tournament to help the players get used to his system, yet two key men were missing; not that it mattered in the end. Victories against the host nation (2–1) and Czechoslovakia (1–0) ensured we won the tournament. Ireland had never won anything at football so, although this was hardly the World Cup, it was a boost; a warm-up to greater success.

I didn't play well against Iceland and after that, even though it was only my third cap, I began worrying about my lack of goals at international level. My role was different, of course. As the runner in Jack's system, I was never going to get as many scoring opportunities as, say, Frank Stapleton. But no matter what the system, a striker is never fully happy unless he is scoring. I missed a straightforward chance to score against Czechoslovakia. Long after my striking partner Mick Kennedy had elbowed a Czech in the face, knocking two teeth out, I earned a penalty. I struck the ball confidently only to look on in despair as the goalkeeper saved it. Frank Stapleton eventually scored to give us the victory, by which time the otherwise likeable Mick Kennedy had been substituted for his misdemeanour.

To celebrate winning the trophy, the Irish lads went out for a drink in the centre of Reykjavic. We had been told Icelandic people couldn't take their drink, which perhaps explained some strange behaviour in one pub. Paul McGrath, for example, ended up in a difficult situation. A local guy seemed to be constantly looking at him. I didn't know if it was because Paul was black, for there were few black people in Iceland. It got worse, however, because the Icelandic man, who, like all his countrymen, was blond, started shouting things at Paul. Never one to accept abuse, especially under these circumstances, Paul approached the offensive character who promptly ran away. I can't recall seeing Paul so livid. Being built like a brick wall, he is not a man with whom you want to argue. Having him in your side was a different matter and I often wonder what Ireland would have achieved without him.

There was an ironic sequel to that tournament in Iceland. Kevin Sheedy ended his Ireland career later with forty-seven international caps. Had he played in those two matches and maybe picked up another cap along the way, he would have qualified for a testimonial. You need ten years' service or fifty caps to get a testimonial with Ireland. Kevin failed narrowly on both counts.

Jack felt we were making progress. Two victories, a draw and a defeat was a useful return from four matches. We felt confident going into our first European Championship qualifying match against Belgium in Brussels on 10 September 1986. We played at the Heysel Stadium which was the scene of thirty-nine deaths prior to the Liverpool–Juventus European Cup final of May 1985. It didn't look as though things had improved around the stadium. It was a bit of a hole, to be honest, and with its crumbling walls certainly not an appropriate venue for an international match. By contrast, the pitch was magnificent – and so too was our 2–2 draw. Belgium had some good players, not least Enzo Scifo, who scored one of their goals, but our system worked well. Trailing 2–1 with a minute remaining, Liam Brady kept his composure to equalise from the penalty spot. Psychologically, it was a good result. Belgium had won the bronze medal for finishing in third place in the World Cup ten weeks before and were hot favourites to qualify from a group that also contained Scotland, Bulgaria and Luxembourg.

It was back to Lansdowne Road for a qualifier against Scotland and this gave me the chance to play against Alan Hansen, the Liverpool defender. The subsequent goalless draw was probably better for Scotland but the feeling in Ireland was that two points from two tough games was a healthy return.

We flew to Warsaw a month later for a friendly against Poland. Ireland always played Poland. I understand the nations are friends in footballing circles, but perhaps the Poles took this a bit too far when we arrived at our hotel in the city centre. Within minutes of opening my bedroom door, the telephone rang. On the other end of the line was a lady who seemed keen to meet me in person. I wouldn't have considered it under any circumstances, but her appeal diminished further when I discovered she was a prostitute. I wasn't the only player to receive such attention. It turned out that prostitutes were swarming around the building. We kept well away, of course, but it was a reminder of how being an international footballer was providing a new set of problems. Playing for Oxford United didn't attract call-girls.

Like all football teams, we had the card schools. But for me, this was on a higher level, for more money. In Poland, I was playing against Niall Quinn, Mick Kennedy, Liam Brady and Kevin Moran. I remember being £100 down playing shoot, which is a subtle variation on pontoon, where you try to get closest to twenty-one. There would be money in a kitty and the players have to beat the banker. A draw wasn't enough; you had to beat him. One by one, as the banker, I beat my four opponents to secure £100 in the kitty. It meant I was quits. I went round again, firstly beating Niall who put his £50 in the kitty, then Kevin who put his £30 in the kitty to make it £180. Liam agreed to bet me £80, which meant I would be quits if I lost or have £260 in the kitty if I won. Incredibly, I won. It was Mick's turn next, and he offered to shoot me for the full £260. Convinced he had good cards, I turned my cards over with a look of trepidation. I had an ace and a two for a total of three or thirteen. I took another card which was a five for a total of eight or eighteen. I didn't want to stick on that so I took another card. It was a four, which meant my total was twelve. My best hope was for a five-card trick which guaranteed victory. I turned another card over, which was a seven, leaving me with a total of nineteen with five cards. I'd won, no matter what Mick had. I asked him to turn over his cards. He had fifteen. He'd been bluffing me.

Mick had no money so he offered to send me a cheque. 'No problem,' I said as I picked up the £260 from the kitty. A week or so later, a cheque for £260 arrived through the post. I'd won £520 which, at the time, was nearly a week's wages. As time went on, and Ireland became more successful, the card schools involved much more money. During one tournament I remember losing £2,000 and during another I won around the same amount. Ever since that trip to Warsaw I got a buzz playing cards for money, even if the games were always friendly.

Our 1–0 defeat in Poland was a minor inconvenience, while my failure to score meant I'd drawn a blank in each of my seven matches for Ireland. It was the same story when we played Scotland in a Euro '88 qualifier at Hampden Park on 18 February 1987. Still no international goals. But more importantly, we won 1–0, and what a victory it was. The performance from Ireland was professional and composed and, had the margin of victory been greater, the Scots could not have complained. Mark Lawrenson, who was by then a team-mate with Liverpool as well as Ireland, scored the goal after I laid the ball through to him. I would have preferred it if the roles had been reversed.

My lack of international goals was becoming a mental barrier, even if I did avoid criticism. The Dublin press overlooked my drought, preferring instead to eulogise Ireland's improvement since Jack became manager. Jack himself was supportive of me. He had asked me to do a specific role and, in his opinion (and that was the one that mattered most), I was making a success of it. One journalist plucked up the courage to ask Jack about my Irish scoring record. 'John is doing what I am asking him to do,' Jack said. 'Whether he scores or not, we're being successful.' The problem was I was doing so much running that by the time a scoring opportunity came my way, I was usually too tired to do anything with it. At the time, I remember complaining that all the chasing around would one day wear my legs down to stumps. The irony was that I felt I was playing some of my best football in an Ireland shirt. I added a new dimension to my game, that of creator, something I'd rarely done before.

Losing 2–1 in Sofia against Bulgaria on April Fools' Day 1987 damaged our hopes of qualifying for Euro '88. It was another good Irish display but this time I felt we were let down by the referee, who didn't seem to be acquainted with the laws of the game. He had a poor game and seemed happy to allow the Bulgarians to get away with some liberal interpretations of the rules. Like the Uruguayans, the Bulgarians seemed to take delight in their ability to spit accurately at us. But we consoled ourselves with the knowledge that Bulgaria would be coming to Dublin for the return game later in the year. We wanted revenge. The defeat in Sofia was followed by a hard-earned goalless draw against Belgium at Lansdowne Road.

This was round about the time David Langan's international career was drawing to a close. David was one of the nicest men I've met, so kind, so inoffensive, with a soft Dublin accent that made conversing with him such a pleasure. He had given Ireland much service and deserves to be highly regarded in the nation's footballing history. David hated flying to away matches and, because of that, he would often be drunk out of his brains when we landed at a foreign venue. Drinking alcohol, he said, was his way of dealing with the fear of being on an aeroplane. A bad back injury forced him to retire from football prematurely, which was sad. He missed out on making some big money with Ireland and is now earning his living as a security guard.

David deserved to be around for games against the likes of Brazil, whom we faced in Dublin that May. Brazil were a tremendous side with skill that took your breath away. Our system made it difficult for them, however, and one of their few chances came when I sliced an attempted back-pass to goalkeeper Pat Bonner. The ball instead fell neatly into the path of Mirandinha, a talented player who would later join Newcastle United. Mirandinha would have scored had Pat not made a fine save. 'You got me out of jail there, Pat,' I said to him afterwards. But within minutes of Pat making that save, I was given a chance to score. Confronted with the seemingly simple task of putting the ball into the goal, the Brazilian keeper blocked the ball with his legs. It was a good save and still I hadn't scored for Ireland. If it was any consolation, I did swap shirts with a Brazilian defender, though don't ask me who it was. I haven't got a clue. Midfield player Dunga, who would captain Brazil to World Cup success in 1994, refused to swap shirts with anyone. Perhaps he couldn't accept that Ireland, a nation that had never qualified for the World Cup, had beaten them 1–0.

We had a great weekend of celebration after that. One afternoon, while the pub was officially closed, there was a band playing for our entertainment as we continued to order drinks. It went strangely quiet for a time until Ray Houghton picked up the microphone and began to sing a medley of Frank Sinatra songs. While the band played, Ray cut a comical figure singing American songs in an Irish pub with a Scottish accent.

After that weekend, we headed for Luxembourg, and it was there I thought I'd scored my first goal for Ireland. As the ball was flighted over from the wing, I seemed to time my run to perfection and, after heading the ball into the goal, ran enthusiastically to the Ireland supporters to celebrate. Though delighted, I wondered why none of the other Ireland players had come to celebrate with me. I turned and found that the game was still going on. To my disappointment, the goal had been disallowed for offside. Not in a million years was it offside but I had to accept the referee's decision. I must have looked the biggest idiot in Dublin as I celebrated alone. I took my frustration out on a defender who had been giving me a tough time. I took some stick from the rest of the Irish players for that incident. Worse still, after twelve games I still hadn't scored for Ireland, though our 2–0 victory at least kept alive our hopes of qualifying for Euro '88. Playing against the likes of Luxembourg is never as easy as it looks. These teams know how to stop you playing and know how to defend.

Being the last game of the 1986–87 season, we went out afterwards. We ended up in a club where they didn't accept cash. Instead they gave you a ticket in which they punched a hole with a machine every time you ordered a drink. Throughout the evening, however, there was no way of telling how much you had spent. When the bill came, some players owed more money than they had in their pockets while others had more cash than they needed. So we ended the night huddled around a table, swapping money, making sure those who were short could leave the club with a clear conscience.

On the flight back to Dublin, we'd heard the Irish press had criticised our display in Luxembourg. One journalist said the margin of victory was inadequate. Liam Brady was incensed.

'Not good enough?' he roared to the stunned media men on the aeroplane. 'A 2–0 victory and you don't think it's good enough. Look at the qualifying table. Look at how well we've done.' That was the first time I'd known the Irish press to criticise the team. And as they were in awe of Liam, they thought better than to criticise us again.

The return game with Bulgaria, on 14 October 1987, was eagerly awaited. The Bulgarians had treated us badly in Sofia the previous April and we were anxious for revenge. The 2–0 victory was sweet and certainly no less than we deserved. We outplayed the Eastern European team from start to finish, picking up another useful two points. We didn't have to lower ourselves to their levels of gamesmanship; better to win the match by playing good football, something we'd done with ease. But it was another blank day for me. Thirteen games for Ireland, still no goals.

There was, by this stage, increasing speculation that my place in Jack's team was in jeopardy. Walsall striker David Kelly was rumoured to be the man to take my place in the team. Before our scheduled game against Israel the following month, Jack approached me and said: 'Aldo, they say you are not going to play. What do you think?' I was baffled and thought it a strange way to behave. When Jack named the team on the coach prior to the match in Dublin, I was shocked to find I had been omitted to accommodate David. Jack was always keen to tell players why they were not in the team and, inevitably, he came to sit next to me.

'Aldo,' he said, 'you are not playing because you are dropped.'

Ireland won the game 4–0 at Dalymount Park and David scored a hat-trick. Israel were poor. I spent the entire ninety minutes simmering with anger on the substitutes' bench. Though pleased for David, I was able to appreciate the irony. He had scored three goals in one match for Ireland, I had scored none in thirteen. Yes, I felt threatened. My only consolation was that

Frank Stapleton's international future was constantly in doubt. Although he was still good for a few goals, he was, at 31, considered too old by many people. There were times when it looked as though he might not play again for his country. Had I been playing for England, one thing is certain: there is no way I'd have lasted thirteen games without a goal. I would probably have been dumped after about seven or eight matches.

The following day, 12 November, was a momentous one for Ireland. Though we were without a game, we knew that if Scotland could win in Bulgaria our place in Euro '88 would be secure. Any other result and we were out. I didn't hold out much hope for Scotland, to be honest, and I remember watching England's qualifying match in Yugoslavia and marvelling at the 4–1 win for Bobby Robson's men. Ray Houghton and I were telephoning each other regularly to find out how Scotland were getting on. So imagine my surprise when Ray told me Scotland had won 1–0 thanks to a Gary Mackay goal. Amazingly, Ireland were in the European Championship finals for the first time. 'You can't trust the Scots,' Jack said afterwards. 'And I mean that in the nicest possible way.' I should have been happier than I was but Jack's behaviour the previous day had left me confused and bewildered. Unable to sit still, I sought the best form of therapy: I pulled on my tracksuit and went for a run.

With hindsight, our qualification should never have been in doubt. We were the best team in the group. We played the best football. We didn't deserve to lose in Sofia to Bulgaria, and really the outcome should have been in our own hands. Though grateful to Scotland for helping us, we should have had our qualification sewn up long before then. Still, it meant we could look forward to the tournament in West Germany to see how far we had progressed in two years. We were drawn to face England, Holland and the USSR. It was a tough draw but they were all tough draws. Our refuge was the hope that our system and never-say-die attitude would make life difficult for our more celebrated opponents.

The 1987–88 season ended on a mixed note for me. Liverpool were crowned first-division champions but then we contrived to lose the FA Cup final against Wimbledon. My penalty miss at Wembley haunted me for a time and I welcomed the diversion that Euro '88 would provide. My only fear was that if Ireland won a penalty, I might not have the mental strength or confidence to take it.

In the run-up to Euro '88, Ireland hit good form. We were devastating against Poland in a friendly match in Dublin on 22 May. The 3–1 scoreline failed to do our performance justice. As in Luxembourg, I thought I'd scored only for the referee to disallow it. Fourteen appearances, still no goals for Ireland.

We were back in Dublin for a behind-closed-doors friendly against an amateur team from Cork. We won 5–2 and I managed to score twice. Although the goals didn't officially count, they were ones that gave me much relief. I might have scored a hat-trick had I not missed a penalty. To my embarrassment, the Cork goalkeeper pushed my kick aside, and the Liverpool players in the Irish squad – Ray Houghton and Ronnie Whelan – spent the rest of the day taking the mickey out of me. It was only two weeks after the embarrassment at Wembley.

Our pre-tournament preparations went well. Aware we were already fit, Jack didn't overtrain us. In fact, he was anxious to make sure we relaxed as often as possible. On a number of occasions he had to shout at players to stop them doing too much exercise. I was jogging one morning and Jack came storming towards me.

'What do you think you're doing, Aldo? Stop running.'

But still I couldn't score for Ireland. We drew 0–0 with Norway in Oslo on 1 June. Fifteen appearances, no goals.

The night before the Norway game, Jack had injured his calf and agreed to let his assistant, Maurice Setters, take training. 'Do what you want with them,' Jack told Maurice. So Maurice arranged a game of keep-ball. The lads were stroking the ball around when Jack, noticing what was going on, shouted over: 'What are you doing, Maurice? You're teaching them bad habits. We stick to a system here. And keeping the ball is not our system.' Jack cut a comical figure. He was wearing a tracksuit but had smart shoes on his feet. He often trained like that. He didn't care how he looked. But that particular incident surprised us because Jack and Maurice were great friends. It was the only time I recall them falling out.

Jack wanted the Ireland players to have a similar bond. That was why he encouraged us to enjoy ourselves. It was common for him to let us go out drinking without stipulating what time we were to be back. So long as we were up for training the next day, he didn't seem to care. He felt it was good for morale for us to be out together. A lot of managers might frown upon that kind of behaviour but, in our defence, I tell people to take a look at our results. Going out never did us any harm. Quite the reverse, in fact. I believe it helped us become close as a squad.

Our days together in Finniston House, a lovely hotel on the outskirts of Dublin, ensured we would be in the right frame of mind for the forthcoming tournament. I even went fly fishing with Jack. We agreed to have a competition to see who could catch the most trout. After a time, I had eight fish but Jack only had five.

'This is too easy,' he said. 'I'm going around the corner.' So Jack left me alone for a time. I ended up catching thirteen and put them in my keepnet. Jack came back to join me and I asked him how he'd got on.

'Oh, I caught loads,' he said. 'But I put them all back.' That was typical Jack. He never liked losing. On our way back to Finniston House, he bought me some fish and chips. I was taken aback. Jack never usually bought me a pint, yet here he was buying me food. I couldn't believe it. Later that night, we cooked the trout and passed them around the squad.

We arrived in West Germany for Euro '88 on 7 June and immediately went clay-pigeon shooting. Though I had never done it before, I was pleased to hit eight out of ten to draw with Jack, who is very good at it. That was a welcome diversion. Once at our base in Germany, we could feel a little of the tension. The Irish media were there, of course, but so too were the English media. This was all new to me. Though I was a Liverpool player, I had never before been involved with this kind of hype. It was almost a relief when our opening match with England kicked off.

Ireland played England in Stuttgart on 12 June. Early on, we sensed England were nervous and it was no surprise to me when we scored inside the opening eight minutes. Kenny Sansom, the England full-back, sliced his clearance and I headed the ball towards Ray Houghton who in turn headed it over Peter Shilton and into the goal. It was a dream start but there was a fear that we'd scored too early. England came at us after that and only poor finishing – Gary Lineker missed three great chances – and some great goalkeeping by Pat Bonner preserved our lead. England were clearly below par. John Barnes, who was by then my Liverpool team-mate, seemed jaded, as did Peter Beardsley; and England's tactics left a lot to be desired. But when the final whistle heralded a memorable victory for Ireland, I immediately thought of Jack's pre-match words. 'They are no different from you,' he had told us. And we proved him right. My other memories were of the Irish support, which was incredible, and the weather, which was much hotter than it looked. I was knackered by the end of the match. We had a great celebration afterwards. We all had to sing a song – my number was 'Liverpool Lou' – and the good cheer flowed as freely as the champagne. On this occasion, Jack wisely insisted we be in bed by midnight.

The following day, we travelled to Hanover to prepare for our match against the USSR. Jack wanted us to relax and he arranged for us to stay in a complex which had all the top facilities. When we got there, however, we realised there was something amiss. I was swimming in the pool when two naked old men jumped in near to me. I was out so quickly, my trunks had barely got wet. A few of us went into a sauna only to be confronted by the sight of an old man and his wife sitting there stark naked. We didn't know what to do. Then we realised we were in a naturist camp. Jack didn't see the funny side of it. He realised, rightly, that if a photographer managed to get film of us in this camp, the story could be turned into something far worse. We were ordered out of the camp and told by Jack that it was out of bounds.

We faced the USSR three days after the victory against England and turned in an even better display. Jack had considered changing our tactics but realised the USSR would probably be fearing Ireland. 'Let them worry about us,' Jack said. We scored an early goal when Ronnie Whelan volleyed the ball into the goal from the edge of the penalty area, and we didn't look like losing. I had a chance effectively to secure the two points when Tony Galvin placed the ball accurately into my path, but my shot was too fierce. The ball flew over the crossbar when a more subtle approach might have brought greater dividends. Nine times out of ten I would have scored from this chance. The USSR were always a threat and they duly equalised with an excellent goal. At the end of the match we were deflated. We might have accepted a point before the match but having played so well, we considered this to be one point dropped rather than one point gained. After the game I was selected for the random drugs test. I was so dehydrated, it took me two hours to pass water.

England lost 3–1 to Holland on the same day which effectively meant they were knocked out. It was a surprise to me because Bobby Robson's men were among the pre-tournament favourites. They had in John Barnes one of the best players in Europe, but when it mattered most, England defended badly and failed to score goals. I later found out that the England players were overtrained and hadn't been allowed to drink. By contrast, Ireland were doing little training and were allowed, encouraged even, to unwind with a few lagers.

We moved to Gelsenkirchen for the crucial match against Holland on 18 June. A draw or better and we were in the semi-final. Defeat and we were knocked out. It was as simple as that. Holland had some players of genuine quality and were emerging from a ten-year period of decline. We had a chance early on when Paul McGrath's header somehow got stuck between the goalkeeper and his post. As I tried to get a toe to the ball, a defender held me off. A goal then and we would surely have got the draw we needed. Alas, we conceded a bizarre goal with seven minutes remaining and lost 1–0, a result which put us out. Television footage suggests the Dutch goal was offside and should not have counted. I am inclined to that view. It was a real sickener for us because, after picking up three points out of four, we felt we had done the hard part and were capable of winning the tournament. 'They had Gullit, Van Basten and they still couldn't hurt us,' Jack said in the dressing-room afterwards.

Kevin Moran arranged a big party in our hotel that night. It was a typical Irish night out: plenty of drink, music and camaraderie. When Ray Houghton and I woke up the following morning, there were ten Irish supporters asleep on our hotel room floor. We didn't know how they got there. That, for me, summed up the relationship between the Irish team and its fans.

Holland went on to beat the USSR 2–0 in the final in Munich, which illustrated how well we'd done. Ireland had given both teams their toughest test in the tournament and, even if we didn't progress, we did enough to suggest we had real international pedigree. That tournament was a watershed in Irish football history.

We flew home the following day to a civic reception in Dublin. As we began our descent, we could see thousands of people congregating in the city centre, waiting to welcome us home. It is one of my most cherished moments. To see how much our efforts meant to them will live long in the memory. I believe we had given Irish fans hope for the future.

I got home to Liverpool on 20 June and stayed in bed for the best part of three days. After a great season with Liverpool and a remarkable two-week spell in West Germany with Ireland, I was shattered. Well and truly shattered. But at least the Euro '88 experience was enjoyable. It enabled me to forget the penalty miss at Wembley a month before. And though I hadn't scored in Euro '88, I regard it as a personal triumph that I should be involved in one of Ireland's greatest periods.

Ireland's failure to qualify for any of the first thirteen World Cup competitions was baffling to anyone who had studied the history of international football. In the 1960s and 1970s, Ireland had produced some quality players. People still talk of Johnny Giles, Liam Brady and Noel Cantwell. Yet these players never appeared in football's greatest competition. For various reasons, Ireland never could produce a team to reach the World Cup finals. And while we were stuck in the shadows, Northern Ireland qualified for the 1982 and 1986 World Cup competitions and made a name for themselves with their fearless style of play.

So when we began our qualifying campaign for Italia '90, we knew history was against us. We were drawn alongside Northern Ireland, Spain, Hungary and Malta. With two teams going forward to the 1990 World Cup, we fancied our chances. Jack decided to arrange our first three games away from home against the toughest teams. It meant a trip to Northern Ireland on 14 September 1988, a trip to Spain two months later, and a trip to Hungary early in 1989. It was a brave move by Jack, one that could have gone horribly wrong. But we had so much confidence following Euro '88 that we felt we could stop any team from scoring.

Playing at Windsor Park, Belfast, was difficult due to the political instability that existed between the Republic and Northern Ireland. The atmosphere wasn't nice and we were glad to get the match over and done with. We drew 0–0 but Tony Cascarino was convinced he'd scored and was disappointed when the referee disallowed the goal. Victory in Belfast would have been a dream start but even a point was welcome. It was my nineteenth game for the Republic of Ireland and still I had yet to score. In the press box after the match, one journalist was supposed to have said: 'I see John Aldridge has kept another clean sheet.' But that remark aside, the Irish press were kind to me. It is doubtful any other group of journalists would have been so benevolent. And the Irish fans had stuck by me, as had Jack. When you are down on your luck, as I clearly was at that time, you find out who your friends really are. Well, there were five million of them in Ireland alone, or so it seemed.

I wasn't surprised to find myself in the team to face Tunisia for a friendly in Dublin on 19 October. Jack was often telling people I was his main man and this gave me a quiet confidence. For sure, I wanted to prove to everyone he was right to have me in the team, but even I was beginning to believe I would never score at international level. The game against Tunisia was one we were always going to win. We were playing well and were in command when Ray Houghton beat two players on the right of the eighteen-yard area. Under normal circumstances, Ray would certainly have scored himself. It was an easy opportunity for him. But instead he cut the ball back into my path. From two yards out I could hardly miss. When my shot beat the goalkeeper and flew into the net I was a man possessed. At last, in my twentieth international for Ireland, I had scored. The crowd's response was amazing. The noise suggested they were delighted for me. I had my hands clasped together when I looked up into the sky as if to thank the heavens. The goal took a great burden off my shoulders, even if the game was little more than a stroll. Ireland won 4–0.

But if that put me in good spirits for the trip to Spain the following month, we were in for a surprise. With a weakened team, and players all out of position, we were over-run by the Spaniards in Seville's Estadio Benito Villamarin. We lost 2–0 but we were outclassed enough for Jack to say afterwards: 'I can't see anyone taking a point from here.' Second-half goals by Manuel Manolo and Emilio Butragueño secured maximum points for Spain and put them in the driving seat in our qualifying group.

We flew to Budapest to face Hungary on 8 March 1989 knowing we could not afford to lose. And we didn't lose, though our 0–0 draw was ultimately disappointing. In a cold and windy Nep Stadium, Hungary showed much in the way of skill and short passing, yet Ireland did most of the attacking. Kevin Moran even suggested we played as if we were the home side, which was a valid comment. 'I am nit-picking if I try to find fault with that performance,' said Jack, though I suspected he was less happy than he looked.

Two points from three matches was hardly the start we wanted to our World Cup campaign, but at least we had key home games coming up. I missed the game against Spain at Lansdowne Road on 26 April because of the Hillsborough disaster. I was still suffering personal turmoil and could not summon up the energy to run, never mind play football. There was too much for me to do in Liverpool at the time, so travelling to Dublin would have been inappropriate and insensitive. Jack was good about it and respected my decision. Less understanding was the Spanish manager, Luis Suarez, who said he could not believe my reasons for missing the game. I found his remarks thoughtless and offensive. His lack of feeling hurt me and I felt he should have kept his mouth shut. I made sure the Spanish press were made aware of my feelings, and even in later years, when I was a Real Sociedad player, I couldn't forgive Luis for his insensitivity. Of course, the Hillsborough disaster affected different people in different ways. My Liverpool team-mates, Steve Staunton, Ray Houghton and Ronnie Whelan, were anxious to get back to playing as soon as possible and they faced Spain in what was a crucial match. We won 1–0, with Michel scoring an own goal early in the match. It was our first goal in the qualifying campaign and it kick-started our bid to reach the World Cup. Touchingly, the Irish players had agreed to donate their match fees to the Hillsborough Memorial Fund and, with the fans playing their part, many thousands of pounds were raised in Dublin that night.

By the time I was ready to play football, Liverpool had a number of big games to negotiate. Two days after the Reds' first-division championship decider against Arsenal, Ireland played Malta in a World Cup qualifier in Dublin on the Sunday. Ray Houghton, Steve Staunton, Ronnie Whelan and I met up at Manchester Airport for the trip to Finniston House. We all played well enough, even though it was our fourth match in nine days, and Ireland won 2–0. We were staying together for the match against Hungary the following Saturday, but after the game, Jack came up to me and said: 'I don't want to see you until Thursday. Go out and enjoy yourself. Relax a bit. You've had a tough time.' I didn't need telling twice. We enjoyed the next few days, drinking Guinness and playing golf. On the Monday night, in the centre of Dublin, Ray and I couldn't find a taxi to take us back to Finniston House. We'd had a few drinks and feared the worst when a Garda car pulled up alongside us.

'What's the problem?' the policeman asked, recognising Ray and me instantly.

'We can't get a taxi,' I said.

'Where are you going?'

'Finniston House.'

'Get in.'

It was a joy to be in a police car for nothing but pleasure. And when I expressed a desire to hear the siren, the policeman duly obliged. Speeding through Dublin with the siren at full blast was a great sensation. When we arrived outside Finniston House, the policeman turned off the siren and drove slowly towards the main building. The rest of the lads would have been asleep and we didn't want to wake anyone up. We invited the policeman in and offered him sandwiches and Guinness.

I decided to begin training again on the Wednesday in preparation for our home match against Hungary on Saturday, 4 June. It was an important match. Victory would give us a great chance of qualifying. Anything less was unacceptable. We played as though our futures depended on it and, thanks to goals by Paul McGrath and Tony Cascarino, we won 2–0. Qualification was now back in our own hands. All we had to do was hold our nerve and we were through to Italia '90. But if we got there, one key man wasn't coming with us.

Alas, Liam Brady's international career was coming to a close. Substituted early in the game against West Germany in September, he vowed never to play for his country again. Jack wasn't convinced of Liam's fitness, and neither was he convinced of his ability to fit in with Ireland's new system of play. But Liam's swansong was a messy affair. The German midfielders were controlling the centre of the field and this infuriated Jack. The crowd were stunned when Liam was brought off and so were the players. Perhaps Liam deserved a better ending to his international career, but Jack had seemed against him for some time. We drew the game 1–1, which was a good result against a strong team. It was also my last game for Ireland as a Liverpool player. I joined Real Sociedad later that month.

We had two World Cup qualifiers left: at home to Northern Ireland and away in Malta. Victory in both would take us to Italia '90. We completed half the job at Lansdowne Road against Northern Ireland, scoring through Ronnie Whelan just before half-time, and through Tony Cascarino at the beginning of the second half. Ray Houghton scored to secure a 3–0 win. I hit the bar late on and cursed my luck. It was my twenty-seventh international for Ireland with only one goal to my name.

For the Malta game, I arranged to meet Kevin Moran, who was also playing in Spain, in Madrid. I had just played for Real Sociedad against Tenerife in San Sebastian so I picked up a taxi after the match. I expected the drive would take around three hours. In fact, it took nearly six. I was all hot and flustered by the time I met Kevin at Madrid's Barajas Airport. Perhaps I should have waited until the following morning and taken a flight from Bilbao to Madrid. Luckily, I didn't have to pay the taxi bill. The FAI covered all such expenses. In the event, Kevin and I spent the night in a hotel, and made our way to Malta the following day. Even that wasn't as easy as it sounds because our Malta-bound flight went via Milan in Italy. Jack wouldn't let Kevin or me train when we arrived in Valletta. 'Conserve your energy,' he said. 'We've got a big game coming up.'

But any fears I had for my international future were soon quashed by my performance in Valletta. Our victory was never really in doubt but when I scored both our goals in the 2–0 win to secure qualification for the World Cup, I was ecstatic. To score for Ireland was pleasing enough but to hit the goals that put us in Italia '90 was special. In the end, we qualified comfortably as runners-up to Spain.

With all my childhood dreams centred around Anfield, the prospect of playing in the World Cup never entered my head as I was growing up. Even when I became a footballer, scoring for Liverpool in an FA Cup final was my ultimate ambition. It was only once the Republic of Ireland had made their mark on football that I thought of the World Cup personally. And when it did happen, it was brilliant.

Our qualification sparked a frenzy in Ireland. Even people not interested in football were discussing what the World Cup would do for the country. The media jumped on the bandwagon they had helped to create. The hype was amazing before and during Euro '88, but for Italia '90 it was something else altogether. You had to be in Dublin to know what it was really like. People in England sensed the reality of it, but they didn't feel it. You had to be there to appreciate the bond that had been created between the players and the populace. Even the media were on our side, something the England squad couldn't boast about their own press.

We were drawn to play England, Egypt and Holland on the island of Sardinia. It was ironic that we should face England again for we had given them such a tough time in Euro '88. To play them again suited us. We knew their players inside out and we also knew they could have problems dealing with our system. They still had quality players in John Barnes and Peter Beardsley, my former team-mates at Liverpool, while Paul Gascoigne was emerging as a world star. Egypt were an unknown quantity but, like all emerging footballing nations, they were bound to be difficult to break down. Holland were another side we had faced in Euro '88. They were the champions of Europe but, despite boasting the talents of Ruud Gullit and Marco Van Basten, were already showing signs of disharmony. We believed we would do well. We had more ability than we were given credit for and the flaws we did have were outweighed by our tremendous team spirit. I don't think teams relished playing against us and that is why we had to be taken seriously. Publicly, we stopped short of suggesting we could win the tournament but there was a quiet confidence within the ranks.

Our pre-tournament preparations took us to Malta. Jack reckoned the heat would be similar to that in Sardinia and would help our acclimatisation. In fact, it did nothing but rain for the first few days we were there, which was something of an embarrassment to Jack. We trained hard, however, and grew close as a squad. Our hotel was nice, ensuring a pleasant atmosphere, and it was difficult not to feel content with life. Ever keen to please his players, Jack allowed us an hour's sunbathing a day – once the sun had decided to make an appearance. We took to the beach with relish, much to the delight of our physiotherapist, Mick Byrne. A father figure to the players, Mick was loved by everyone. If you had a problem, you went to see Mick. He had a way of doing things that made you laugh, even if he didn't mean to be funny. That was Mick's way. But even he took us by surprise when he tried to get undressed at the side of the hotel swimming pool. Mick was facing us as he eagerly began peeling off his shorts, so he couldn't have known that two old ladies were sunbathing behind him.

'Mick, behind you,' we shouted in unison. Thinking we were winding him up, Mick continued to strip. 'Mick, behind you,' we shouted again, this time with more urgency.

'You're winding me up,' he said. 'You don't get one over the silver grey fox.'

So when Mick's shorts finally came down, these two old ladies had a wonderful view of his white backside. We fell to the floor as one, creased up with laughter. It was only when the women screamed that Mick realised we had been right all along. I have never seen a man pull up his shorts quite so fast.

Even when there was a wall behind him, Mick wasn't safe. After training, we would usually go to do some work in the gym. While Ronnie Whelan, Kevin Sheedy, Kevin Moran and I pumped iron, Mick was enjoying a session on the fly press machine. He was happily burning calories when one of the wires on the machine snapped and smacked him in the face. It might have turned sour had Mick carried out his threat to sue the hotel. Later that day, we found out he needed three stitches in a cut above his eye.

During our stay in Malta, we had a game against the national team. It wasn't an official international match but we took it seriously enough, winning 1–0. While I sat on the substitutes' bench, Frank Stapleton scored the goal, which would have been his twentieth for Ireland had the match counted for the record books. So the FAI contacted FIFA, the world's football governing body, and asked if the match could be made official. FIFA agreed and it meant Frank was Ireland's all-time record goalscorer, beating the record held by Don Givens. We were all pleased for Frank. I didn't know it then, of course, but his goal that day became a thorn in my side, as we shall see.

During that pre-World Cup period, we drew 0–0 with Turkey in Izmir. At the hottest part of the day, we failed to raise our game. The locals were laughing at us. They wouldn't even stand in the sun at that time of day, never mind play football. It was 114 degrees, and here were these predominantly white-skinned footballers from Ireland running around like idiots. Little wonder the match finished goalless. The heat was so debilitating it looked as though we weren't making any effort. But we had to question the wisdom of playing a match in such conditions at that time of day. It was a waste of time.

Relieved for the match to be finished, I showered and got dressed. I searched in my tracksuit trouser pockets for my watch, gold bracelet and wedding ring. My heart stopped; the items were gone. I looked everywhere for them, still no sign. The chap in charge of the dressing-rooms was called out and he pleaded ignorance. Jack was by this stage getting angry. The police were called and they seemed to be pointing the finger at the dressing-room attendant. I was told not to worry; the items could be claimed back on the insurance. When we returned to the hotel, I noticed there was something at the bottom of my tracksuit trousers. Closer inspection revealed a watch, a gold bracelet and a wedding ring. It turned out there was a hole in the pocket and the items had slipped down the trousers. I told Jack, who chased me around the hotel and would surely have thrown a punch had I not been too fast. At least the dressing-room attendant was cleared.

We moved on to Palermo and settled in a pleasant hotel near the beach. Our first game was against England on 11 June in Cagliari. It was a tense affair with little excitement for the millions of neutrals around the world watching on television. On a pitch which seemed to me to be too small, both sides turned the affair into a game of cat and mouse. It was as if there was too much respect between the players. To make matters worse, there was an electrical storm late in the match. Gary Lineker gave England the lead early on and, after Steve McMahon had lost control of the ball, Kevin Sheedy equalised with a devastating left-foot shot from the edge of the penalty area. It was a typical Kevin Sheedy goal – he had one of the best left feet in football – and the eventual 1–1 draw was probably a fair reflection of the game. I'd had a tough battle with England defender Des Walker. We'd been niggling each other throughout the match but I did feel a little guilty when I accidentally pushed him over the advertising hoardings on the touchline. He must have hurt himself. Not that I stayed on the field to apologise; I was substituted later on. Jack felt my role in the team meant I tired after an hour or so. I couldn't have disagreed more. I was fitter than Jack gave me credit for and my career records show a high percentage of my goals came late in matches when defenders were tiring. I had no problems playing for ninety minutes, even in the cauldron of the World Cup.

Still, we were reasonably happy with the point. We celebrated with a few drinks and immediately began our preparations for the Egypt match in Palermo the following week. More and more Irish fans were arriving in Palermo at this stage. Even the day after the England match, some of them had T-shirts with 'Kevin Sheedy scores against England' written on them.

Egypt surprised most people by drawing 1–1 with Holland in their opening match so the North Africans were clearly a strong side. When we kicked off, it soon became obvious how defensive they were. They seemed content to put men behind the ball and make it difficult for us to break them down. Egypt also had one major advantage: the heat. They were used to humid conditions, we were not. It meant they seemed more comfortable as the match went on. We still should have won, however. Ray Houghton was given a great scoring opportunity late on but he was denied by the Egyptian goalkeeper. The match finished goalless but this time we were far less happy than after the England match. Again I was substituted late on.

By that time, Joan and Paul had travelled over with my mother. My father didn't like flying so he stayed at home. But the morning of the Egypt match, Mick Byrne knocked on my door.

'Wake up, Aldo, your mates are here and they are in trouble.' Apparently, four of my friends had broken the usually tight security and ended up going for a swim in the hotel swimming pool. It was only when one of them found a rifle pointing in his face that the lads realised there was something wrong. My friends were told by security guards to get out of town, but they did return to the hotel later in the tournament to enjoy drinks with some of the Ireland players.

The wives came to join us in the hotel after the Egypt match but Jack insisted they go back to their own hotel until after the Holland match four days later. Joan wasn't happy about that and neither was I. It was a bit of a depressing atmosphere. But things lightened up the following day – and it was thanks to Mick Byrne. We were all sitting around in the lobby when Mick came towards us.

'Cheer up, you lot,' he said. We ushered him away; we were too depressed for humour. Mick was undeterred, however, and as he began singing 'The Lambeth Walk', he stepped backwards towards a table which had a beautiful crystal ship on top of it. As Mick carried on with his song, he hit the table and the ship started to slip towards the floor. Mick tried to grab the ornament but missed it completely. While we fell into laughter, this crystal ship crashed to the floor. The hotel manager rushed over and complained to Mick.

'Me sorry,' said Mick at least six times in what just about passed for an Italian accent. But still the hotel manager complained. 'Listen,' Mick said to him, 'me no sorry any more.' That was the kind of encore only Mick could provide.

We faced Holland in Palermo on 21 June knowing victory would effectively confirm our passage into the second round. I had a goal ruled out early on when I was convinced it should have been allowed. Then Ruud Gullit wove his magic to put Holland a goal in front. I was substituted for the third successive World Cup match and we equalised soon after when Niall Quinn took advantage of a mistake by Dutch goalkeeper Van Breukelen to score. When the news came through that England had scored against Egypt, Ireland felt it was essential to beat Holland to finish in second place in the group. So we spent the final ten or so minutes going all out for victory. It made no difference. The match finished 1–1. It meant that both Holland and Ireland were through to the second round but as we boasted identical records, we had to draw lots for second place. We were successful and were drawn to play Romania in the second round. Holland were given the tougher game against Germany and subsequently lost 2–1.

We flew to Genoa to face Romania on 25 June and felt confident of victory. But after half-an-hour, I felt a muscle go at the bottom of my calf. I remember having a similar injury before Real Sociedad's game against Zaragoza the previous February, and I was worried the recurring trouble might prematurely end my World Cup. In my absence, Ireland fought hard and secured a goalless draw after extra time. Romania's main threat had been through Hagi, who had a number of long-range shots saved by Pat Bonner. The penalty shoot-out that followed was tense. The first eight kicks were fired home, but Romania missed their fifth. I knew Daniel Timofte would miss. His run-up was so casual you wondered how he ever thought he would get power into his shot. Pat's save was inevitable. Now it was left to David O'Leary to secure Ireland's place in the quarter-final. With great composure, David scored and we all dashed towards him in celebration. Now, only Italy stood between Ireland and a place in the semi-final.

We didn't need any more inspiration than a game against the hosts but we got it anyway. Before the Romania game, it was suggested that, if we did go on to play Italy, Jack should arrange for us to meet the Pope in the Vatican. Jack agreed. So when our game against Italy in Rome was confirmed, we asked Jack if he would fulfil his promise. 'No problem,' he said. So there we

were, a collection of footballers from Ireland, off to meet the
Pope. It was a memorable experience for more reasons than
one. Most people don't get to meet him so that was a novelty
in itself. But actually being in the room as he introduced himself
to us was something special. My mother was proud. I know I
won't forget the moment; nor will I forget the nerves that nearly
overwhelmed me as the Pope moved from one player to the next.
Then he offered me his hand and smiled. I still have photographs
of the Pope shaking hands with me. As a Catholic, it was a
life-enhancing experience for me and another example of how
football had given me wonderful opportunities in my life. Jack
was equally impressed, though he has since admitted that he
fell asleep just minutes before the Pope shook his hand.

Two days before the Italy match, Guinness put a temporary
bar in our hotel. We were sitting around reading when Jack
approached us, drinking Guinness from a pint glass.

'How would you like one of these?' he asked, sipping his
drink. 'You haven't had a pint for five days, have you? Tell
you what, Aldo, get all the lads together and you can all have
a Guinness.' We took to our task with relish. But one pint led
to two, two to three. We ended up having four pints each.
'I'd rather you drink Guinness than Coke,' Jack said, justifying
his actions. There were Italian policemen gathered around us
and they couldn't believe we were preparing for a World Cup
quarter-final in this way. We ended that evening playing a game
where you lick a coin, stick it on your forehead, and see how
many times you have to hit the back of your head to knock the
coin off. Usually it would take four goes. But on one occasion,
I licked my finger and pressed it against Jack's forehead. He
didn't know there was no coin there. He whacked the back of
his head twelve times before he realised he had been conned.
We had been nervous at the prospect of facing Italy; Jack eased
the tension by letting us drink Guinness, and helped us relax by
encouraging us to play games as a squad.

I had a fitness test on my calf the day before the match and I
was delighted to be cleared to play against Italy. It turned out I
had nothing more than a tired muscle. All it needed was a couple

of days' rest. It gave me a surge of energy for the game against Italy in Rome's Olympic Stadium the following day. The game was always going to be hard. Not only were Italy hosts, they were also the favourites. They were playing good football and had found, in Salvatore Schillaci, the star of Italia '90. But we sensed they feared our spirit and ability to stop even the best sides from playing their natural game. It was a tight contest and it was always likely that a single goal would win the match. That was how it proved, but it was Italy who scored it. Kevin Sheedy tried to pass the ball to me but it was intercepted by Paolo Maldini who in turn passed the ball to Roberto Donadoni. Donadoni made ground and fired a shot which Pat saved. The ball came out to Schillaci who scored with a right-footed shot. Jack went berserk at Kevin because it was not our style to play balls into feet like that. We were punished for it. Italy won 1–0 and on the balance of play, probably deserved it. But we gave a good account of ourselves and the rest of the world were able to appreciate just how close we had come to going further in the tournament.

I often thought we could have won the World Cup. Had we beaten Italy we would have faced Argentina in the semi-final. The South Americans had been dour throughout the tournament and had they played us it would have been a guaranteed 0–0 draw. Then the game would have gone to penalties and anything could have happened. Argentina beat Italy on penalties and reached the final only to lose 1–0 to West Germany. It hadn't been a great World Cup overall, but it was a success where Ireland were concerned. Our fans had been brilliant throughout and, as after Euro '88, we returned to a heroes' welcome. The pilot changed his route on the return to Dublin so we could see the crowds congregated in O'Connell Street, waiting for our appearance. It was yet another memorable day. It seemed as though half of Dublin were there to see us. The other half must have watched it on television.

On a sour note, Michael Robinson, the former Ireland striker, was reported to have criticised our performances in Italia '90. Commentating for Spanish television, Michael probably didn't think anyone in Ireland would find out. But when I returned to San Sebastian after the summer, my Real Sociedad team-mates told me what he had said. That disappointed me. Ireland had produced some of the best displays in their footballing history, yet still we couldn't satisfy everyone.

Looking back on it, I don't care what the critics said. We went to Italy to do a job. We went further in the tournament than many people expected. We had done what no other Irish team in history had done. And being part of that Irish team makes me more proud than I can express in words.

— 8 —

KING'S COURT

T HERE are some international footballers who wouldn't touch a small club with a barge pole. It's as if they believe slipping out of the top flight of a major league really means falling off the edge of the world. If I had the same view, I would never have considered joining Tranmere Rovers. But I was lucky. I'd seen all levels of football, spent six great seasons in the lower divisions, and realised that there is a life away from England's Premier League.

The most successful people usually have one thing in common: they have at some point in their lives taken a risk. If you play it safe, you can only go so far. You sometimes have to back your instincts, even if logic suggests you take the easier option. That is why I smile to myself when I consider the reaction of the top-flight managers in England when I became available for transfer from Real Sociedad in the summer of 1991. Howard Wilkinson of Leeds United had a look but reckoned, at £400,000, I was too expensive, especially given that I was approaching my thirty-third birthday. Some managers made inquiries but not one from the top flight made a tangible bid. For sure, I was a risk – but after scoring forty goals in two seasons in Spain, I was surely a risk worth taking.

So when Tranmere Rovers came in with a £250,000 bid I had to be realistic. Their chairman, Peter Johnson, knew I was anxious to return to my Calderstones home in Liverpool and he cleverly pursued me, as did the club's manager, John King. I cursed the top-flight managers for not wanting to take a risk with me, yet I knew that if I joined Tranmere I would be taking a professional risk. I couldn't have it both ways. Tranmere had earned promotion from the third division the previous May and were, thanks to the chairman's wealth and expertise, clearly a club on the way up. In a sense, they were like Oxford United in the mid-1980s: unfashionable, perhaps, but ambitious, with the potential for drastic improvement.

I could see that joining Tranmere had many advantages. Maybe it wasn't the move of my dreams but it was one that would, once and for all, allow my family to be settled in Liverpool. That had to be my priority. After putting Joan and the kids through too much domestic insecurity in Spain, I now decided that professional ambition and financial considerations were minor issues compared with the happiness of my family. We had done well financially in Spain so a drop of ninety per cent in salary at Tranmere was not considered a hardship. In any event, money had ceased to matter. Contentment was far more important.

Though Real Sociedad manager John Toshack was hoping to sell me to Leeds United for £400,000, he knew Tranmere would not increase their offer of £250,000. So he accepted Peter Johnson's bid – and so did I. After two years in a foreign country, I was going back to Merseyside, hopefully forever. I found going back to my roots an exciting prospect. We felt it when we packed our belongings and left San Sebastian for the final time. Liverpool isn't exactly the centre of the universe but to us it is home. Always has been. Returning to Calderstones was a relief.

It wasn't long before it became clear that returning to Liverpool was the most important decision of my life. During the summer, my father suffered a stroke that for a time left him bound to a wheelchair. It was a shock to us all, particularly my mother, who found it hard to accept my father in his debilitated condition. I was able to visit him regularly and provide much help to my mother. The situation would have been much more awkward had I still been in Spain. My return to Liverpool was a blessing;

an act of fate that allowed me to be near my loved ones at a difficult period. Though he was later able to walk, my father was never the same after the stroke. He'd lost that sharpness and quick wit that made him such a pleasure to be with. I still enjoyed his company, of course, but it upset me that he could change so quickly.

Football was a welcome diversion. I was determined to make sure I fitted in quickly at Tranmere. The club had never spent so much money on a player and the fact that I had played for Liverpool and for Ireland could have thrown up barriers between myself and some of the other players. So my plan was simple: to go out with the lads regularly and show them that I liked a pint and a laugh just like them. Initially, I think some players stood off, not really knowing how they should treat me. But it wasn't long before I was fully integrated and I became especially friendly with the likes of John Morrissey, Dave Martindale and Eric Nixon. After two years in Spain, it was nice to hear so many Scouse accents.

We began our pre-season programme on the beach at Moreton. Five days of sheer agony which was, in a perverse way, essential. I hadn't had a full pre-season for two years so running up and down the sand dunes provided me with a welcome change. There was a feeling that though Tranmere were considered a small club, they were anxious to adopt a professional attitude. They did most things well, yet there were times I questioned their wisdom.

We were due to play away at Brighton and Hove Albion at the beginning of the 1991–92 season and we travelled the night before, staying in a nice hotel in the town. I was surprised to learn that manager John King encouraged the players to go out, providing they were back at the hotel before half-past eleven. The camaraderie reminded me of my days playing for Liverpool. John had provided steak sandwiches for us, something I found baffling after the years of eating the correct food. In my early days at Tranmere, I found myself drinking more wine than lager simply because that was how they did it in Spain. Overall, Tranmere was a bit of a culture shock for me in those summer days of 1991, though fitting in was a pleasurable experience.

The thought that this was a lower level of football never entered my head. I was signed to score goals and that was all I had on my mind when we took the field to play Brighton at the Goldstone Ground on 17 August. Inevitably, I had built up a reputation over the years, a reputation opposing fans seemed desperate to tarnish. So when I heard the Brighton fans chanting 'What a waste of money' every time I went near the ball, I knew I had to justify Tranmere's faith in me. By half-time, I had scored twice and we were never going to lose after that. I was glowing with delight at the end and the 2–0 victory was deserved. I had to get used to opposing fans questioning Tranmere's decision in bringing me back to England, but I found this kind of criticism the perfect incentive. Of all the fans, those at Reading and Swindon are the ones I found the worst. It had a lot to do with the fact that I had done so well at Oxford. They couldn't cope with that.

After the disciplines of Spanish football, Tranmere's attack-minded style of play was pleasurable for a centre-forward. John's idea was to get the ball out wide as quickly as possible and create chances for either myself or big Jim Steel, my striking partner. It meant we were always guaranteed to score goals, even if the flipside of the coin ensured we would concede our fair share, too. To get his system to work, the manager needed specialist wingers. John Morrissey, a former Everton and Wolves player, occupied the role down the right and, for his ability down the years, deserves to be regarded as a Tranmere great. I've lost count of the chances he has created for me; he has provided me with more scoring opportunities than any player with whom I have played. John Morrissey would always get the ball over early, something strikers like. For sure, he had skill in abundance, and he was a tough tackler, but his ability to put over accurate crosses no matter what the angle made him the player he was. Off the field, he was good company. Whenever John Morrissey was around there was always laughter. And that is why I was so keen to keep him at Prenton Park when

I became manager of Tranmere. Players like him are good for morale.

The same can be said for Eric Nixon, the goalkeeper. After the Brighton game, he arranged a party to welcome me to Tranmere. It was a kind of initiation ceremony, something I appreciated. Eric was among the best shot-stoppers I have either played with or against. He had certain flaws – don't all goalkeepers? – yet you always felt he had a chance of saving any shot. He wasn't too far off being one of the best in the country at that time.

In any case, the players at Tranmere felt that, no matter how many goals we conceded, we would always score more. It was true when we played Halifax Town in the League Cup second round first leg and won 4–3, and again in the second leg when we repeated the scoreline. We also played out 2–2 draws against Bristol Rovers and Grimsby Town. I enjoyed those first games for Tranmere, particularly as I had chipped in with nine goals – nine goals and September hadn't yet arrived!

It was during the opening Halifax game that I witnessed for the first time John King's ability to keep his cool. I remember Dave Higgins, a defender, giving the manager a mouthful of abuse. It was relentless, yet John shrugged it off as if absorbing insults was part of his job. I was stunned at first. It would never have happened at Real Sociedad or Liverpool, while even my managers at Oxford United and Newport County let you know how far you could go with your temper. It wasn't long before I realised that John never fought fire with fire, preferring instead to remain calm and collected. Dave, on the other hand, wore his heart on his sleeve and was, like John Morrissey, a charming, bubbly character; very much part of the fabric of Tranmere Rovers.

Our failure to keep it tight at the back proved our undoing, however, and we never really threatened to gain promotion to the top flight. I appreciated that John wanted to put the emphasis on attack and, of course, it suited me. But I remember enduring periods of frustration at the goals we were conceding. 'Bloody hell,' I said to myself, 'I am doing exactly what I was signed to do yet we seem to be letting them in as quickly as we are scoring them.' Jim Steel, my striking partner, was getting his fair share of goals, while the midfielders were equally productive, but somehow we didn't quite have the right players to allow for such a system. As the season wore on, it was obvious we needed a bit more strength in defence. I noticed it after our 6–6 draw against Newcastle United in the Zenith Data Cup at Prenton Park. It was an amazing night for the fans; Sky Television, who covered the game live, often repeat it as a 'Great Sporting Moment'. But even though I scored a hat-trick and we won the tie 3–2 on penalties, the night left a bad taste. No self-respecting team likes to concede six goals, even if the tournament was more of a stocking filler than a cherished present. What did make me laugh was that Eric Nixon earned a man-of-the-match award. Man of the match, after conceding six goals? What was the world coming to?

Beating Chelsea 3–1 in a League Cup third-round replay at Prenton Park gave Tranmere some welcome national acclaim. The Londoners had Dennis Wise and Vinnie Jones, two players with whom I had competed in the 1988 FA Cup final. It was nice to get some kind of revenge, particularly against Dennis. As in the Liverpool–Wimbledon game at Wembley three years before, he shouted abuse at me as I prepared to take a penalty. This time I scored, though my one-fingered salute to the crowd was misinterpreted by the Chelsea goalkeeper. Thinking I was undermining his credibility, he chased after me and, as a host of other players joined in, it was some time before order was restored. Chelsea had two black defenders that night, Paul Elliot and Ken Monkou. Paul was of Caribbean extraction, while Ken had his roots in Africa. So whenever Paul thought he should clear the ball with his head, he would shout 'Jamaica', and whenever Ken thought he should clear the ball with his head, he would shout 'Africa'. I found this amusing, but I wasn't prepared for Dave Higgins' response. Dave was from the Old Swan area of Liverpool and when he jumped to head the ball clear, he shouted 'Old Swan'. I didn't know whether anyone else noticed because I was too busy laughing.

I was scoring goals at an amazing rate, hitting the nineteen mark with a hat-trick against Grimsby Town in a 5–1 win against

Family portrait – with my wife, Joan, son Paul and daughter Joanne

At the Vatican – meeting Pope John Paul II during the 1990 World Cup

Smith (*left*) and John Toshack –
men in my career

n King (*below*) and John Barnes
ersey marvels

Jack Charlton – a legend in Ireland

Paul McGrath (*left*) and Ray Houghton – great players and great friends

Flashpoint – the infamous touchline row during World Cup 1994

Real Sociedad, circa 1990 – I am third from left, centre row

My only World Cup goal – against Mexico in 1994

the ball – in Tranmere colours, July
'95

tening ear – with Jack Charlton,
field, December 1995

iking out – for Ireland against
lland, Anfield, December 1995

Into the sunset – at the end of my playing career, Prenton Park, May 1998

Best friends – with my family, 1998

them on 22 October. After going out of the League Cup with a 3–1 defeat at Leeds United, I scored the winning goal in the win at Derby County. Scoring against the bigger teams always gave me pleasure, especially at a time when some observers were questioning my ability to perform at the top level. I broke new ground, too. My two goals in the 3–0 win against Runcorn in the FA Cup in November saw me surpass the three-hundred-goal mark in my career.

I would suffer for that hat-trick against Grimsby. Paul Futcher, one of their defenders, didn't have the best of times that night so when we faced them in the second division later in the season, he was determined to keep me under control. The problem was he did his job with far too much enthusiasm. He fouled me once too often and I turned to face him, elbowing him in the nose. Paul was sent off for his foul. But though the referee had not seen my retaliation, he took one look at the blood pouring out of Paul's face and dismissed me also. Fair enough, I deserved to be sent off. But the referee was wrong to base his decision solely on the damage to Paul's face. That in itself didn't suggest I'd been guilty.

Old failings still haunted Tranmere. The 4–0 defeat against a strong Ipswich Town side later in November illustrated how far away we were from being a title-winning side. The pleasure of playing for Tranmere could not conceal my disappointment at our lack of consistency. I was as determined as anyone to see the club earn a place in the top flight of English football, yet I knew we were three or four players away from being a top team. We were talented and exciting to watch, but that is often different from being strong. After losing 2–0 to Nottingham Forest in the Zenith Data Cup, we were denied a good run in the FA Cup when Oxford United beat us 3–1 at the Manor Ground.

With little for the team to play for except pride, I concentrated on scoring as many goals as possible. I knew nothing of the club's goalscoring records but during the season, Tranmere director Fred Williams put £1,000 at 25–1 on me to score forty league and cup goals that campaign. I hit the thirty mark in the 1–1 draw against Sunderland at Roker Park on 11 February and fancied my chances. A hat-trick in the thrilling 4–3 win against Derby County at Prenton Park a month later put me on thirty-six goals, with thirteen games of the season left. That should have encouraged me but it had the opposite effect. I lost form and only managed two goals in the next eleven games. A goal in the 1–0 win against Charlton meant I needed another in the final match to give Fred a £25,000 cheque. Ironically, we faced Oxford United at Prenton Park. And I had mixed feelings. My duty was to Tranmere, of course, yet Oxford needed to win to avoid relegation. I did not want to see my former club slip into the third division, especially as I had helped them earn promotion to the second division seven years before. Tranmere had nothing to play for except pride and Oxford's determination was always going to make it difficult for us. They won 2–1, playing as if it were a cup final, though I at least had the pleasure of scoring our goal – my fortieth of the season. While Oxford earned themselves another season in the second division, Fred celebrated his £25,000 win. He donated most of it to charity and gave the rest to the players for a night out. We enjoyed the proceeds of Fred's generosity, drinking long into the early hours of the morning, bonding together like old friends.

It had been an enjoyable first season from a personal point of view. Beating Newcastle United 3–2 at St James' Park was among the highlights, especially as Kevin Keegan had not long taken over as manager of the North East club. I scored twice, giving further credence to the view that I was still at my peak.

John King was busy in the transfer market in the summer of 1992, anxiously trying to give Tranmere the players they needed for an assault on the divisional championship. The English game had been reshaped, with the top-flight clubs forming the new FA Premier League. Tranmere were now in the restructured first division and we believed success was just around the corner in the 1992–93 season. Winger Pat Nevin was signed on a permanent basis from Everton after a successful loan period, while we also snapped up Ian Nolan, a full-back with lightning pace, from Marine for next to nothing. Pat's skills were obvious from day one, yet it was Ian who made the greater

184

impression, turning himself into a good player in what seemed no time at all. The younger players were coming on, too. Shaun Garnett, a central defender, was growing in confidence, as were midfielders Ged Brannan and Kenny Irons. Striker Chris Malkin was also hitting good form. I always felt Chris was underrated. Some observers suggested his touch wasn't good but his pace and workrate turned him into a useful partner up front. If my spell at Tranmere could be called successful, it is partly because of people like Chris.

The emergence of young players seemed to be the feature of the 1992–93 campaign. The club's youth policy, one of the most successful in the country, was saving Tranmere thousands of pounds and much credit deservedly went to Warwick Rimmer who helped nurture the apprentices.

Young players are great to have around, and they are always guaranteed to try things most of the older players wouldn't consider. At Derby County, for example, we arrived an hour or so before our scheduled pre-match lunch so the team went for a walk. Desperate for any form of entertainment, we passed a massage parlour and, inevitably, a couple of the younger players decided to make use of the facilities. They returned not long after and insisted they'd had nothing more than a massage. Few of us believed them; it was easier, and funnier, to suggest they'd enjoyed something far more erotic. As they walked towards the dressing-rooms to get changed, their shoes made a funny squelching sound.

'Oh, that's the massage oil,' one of them said. 'It has dripped down into our shoes.' Somehow it was inevitable that these two should be among our best players that day.

Tranmere began the new season well, beating Cambridge United 2–0 at home and Blackpool 3–0 in the League Cup, and after hitting three of those opening five goals, I continued to feel on top of my game. But this time the view that we were still short of being a good team came early on. We lost 1–0 to Sunderland in our second league match and then, inexplicably, we bowed out of the League Cup following a 4–0 defeat at Blackpool. Trevor Sinclair had a good match for Blackpool that night but, without taking credit away from our opponents, it was Tranmere who deserve blame for the result. There was no excuse for our performance. We were terrible. Had we won the first leg 6–0, I am sure we would have lost the second 7–0. There was an inevitability about it all, though the fact that we could play so poorly and be so cleanly exposed by an inferior team suggested we had not learned our lessons from the previous season.

Looking back on the 1992–93 season, I have to say it wasn't my most memorable. The goals were still going in – I'd bagged twelve by the start of November – but I had my moments of frustration. For a start there was the Anglo–Italian Cup – football's equivalent of a jail sentence. We qualified to face AC Reggiana, a *Serie B* team, and flew out to Italy the day before the match. Talk about boredom. You couldn't motivate yourself for anything, never mind a game of football. Even ordering drinks at the bar seemed an effort. I'm sure Tranmere's fans enjoyed their first taste of European football and, of course, the trip to Italy provided them with a great excuse for a party. But the match itself was meaningless and the goalless draw failed to give pleasure to much of a crowd measured in dozens rather than thousands. As I looked around the empty concrete bowl of a stadium, I considered how much fun it would be to mow the lawn in my back garden. Walking the dog suddenly felt like a viable option. Fortunately, it was my only trip to Italy for an Anglo–Italian Cup match. The rest of the Tranmere players still had many more to endure.

Our inconsistency added to my frustration. We lost 1–0 to Newcastle United, a result that showed how much things had improved at St James' Park under Kevin Keegan. We played well that day and were equally impressive against Birmingham City, whom we beat 4–0. But while we were capable of playing marvellous football, we were also capable of underachievement. Like the time we lost 3–2 at Watford and 4–0 at Portsmouth.

We ended the year in impressive form, however, beating Derby County 2–1 at the Baseball Ground (I scored twice), West Ham 5–2 at Prenton Park (I scored a hat-trick) and Wolves 3–0 at Prenton Park (I scored another hat-trick). So when I tore muscles in my stomach after scoring twice in the 4–0 win against Oxford on 15 January 1993, I cursed my luck. I had an operation which might have worked had I not begun training too quickly, doing sit-ups when I should have been resting. Though I knew the injury hadn't healed properly, I played against Luton Town at Prenton Park in late February and hated every minute of the 2–0 defeat. After reluctantly agreeing to have several injections, I also played in our 1–0 defeat at Bristol Rovers and it was then I realised I needed more treatment. I was sent to a specialist in Crosby, north of Liverpool, and had two months out of the game. But this time the treatment was successful and my stomach gave me no further trouble.

Jimmy Greaves, the England striker-turned-television pundit, was giving me trouble. He seemed to be making a big issue of my new style of taking penalties. Just before striking the ball, I would tease the goalkeeper by shuffling. It brought great dividends until the media turned it into a story, and I started to lose confidence. I missed three penalty kicks in successive games during the season, a situation that bothered me.

I consoled myself in the performances of the team. Tranmere bounced back and ended the season in consistent form, qualifying for the play-offs following a 1–1 draw at Peterborough which was notable for the sending-off of goalkeeper Danny Coyne on his debut.

We were drawn to face Swindon Town over two legs for the right to play in the final at Wembley. I had never been a fan of Swindon. Earlier that season I had scored twice against them at the County Ground before the floodlights failed, causing the match to be abandoned. Throughout my career, their fans took delight in putting me down. They were relentless in their abuse. To make matters worse, they had Glenn Hoddle as their player-manager. I have never really taken to Glenn. I appreciated his skill and ability to cut defences open with long, raking passes, but he was usually the first to disappear if games got physical.

Bad defending allowed Swindon two early goals in the first leg at the County Ground and we knew we had to bounce back quickly. So when I headed the ball into the goal I did not expect the referee to disallow it. Even to this day I don't why it didn't count, but I believe it proved crucial. At 2–1 down we would have fancied our chances of forcing a draw. But when Swindon made it 3–0 later in the game, we were always up against it. Only a late John Morrissey goal gave us a chance of pulling it back in the second leg at Prenton Park three days later.

We knew we had to get the crowd on our side in the return leg, so Steve Mungall, our veteran defender, circled the pitch, whipping the fans up into a frenzy. It must have been one of the best pre-match atmospheres witnessed at Prenton Park and certainly one that would affect Swindon. And it worked. We outplayed our opponents for long periods but, alas, conceded two goals at crucial stages of the match. We won 3–2 but lost the tie 4–3 on aggregate. Glenn Hoddle had got on my nerves throughout both games. His efforts to get me booked finally bore fruit at Prenton Park and that summed up a miserable night for me. Even when we won a penalty, I allowed Kenny Irons to take it. My confidence with penalties had, for a short time, disappeared.

Much to my chagrin, Swindon won at Wembley to confirm their place in the Premier League. All we could do was plan another first-division campaign. We had improved during the course of the season but we still lacked the consistency all teams need to mount a serious promotion challenge.

That was the summer Tommy Coyne's wife, Alison, died in tragic circumstances. Tommy had signed for Tranmere from Celtic for £350,000, on my recommendation. A Republic of Ireland team-mate of mine, he was a hard-working, versatile player who would have been a great favourite at Prenton Park had he stayed long enough. But his wife never settled on Merseyside, became depressed, and died following a drug overdose. Tommy was never going to stay at Tranmere after that and he signed for Motherwell later in the year. I felt so guilty. Had I not been so keen to see Tommy at Tranmere, his wife might still be alive. The player himself showed great dignity throughout the unfortunate affair. As honest a person as you could wish to meet, he bounced back to become a great hero in Ireland's World Cup campaign of 1994, playing with courage under difficult circumstances.

Tranmere began the 1993–94 season with a goalless draw at Crystal Palace and a 1–0 win against Leicester City. We didn't know it then, of course, but these two sides would end the season gaining promotion to the top flight. For us it would end in more frustration.

That was the season the Inland Revenue decided to look into my affairs. They had been made aware of how much money I had brought into Britain from Spain in 1991 and felt sure they could issue me with an invoice. They had no grounds for such a demand. I had done everything correctly and, though they ended up dropping the matter, I was left with a £20,000 accountancy bill. The taxman who gave me most hassle was a Birmingham City fan and his last words to me were: 'I look forward to seeing you at St Andrews.' At St Andrews, I scored twice in our 3–0 win.

I don't look upon that domestic season with much affection, however. I failed to score in any of the first five matches – my worst start to a campaign – and I began to suffer a number of niggly injuries that worried me. The first came in the second of two matches in five days against Oxford United in September. We beat my former club 5–1 in the Coca-Cola Cup, a game memorable for a Pat Nevin hat-trick. I scored two that night and still believe one of Pat's should have been accredited to me. In the second game, I limped off with a thigh injury during the first half of our 2–0 win. The damage wasn't serious but it was enough to keep me out of action for a month. By that stage, Tranmere had replaced physiotherapist Alec Muir with Les Parry. Les came on good recommendation and, when I became manager of Tranmere, he was one of the men I was glad to have around.

I returned to action at the end of October and scored twice in the 4–1 win against Grimsby Town in the League Cup at Prenton Park. When I hit the winning goal against Luton Town in mid-December, I had scored eight goals in six successive matches. But though I felt I was getting my touch back, Tranmere were throwing away too many points – a contrast to our form in the Coca-Cola Cup, where victory against Premier League team Oldham Athletic gave us a quarter-final tie against Nottingham Forest.

No longer managed by Brian Clough, Forest were enduring a rare spell out of the top flight. They hadn't quite lost their way but they were no longer the force of previous seasons. Although they had already beaten us in the first division, we fancied our chances of knocking them out, and such optimism was well in order. We may have been prone to inconsistency, but Tranmere were capable of beating any team in England. We had a good, attacking formula, with the younger players – such as Tony Thomas, Ian Nolan, Ged Brannan, Shaun Garnett and Kenny Irons – starting to hit peak form and older players such as myself, Eric Nixon and Pat Nevin maintaining a high level of performance. Liam O'Brien, a Dublin-born central midfielder, had been signed from Newcastle United to add composure to the engine room. So we were not surprised to get a 1–1 draw at Forest on 26 January 1994 and force a replay at Prenton Park three days later. We completed the job in front of our own fans on the Saturday, winning 2–0 to confirm our semi-final place against Aston Villa.

The Tranmere squad went to Dublin to spend the rest of that weekend celebrating. It was the perfect response to what had been a difficult period and the players appreciated the gesture by manager John King. Liam took us to the Lansdowne pub and we spent hours drinking and singing, conveniently forgetting that we were due back in England the following day. A few of the younger players, particularly Shaun Garnett, took delight in singing pro-English songs, while Liam and I reacted by singing some of the Irish songs we knew. The evening got even better when a few of Liam's Dublin-based friends came to join us. They were big, tough men and were keen to have a laugh. When Shaun Garnett went to the toilet, Liam's friends decided it was time for a practical joke. They followed the Tranmere defender and complained that his singing was causing offence and was bordering on the blasphemous. Shaun, as nice a man as you could wish to meet, was apologetic but his efforts to diffuse the situation fell on stony ground. A few minutes later, he emerged from the toilets wearing nothing except a pair of underpants. My friends, pretending they hated the English, had stripped him. It was only when the rest of us fell about laughing that Shaun realised he had been conned.

We faced Villa in the semi-final first leg at Prenton Park on 16 February and I was able to appreciate a host of ironies. My last appearance at this stage of the competition was for Oxford United against Villa. In the Villa side to face Tranmere there were six players with whom I had played in recent seasons. They had Irish internationals Steve Staunton and Ray Houghton, both formerly of Liverpool, Dalian Atkinson and Kevin Richardson, both formerly of Real Sociedad, and Paul McGrath and Andy Townsend, two more Irish team-mates. That went in our favour, as did our performance. From start to finish, we outplayed Villa, playing a brand of football rarely seen outside the Premier League that season. Ian Nolan, Mark Hughes and I scored to give Tranmere a three-goal lead and a virtual passage to Wembley, or so we thought. In the last minute, Dalian scored to bring Villa back into the tie. Psychologically, it was a good goal for Villa, and one that should never have been allowed to stand. There had clearly been a foul on a Tranmere player just before Dalian scored, a fact confirmed by the referee when he contacted John King soon afterwards to apologise. Our 3–1 victory was welcome, of course, but I couldn't help thinking Dalian's last-gasp intervention would prove our undoing.

Shaun Garnett had played well for Tranmere in the first leg but he was surprisingly dropped for the return game at Villa Park. I later found out from Ray Houghton that the Villa management team expressed pleasant surprise when they saw that Shaun had been dropped. Handed another psychological boost, Villa quickly went into a two-goal lead to pull the scores level on aggregate. We could have crumbled then but we showed great character and professionalism to keep our composure. I was fouled by Villa goalkeeper Mark Bosnich inside the eighteen-yard area and was delighted when the referee pointed to the penalty spot. As the rules stood then, Mark should have been sent off. There was no doubt about it. But my feeling at the time was that the penalty was compensation enough for Tranmere. Besides, you don't like to see an opposing player sent off when there is no malice involved. I duly scored to put Tranmere 4–3 in front on aggregate and that was when we tightened it up at the back. We survived until the last minute when, much to our disappointment, Villa pulled the scores level again to take the game into extra time. Though we were getting tired, we created a glorious chance towards the end of the extra period when Liam O'Brien struck a shot which hit the inside of one post and rolled across the goalline towards the other. Seconds later, the referee blew his whistle to signal the end of the match. A penalty shoot-out would decide which team went to Wembley.

At times like that there is little you can do, apart from making sure you score your own penalty. The whole affair is something of a lottery but as nobody has suggested a better alternative, we are stuck with it. I had been involved in penalty shoot-outs before but none as tense as this. It was surely the most crucial moment in the history of Tranmere Rovers FC. Somehow we were never meant to win it. Liam O'Brien had a chance to put us through but missed. And then Ian Nolan missed to confirm Villa's victory. It was no consolation to me that my own penalty kick was among the best I have taken. As Villa celebrated, I felt as low as I had done six years before when I missed a penalty in Liverpool's FA Cup final defeat against Wimbledon. Aston Villa went on to beat Manchester United 3–1 at Wembley to win the Coca-Cola Cup.

The coach journey back to Merseyside was depressing. Shaun and Tony Thomas, both of whom had been dropped, were particularly low. Indeed, Tony's relationship with John King was never the same after that day and he subsequently slapped in a transfer request. There was a kind of eerie atmosphere when we arrived in the players' lounge at Prenton Park. Most of us got drunk and the evening ended with a few players arguing. Some framed photographs on the wall ended up smashed but the incident was nowhere near as big as has been suggested.

The hangover came when we played Grimsby Town at Prenton

Park. Trailing 1–0 when the half-time whistle sounded, a small section of supporters took it upon themselves to boo us off the field. After our efforts against Villa, we considered it a nerve that people should want to criticise us. The majority of fans were on our side; we knew that. But it only takes a few hundred people to create a negative atmosphere. We lost to Grimsby 2–1 and it was some time before the depression among the players and supporters lifted.

We played enough good football in March and April to get ourselves back in with a chance of promotion and our 2–0 win against Charlton Athletic at home on 26 April confirmed our place in the play-offs for the second successive season. It hardly mattered to us that we lost our last two matches of the season, 3–2 against Sunderland and 2–1 against Birmingham. The defeat against Birmingham was significant for our opponents. Anything less than three points would have consigned them to relegation from the first division.

Standing between Tranmere and a place in the play-off final at Wembley was Leicester City. We should have beaten them, as we had done at Prenton Park earlier in the season. This time we failed to rise to the occasion, drawing 0–0 at home and losing 2–1 away. In the defeat at Filbert Street, David Speedie scored the winning goal late on, after which goalkeeper Eric Nixon was dismissed for racing half the length of the field to join a ruck of players before punching David square on the chin.

Yet again, Tranmere had missed out on success by the narrowest of margins. I was overwhelmed by frustration but at least I had the World Cup in the USA with the Republic of Ireland to look forward to. The rest of the Tranmere players had a whole summer to reflect on what went wrong.

Our preparations for the 1994–95 season took us to the Isle of Man for a mini tournament. I had just returned from the World Cup and needed a rest. But I recalled the happy times in Douglas as a child and reckoned returning there with the Tranmere players was just what I needed. I don't remember much about the football but I do remember the quality nights out with Eric Nixon.

Back on the British mainland, full-back Ian Nolan was sold to Sheffield Wednesday for £1.5 million. His departure was inevitable. He had been seeking a big move for some time and rightly thought his ability warranted a position with a Premier League club. We were sorry to see him go. He forged a useful partnership with Pat Nevin down the left flank and earned more than his fair share of man-of-the-match awards. In time, he would be replaced by Gary Stevens, the former Everton and England full-back, who was signed from Glasgow Rangers for £350,000. Gary for Ian was an acceptable swap and Tranmere were not weakened. And with another year's experience behind us, we saw no reason why we couldn't secure that dream spot in the Premier League. With Peter Johnson taking over as chairman at Everton, Tranmere appointed Frank Corfe as his replacement. Frank's first job was to oversee the refurbishment of Prenton Park. Three of the four stands were totally rebuilt in 1994. And with more money than ever coming into the English game, Frank knew Tranmere had no choice but to mount a serious assault on promotion to the top flight.

We began well enough and seemed to be showing more consistency than in recent seasons. Personally, things went well, too. My second goal of three in the 4–2 win against Luton Town on 30 August 1994 was my hundredth for Tranmere. I had no idea I'd scored so many goals for the club and it was only when the public address announcer revealed that information that I realised I had joined a handful of club strikers in surpassing one hundred goals. It was a special moment, but nothing compared with the four goals I scored in the 6–1 win against Barnsley at Prenton Park on 1 November. It was something of a balmy night. I remember the *Liverpool Echo*'s match report revealing that Barnsley had enjoyed (if that is the right word) twenty-five attempts on goal while Tranmere had nine. Everything seemed to go well for me that night. In addition to my four goals, I had a hand in the other two.

I might have smiled afterwards had I not limped out of the dressing-room with intense pain in my right foot. It was agreed that I would have surgery three days after our game against

Stoke City on 17 December, by which time the pain was so bad I needed an injection. Doctor Mike Azurdia gave me the jab but it served only to deprive me of all feeling in my foot. We lost 1–0 and I don't recall having a touch of the ball. The operation kept me out of football for another month but, on my return against Wimbledon in the FA Cup, I injured my thigh and missed another four weeks of action. Even when I returned, I found myself out of the team. I asked for a chat with John King. 'If you're not going to play me, I'm going to look for a team who will,' I told the manager. I was out of order to allow my frustration with not playing to show through. I should have adopted a more professional attitude, especially as Tranmere had done well in my absence. Still, when I returned to the starting line-up we had the look of potential champions.

The word 'potential' is rich in significance because we contrived to cock it up. After beating Bolton Wanderers 1–0 on 14 April 1995, we were installed as first-division title favourites. We needed to win only three of our last five matches to secure promotion to the Premier League, which was well within our capabilities given the form we were in. So it is with some embarrassment that I recall the circumstances surrounding our failure. We lost 5–0 away at Derby County, 2–0 at home to Southend United, and 5–1 away at West Bromwich Albion. This was relegation form. Draws against Wolves and champions Middlesbrough secured a place in the play-offs for the third successive season, but this was hardly an achievement given our position after the Bolton game.

Still, we just had to beat Reading over two legs to earn a place at Wembley. Deep down we thought, as we had beaten them twice in the first division that season, that this was our best chance of qualifying. How wrong we were. Reading took us to pieces at Prenton Park, winning 3–1 with a display of controlled football. They dominated the midfield to such an extent that we were lucky to emerge from the match with only a two-goal deficit. Before the return leg at Elm Park, John King arranged for us all to have some team therapy in the hotel. A guy came to see the squad and he had us doing a range of things including mock war. I was surprised none of us got hurt. It seemed a stupid way to prepare for such a crucial match and, in truth, we were baffled. We drew 0–0 against Reading in the return leg but the damage had already been done.

Our failure that spring reminded me of Newport County's failure in the third division in 1983. The pain was comparable, and both times the consequences were grim. Newport were never the same and left the Football League altogether five years later. For John King, it was his last chance of promotion with Tranmere. We had crumbled so badly towards the end of the season that I didn't think we could recover. He had many good points and he is still the most successful boss the club has had. I always had respect for him but I'd heard a couple of players say they didn't feel the same way. I think some questioned his tactics and his ability to man-manage. Often in team talks he spent more time discussing the virtues of the opposition instead of motivating his own players. Strangely, that was the opposite philosophy to Bill Shankly, on whom I know John King tried to model himself. As Tranmere grew in stature, maybe the job became too big for him.

Before our game against Bristol City at Ashton Gate in April, I called the squad into my room in the hotel for a meeting. I remember my words clearly. 'Even if you don't want to win for John King, why not do it for Tranmere? And if you don't want to win for Tranmere, why not do it for yourselves?' Even self-interest failed to help our results in the end, though I have to make it clear I wanted to be successful at Tranmere as much for John King as I did for myself.

John showed he meant business in the summer of 1995, breaking Tranmere's transfer record to sign defender Shaun Teale from Aston Villa for £450,000 and bringing in striker Gary Bennett from Wrexham. He also allowed strikers Ian Muir and Chris Malkin to leave, believing that young Ian Moore, son of Tranmere coach Ronnie, would come good. For a time, it looked as though everything would click into place. Gary and I forged a useful striking partnership, Ian looked promising in his rare run-outs, Shaun was solid at the back, and Danny Coyne looked an able deputy for the dropped Eric Nixon. We won our first three matches of the season to sit proudly on top of the first-division table. Could this be our season? Alas, no. Old failings still haunted us. For every memorable victory, such as the time we beat Derby County 5–1 at Prenton Park, there was a shock like the 3–2 defeat at Watford.

My own form was acceptable. I had scored sixteen goals by the turn of the year, two of them coming against Oldham Athletic on a difficult pitch at Prenton Park on Boxing Day. I always seemed to do well against Oldham, except for one notable exception. After being sent off in a disappointing match at Boundary Park, I later received a bill after my anger got the better of me and I kicked a hole in a dressing-room door. It was the only thing I had hit right all afternoon, and they invoiced me for it! Though I never saw the funny side of that incident, Ged Brannan clearly did. He was in the dressing-room receiving treatment for an injury when he saw my foot crash through the door. Ged, who couldn't see whose foot it was stuck in the hole, let out a huge laugh when the unidentified man struggled to wriggle himself free. But in the Boxing Day match I was especially certain of a good game. On Christmas Day, I managed to score eight goals in five minutes during training. I was buzzing and it showed the following day.

So why John King considered off-loading me is anyone's guess. For the first time since my move to Tranmere I was beginning to feel insecure. There was talk around Prenton Park that John wanted to pair Ian Moore and Gary Jones up front. Apparently, the club wanted to be relieved of my salary. Ian had done well up to a point, scoring eight goals in eight matches, while Gary showed himself to be talented and versatile. I could accept that the club had to look towards the future, but my goals suggested I was hardly any closer to retirement than when I moved to Prenton Park. There was also talk that Cardiff City wanted to take me on as a player-manager, while an official from the Major League Soccer in the USA asked if I would be interested in crossing the Atlantic for a two-year contract. My contract with Tranmere was due to end in May 1996 and there was no suggestion that John or Frank Corfe wanted to renew it. When they offered me a testimonial, it looked to everyone as though it was a sweetener, a gift to cushion the blow of my impending departure.

Worse still, Tranmere were slipping down the first-division at an alarming rate. Suddenly, after beginning the season among the title favourites, we were now relegation material. By the end of March, Ian Moore had lost his form and was a shadow of his former self; Gary Bennett and I, for all his pace and workrate, were not hitting it off up front; and Shaun Teale picked up a number of injuries which diminished his strength in the defence. Shaun was exposed badly when we lost 6–2 against Derby County at the Baseball Ground on 8 April 1996. After the match I spotted my old friend Jim Smith, the Derby manager, talking to John King. As I passed Jim, I shouted to him: 'If you need a twenty-goal-a-season man, why not sign me?' Jim laughed.

I liked John. He had signed me at a time when most other managers were debating whether I could still play the game; and, as all Tranmere supporters know, he played a major part in turning the club around. Without John there might not be a Tranmere. But in this game, as in every other, you have to put yourself first. I know John would agree with that.

After the defeat against Derby, I did not expect to be playing under John King for much longer, but even that didn't prepare me for the telephone call I received at eight o'clock in the morning on Friday, 12 April 1996.

'Hello, John. It's Frank Corfe.'

'Hello, Frank, how are you?'

'I'm fine, John. Can you come up to meet me this morning?'

'Yes, what for?'

'I'll discuss it with you in person.'

I showered and dressed within twenty minutes and was sitting with Frank in his office within the hour.

'I'll get straight to the point. John King will no longer be manager of Tranmere Rovers FC today and I want to know if you're interested in the position.'

'Position?'

'Yes. I want you to be the player-manager of Tranmere. Interested?'

'But . . .'

'I have another person in mind who will be offered the job if you don't take it. It's as simple as that. Do you want to be player-manager of Tranmere?'

'I need to phone my wife.'

'Of course, but I'd like a decision soon.'

I telephoned Joan, who expressed her surprise. Like myself, she though Frank had called the meeting to tell me my contract would not be renewed and that I would be leaving Tranmere that summer. Suddenly, without the time to prepare for it properly, we were being confronted with an offer that would change our lives. Joan said she would back my decision whatever it was. I had feelings of elation and feelings of guilt. I genuinely felt sorry for John King but, whether I took the job or not, I could not save his position at Tranmere. I replaced the telephone receiver and faced Frank.

'OK, I'll take the job,' I said.

'Good,' Frank replied, offering his hand.

We discussed terms immediately. My contract would take me to the end of the 1997–98 season but would not involve a wage rise. I didn't even raise my eyebrows. I knew Tranmere were short of cash and, besides, money was irrelevant. The security of a two-year deal plus the novelty of becoming a football manager dominated my thoughts. Frank and I shook hands again and as I left his office to join the players at training, the chairman asked if I would keep the news confidential for a time.

I trained with the players as normal and smiled to myself as Ronnie Moore and Kenny Jones, the kit man, laid out cones for a session of sprints. They knew nothing at that point. Few people asked why John King wasn't at training. After we had showered and dressed, Frank emerged and asked us all for our attention.

'There is a change I wish to inform you of,' he said. 'John King is no longer manager of Tranmere Rovers. His replacement is somebody known to all of you. Would John Aldridge please come to the front.'

I was a little self-conscious as I left my seat and stood next to Frank. There was silence for a few seconds as everyone in the room waited for my first words as Tranmere's player-manager. I'd already planned what I was going to say.

'I know this is a surprise to you all, but it was also a surprise to me. All I will say is this: if there is anyone who doesn't want to play for me, doesn't want to give me one hundred per cent, will you please leave the room now.' Nobody left the room. I began speaking of the subtle changes I intended to introduce before I asked the players if I could talk to them on an individual basis. I told everyone that Ray Mathias, Tranmere's longest serving player and already on the coaching staff, would be my right-hand man. Then I went to Prenton Park for a press conference and a photocall. I arrived home in the early afternoon and thought my head might explode. For the rest of the day, the telephone did not stop ringing. I received a number of telegrams and goodwill messages from friends and supporters. Kevin Keegan's telegram was the funniest. 'Welcome to the grey-haired club,' he said. That summed up a special, if tiring day. I would like to have relaxed but we had to prepare for the game against Leicester City at Prenton Park the following day.

I didn't want to make changes for the sake of it but I knew certain things had to be done. I adopted a new system of four defenders with Liam O'Brien in front of them, and four midfielders with one striker – myself – in front of them. I didn't mind playing alone up front providing the midfielders supported me at every available opportunity. The problem was the tactics didn't work out too well in the first half of the game against Leicester and I was a worried man at half-time. We drew the game 1–1, which was a relief, and I spent an hour after the match giving interviews to the media. I was positive, telling the journalists that much good had come out of the game.

I stuck with the tactics for the home game against Ipswich Town the following midweek and watched everything go according to plan. We won a thrilling match 5–2 and played our best football of the season. Kenny Irons had an inspired game, scoring twice and dictating play as I'd hoped. The fact that the midfielders all played well suggested my new formula had given them more freedom and flexibility. That night I met my friend and former Liverpool team-mate John Wark and offered him a coaching position at Tranmere. He agreed to give it thought but decided his family were settled in Ipswich and might not appreciate a return to Merseyside. I respected his decision and enjoyed a memorable drinking session with him in a bar in the Moat House Hotel. John could drink anyone under the table but trying to keep up with him was always good fun.

Further draws against Port Vale, Grimsby Town and Charlton Athletic confirmed our first-division status and we were relaxed as we beat newly crowned champions Sunderland 2–0 at Prenton Park in the final match of the campaign. Sunderland had come into the match on the back of an eighteen-match unbeaten run.

When the season ended, I reflected on the events of the previous month. After fearing my days at Tranmere were coming to a close, I was now part of the fabric of the club. The club's immediate future was, in a very real way, in my hands. The downside was that I had little free time. I was already involved in a sports kit manufacturing firm, US Athletic, which was run by my friend, Brian Omar. On top of that, I had two full-time jobs, not to mention a family and hectic social life. Twenty-four hours were no longer enough each day. As I tried to get to grips with the job, I felt myself growing increasingly tired; but as my mind was active, I was sleeping less and less. I was beginning to see why Kevin Keegan mentioned grey hair in his telegram. This really was a tough job and I hadn't even tasted the bad times. I decided I would give it two years, after which I would retire as a player and decide if I was cut out to be a manager.

Ronnie Moore had to go. He had served John King for a decade as assistant manager but he was not my kind of man. Ronnie accepted my reasons for dispensing with his services. To his credit, he agreed to stay on and help me until the end of the season. Kenny Jones, by contrast, disappeared off the face of the earth. I was never given the chance to tell him his services were no longer required, and neither was I able to shake his hand. I haven't seen him since.

The Sunderland game wasn't quite the end of the season. On 10 May, I brought together most of the Liverpool players from the 1987–88 season to face Tranmere for my testimonial match. I diplomatically decided to play forty-five minutes for each side. More than 12,000 people turned up to make it a memorable night. The scoreline was irrelevant and I was anxious to make sure a host of charities benefited from the proceeds.

When it was all over, I breathed a sigh of relief. But if I thought the hard part was done, I was in for a shock. The most difficult times were just around the corner.

— 9 —

FOREVER YOUNG

T HE Republic of Ireland emerged from Italia '90 as one of the world's leading footballing nations. By the start of the 1990–91 season, we were ranked as the seventh best nation on earth, having raked in £1.2 million profit from the World Cup. The FAI was now bankable for the first time in years and, at long last, a respected force in international circles. No longer were we regarded as underdogs. Jack Charlton had brought in good players to fit an effective system, producing a team that stood a chance of beating any other country. Most importantly, we had given the Irish people a new footballing identity. With their easygoing nature and enthusiasm for partying, Irish fans were now as famous as their players. Suddenly, they were making news just for being Irish.

The immediate post-Italia '90 period was the best time to be an Irish footballer, so you can imagine how I felt to be involved. I might have been from England but I felt as Irish as any of the five million or so who lived in the Republic. I had an affinity for the country and there was clearly a mutual affection. Whenever I was in Dublin, people wanted to talk to me, buy me drinks, or just shake my hand. It was incredible that they should have so much time for me. They could sense my enthusiasm for all things Irish and I suppose they could relate to that.

So when I began the 1990–91 international season by scoring a hat-trick for Ireland against Turkey at Lansdowne Road, I could hardly have been more pleased. Anxious to prove to my critics that I could succeed at the highest level, the goals were well timed and doubled my tally at international level to six. They were important goals; they helped us beat the Turks 5–0 to kick-start our Euro '92 campaign with two vital points. Also in our qualifying group were England and Poland, with only one nation going forward to the finals in Sweden. It was a tough task but, because we played so well and remained unbeaten, our eventual failure to reach the finals was disappointing. Our destiny was in our own hands for most of the time and we only had ourselves to blame when England finished top of the group and secured a place in Euro '92.

To be fair, England played well against us at Lansdowne Road on 14 November 1990. Though new manager Graham Taylor surprisingly dropped Paul Gascoigne, England outplayed us for long periods and probably deserved to win. We never came close to fulfilling our potential so we were pleased to finish with a 1–1 draw. The return game at Wembley in March was a different story. Turning in one of our best displays of the campaign, we outplayed the opposition. At times, England struggled to get the ball out of their own half, yet somehow they scored fortuitously when Lee Dixon's shot was deflected into the goal off Steve Staunton. We equalised soon after through Niall Quinn and had a great chance to win the game when Ray Houghton went through on goal only to miss. Again we drew 1–1, though this time it was Ireland who felt the frustration of missed opportunities.

The failure to win at Wembley wouldn't have been too much of a problem had we taken our chances in two games against Poland. Drawing 0–0 with them at Lansdowne Road was another blow, but letting a 3–1 lead slip against them in Warsaw was what really proved crucial. I was a substitute that night and marvelled at our performance for eighty minutes. But sustaining it for a further ten minutes proved beyond us, though we were hardly helped by an injury to Steve Staunton. We drew the game 3–3 and the atmosphere in the dressing-room afterwards was as if we'd been beaten. We were no longer in control of our destiny.

By this time I was a Tranmere Rovers player. Moving to Prenton Park seemed appropriate after the unsettling two-year period in Spain, yet it could have spelled the end of my international playing days. While I was playing top-flight football I always felt confident Jack Charlton would keep me in his plans. But with Tranmere outside the top division, there was a thought at the back of my mind that Jack might dispense with my services. I'd certainly taken a risk. But Jack persevered with me and, if anything, my form for Ireland improved as the years went on. Incredibly, it was as a Tranmere player that I turned myself into a prolific international goalscorer.

Our Euro '92 fate would be decided on 13 November 1991. We needed to beat Turkey in Istanbul and hope England would slip up in Poland. I hated Istanbul. We went for a pre-match stroll and were distressed to see chained bears walking around in pain. There was a horrible atmosphere in the city, a sense of doom, a feeling of belligerence. We couldn't wait to get out of the place. Our mood did not improve when we tried to enter the stadium. Hundreds of Turkish supporters were hanging around and they proceeded to spit at us as we got off the team bus. Thankfully, John Byrne was in good form and he scored twice in our 3–1 victory. But when Gary Lineker scored for England in Poland, thus forcing a 1–1 draw, our hopes of qualification were in tatters. It was only late on that we realised England had qualified. One look at the glum faces on the Irish substitutes' bench confirmed our worst fears. It was a depressing day all round.

Chris Hughton, the Tottenham Hotspur full-back, came closest to summing up the disappointment. As we tried to console each other, Chris lit a cigar and started to smoke it. No words were necessary. The look in his eyes suggested he knew his international career was over. I was more disappointed for him than for anyone else. Most of us still had a future in the Irish squad and knew there might yet be more games at the highest level. The same could not be said for Chris. As he casually puffed his cigar, he was savouring his last moments as an Irish international.

In my opinion, we were the best team in our qualifying group and should really have qualified instead of England, but the best teams don't always get their just rewards. We were perhaps lucky to qualify for Euro '88, yet now, with a better team, we failed to qualify for Euro '92 when a place in Sweden was ours for the taking. To add to our frustration, England failed miserably in the tournament, finishing bottom of their group and going home long before Denmark beat Germany 2–0 in the final in Stockholm.

The rest of that 1991–92 season was an anti-climax for Ireland. We lost 1–0 against Wales at the Royal Dublin Society Showground. Why we played there I'll never know. The pitch must have been about 140 yards long and would never have met with official approval had the match been in a recognised competition. The RDS Showground is usually used for horseracing and concerts, not football. We won games against Switzerland and the USA in Dublin before beating Albania 2–0 in a World Cup qualifying match at Lansdowne Road in May. I scored in that game, taking my tally for Ireland to eight in forty-five matches. But I remember being tired for most of that match. Four days before, I had returned from the Tranmere Rovers players' holiday in Magaluf. Eager to burn off the excesses of the trip, I tried to do a bit of training when I got to Dublin. 'No way, Aldo,' said Jack. 'I want you resting.'

My own form had been excellent that season and, after scoring forty goals for Tranmere Rovers, and playing some of the best football of my international career, the media voted me the Irish Sportswriters Player of the Year. These days, there are awards for everything. Yet the Irish award of 1992 was special and remains among my proudest possessions. After my early scoring record for Ireland, the Dublin press had every right to criticise me. They chose not to, however, preferring instead to encourage me. So when the good times came, and I was scoring regularly, I was happy to regard many Irish journalists as my friends.

Then it was off to America for the four-nation US Cup tournament alongside Italy, Portugal and the host nation. I love America; always have done. There is something special about the atmosphere in all the main cities. The belief that in America anything is possible is something of a cliché, but it is true. We were based in Boston, which is a particularly lovely place and boasts one of the largest Irish communities outside Dublin. And so, although the US Cup was the tour we supposedly did not need, we were welcomed with open arms by those who claimed Irish blood – which seemed to be everyone. Indeed, most of the players were happy for the opportunity to check out the numerous Irish bars in the area, and with the pressure off, we turned the trip into something of a working holiday.

It was in Boston that I really felt I'd finally made my mark in the world. Lining up for the national anthems before the Italy game, Gianluca Vialli, the Italian striker, approached me. 'John,' he said in an authentic Italian accent, 'after the match, my shirt, my shorts, my socks, for your shirt, your shorts, your socks.' The rest of the Irish players looked at me in disbelief. Gianluca was then among the best players in the world, yet there he was anxious to acquire souvenirs of the day he played against me. My ego came in for a good massage on that occasion. All I needed was a big chair, a fat cigar and a pair of slippers to fully lap up the boost to my credibility! I'd played against Gianluca in a friendly match at Wembley the previous summer. I was with Real Sociedad, he was with Sampdoria. Presumably he remembered me from that.

But the feeling of goodwill disappeared once the match in Boston kicked off. The referee was atrocious, sending off Pat Bonner for a foul when none seemed to be committed, and giving the Italians a debatable penalty. To make matters worse, Franco Baresi and I spent most of the match niggling each other. Great player though he was, Franco was someone I found arrogant and far too self-assured. Perhaps this was essential to the way he played but he didn't strike me as being a particularly nice person. To add to my disappointment, Italy beat us 2–0, though they could hardly have been pleased with the manner of their victory. Ray Houghton and I were fuming after the game. We approached the referee, who looked Italian.

'Are you Italian?' I asked.

'No, no, I am American.'

'Is your dad Italian?'

'Yes.'

'Oh, so you're Italian, aren't you?'

'I was born in Italy but I came to America when I was ten.'

Ray and I told Jack and he in turn informed the FAI. We couldn't believe a person with strong Italian connections could be asked to referee a match involving the Italian national team.

Niall Quinn, our striker, had injured his back in the match and had to be carried on to the plane for the flight to our next match. As if that wasn't enough, he ended up drunk and was soon in a terrible state. Quinny was good to have around, even if he once cost Steve Staunton and I £12,000 each on a horse he had advised us to invest in. I recall, too, the time Niall slipped away after a light lunch during a get-together with the Irish squad. I managed to catch up with him at a Chinese restaurant in our hotel and was surprised to see him tucking into two main courses. Nobody could eat like Niall Quinn.

Having already lost 3–1 to the USA in Washington, it was important we beat Portugal in our last game. We did just that, though the Portuguese were a young team who showed great talent going forward. The victory at least gave us some credibility and much confidence for the mammoth World Cup programme that would dominate the 1992–93 international season.

Having already beaten Albania 2–0, we were off the mark in a group that contained Denmark, Spain, Latvia, Lithuania and Northern Ireland. With new players coming through the ranks, we felt we had a great chance of qualifying for the 1994 World Cup. Roy Keane, then with Nottingham Forest, had emerged almost from out of the blue and he was an excellent midfield player, but experienced players such as Paul McGrath, Kevin Moran, Andy Townsend, Ray Houghton and myself were still very much the backbone of the side.

My former Liverpool team-mate Ronnie Whelan was still around and he turned in a fine display as Ireland beat Latvia 4–0 in the second World Cup qualifier. Though suffering with various injuries, Ronnie dominated the midfield against tricky opposition. Kevin Sheedy scored our first goal in the opening forty-five minutes and I secured the victory by scoring three times in the second half. It was my second hat-trick for Ireland and now my international tally was eleven in forty-eight appearances.

We followed that up with two marvellous goalless draws against Denmark in Copenhagen and Spain in Seville. The Danes were the newly crowned European champions and had, in Brian Laudrup, one of the best players in the world. He was in devastating form against us but Ireland had chances to win. Indeed, in the last minute, substitute David Kelly came close to scoring with a header. In Spain a month later, we also had chances to win. I actually put the ball into the net only to have my effort disallowed. Why, I'll never know. The Russian linesman flagged Niall Quinn for offside as I rounded goalkeeper Zubizarreta to score. Even Diego Maradona, watching from the press box, said the goal should have been allowed to stand. Diego, once the world's greatest player, had not long signed for Seville and was an interested spectator. I understand he was impressed with Ireland's display and particularly that of Roy Keane.

During that trip to Seville, I received much attention from the Spanish press after my spell in San Sebastian. I also met up with Goicoechea, my former team-mate at Real Sociedad. It was nice to know I wasn't forgotten, even if our draw in Seville was a blow to Spain's hopes of qualifying for the World Cup.

I was recovering from an operation for a torn stomach muscle when Ireland played host to Northern Ireland at Lansdowne Road in our fifth World Cup qualifier. With the political situation still delicate between the two nations, protocol dictated that only the Republic's national anthem, 'Amhran na bh Fiann', be played. With Ray Houghton in fine form, Ireland won 3–0 thanks to goals by Andy Townsend, Niall Quinn and Steve Staunton.

The World Cup campaign soon became a three-horse race between ourselves, Spain and Denmark, with the top two teams qualifying. Our 1–1 draw with Denmark in Dublin on 28 April 1993 might have been a bad result for Ireland on paper. But given that Denmark played so well, and we equalised late on through Niall, Jack was delighted that we picked up a point. We were still unbeaten and had our destiny very much in our own hands.

Going to Albania the following month was an education. One of the poorer and more mysterious nations of Europe, Albania was everything we expected it to be. Everywhere we looked there seemed to be people with arms or legs missing, begging for food. Poverty was rife. There was an atmosphere of despair hanging in the air and there was no escape. Our hotel was of a poor standard, with homeless children always hanging around. England had gone to Albania not long before and we'd heard a story of how Paul Gascoigne had cut up Mars Bars and thrown them to the children to eat. They were delighted and took to Gazza, as most people do. We found the kids in Tirana to be equally keen to meet us yet it was hard not to feel sorry for them. They had nothing except their smiles.

Winning a difficult game 2–1 kept our World Cup hopes alive, as did winning 2–0 against Latvia in Riga, and 1–0 against Lithuania in Vilnius. It ensured our three-game Eastern European tour was successful. A further 2–0 victory over Lithuania in Dublin – I scored the opening goal to take my tally for Ireland to thirteen – set us up nicely for the home game against Spain in October.

And what an anti-climax it proved to be. I was already ruled out of the match with a thigh strain and I watched as Spain took us apart. Despite boasting a five-man midfield, Ireland couldn't get control of the midfield in the first half and Spain went three goals up. Reverting to a more familiar system, Ireland improved in the second half but could only pull one goal back, through John Sheridan. We lost 3–1 and I felt as bad as I did when Liverpool lost the first-division championship decider against Arsenal at Anfield in 1989. I really did feel our World Cup dreams were over, although as it turned out, John's strike, which seemed at the time to be a consolation, would prove vital at the end of the qualifiers when goal difference was added up.

Our fate would be decided in Belfast on 17 November 1993 when we faced Northern Ireland. We knew that victory would take us to USA '94, while a draw would be good enough only if Spain's game against Denmark did not finish all square. Defeat and we were out.

But if the mathematicians were working overtime trying to figure out the various permutations, the politicians were anxious to be diplomatic. The game was played against a backdrop of political uncertainty and, thanks to Northern Ireland manager Billy Bingham, there was a lot of rubbish flying around in the press. Billy had gone on record before the match calling the Republic of Ireland players carpetbaggers and mercenaries. This was wrong, insensitive, and way out of order. My career with Ireland made me proud and had nothing to do with the pursuit of money. I'd have represented my adopted country for nothing and I believe others in our squad would have done, too. If Billy didn't like the fact that English-born players could represent Ireland, he should have complained to the world's governing body, FIFA. We were acting within the rules.

We were on the team coach, travelling to Windsor Park, when we realised the full extent of the political instability. There were security men on motorbikes both in front of the bus and behind it, while above us helicopters kept watch. As we turned off the main road a hundred or so yards from Windsor Park, a woman and her two children were waiting to cross the road. Knowing the Irish players were on the coach, she turned her back and made sure her kids' backs were turned, too. She didn't want them to see Catholics from the Republic. Such a simple act yet so significant. It made me realise how deep-seated the problems are in the north.

The game itself was intense but far too tight for it to be entertaining. The first half was a virtual non-event, even if we were the dominant side. I don't think I had a chance in the opening forty-five minutes. The second half was more open but my heart sank when Jimmy Quinn scored superbly from twenty yards in the seventy-third minute to give Northern Ireland the lead. Three minutes later, one of our substitutes, Alan McLoughlin, equalised with an equally sweet shot. After the match I heard a story that Alan wasn't even supposed to have been on the field. Apparently, Tony Cascarino was supposed to have replaced Ray Houghton but wasn't wearing an Ireland shirt. Instead of waiting for him to put one on, Jack sent Alan on to the pitch. Whether or not the story is true, it was an inspired substitution. We held out for the remaining fourteen minutes and threw our arms into the air when the final whistle sounded. It wasn't quite the end of the story because Spain's game against Denmark still had three minutes to run. Spain were leading 1–0 but if Denmark were to equalise, it meant we were knocked out. Denmark had two great chances but could not convert them. The final whistle in Seville confirmed that we had qualified for the World Cup finals in the USA.

The celebrations afterwards were typically memorable; I was the only sober one there. I'd been suffering with flu and nearly didn't play in the match. I felt weak, didn't have a good game, and watched as everyone else got drunk. I had mixed feelings as, one by one, the rest of the lads stumbled back to the hotel at around seven o'clock in the morning. In the months leading up to USA '94 I began to have more feelings of insecurity, which were confirmed when Jack called me for a chat.

'Aldo,' he said, 'I've had a word with the doctor and he's told me the warm conditions in America won't suit you at your age. Perhaps it's time for me to look for a younger man, and I am looking towards playing Tommy Coyne in the World Cup.' I was understandably gutted and wondered whether I'd even make the twenty-two-man squad for the tournament. But when, on 1 June 1994, Jack announced his squad, I was delighted to find my name on the list at number nine.

It was a new-look Irish squad that boarded the flight from Dublin to New York for USA '94. Young players like Jason McAteer and Phil Babb had matured in a short space of time and were essential to Jack's style of play in America. Like myself, Jason was born on Merseyside but had Irish blood. When Jack offered him the chance to play for Ireland, he had no hesitation in saying yes. It was a boost because the Bolton Wanderers midfielder was versatile, had an abundance of energy, and was clearly set for a promising career. Phil was a versatile player, too. He could perform well in any defensive role and had pace, which would be essential at this level. We also had a young full-back in Gary Kelly of Leeds United, yet the average age of the squad was no younger than in 1990. Veterans such as myself, Pat Bonner, Ray Houghton, Paul McGrath, Kevin Moran and Andy Townsend were still around and still very much part of Jack's plans.

We went into the finals on the back of victories against Holland and Germany, results which gave us confidence for the tournament. We had been drawn in what the press called the Group of Death, alongside Italy, Norway and Mexico. Italy had some of the best players in the world and were among the tournament favourites; Norway had knocked out England and were a growing soccer force; and Mexico, though prone to underachievement on the world stage, would find the hot, humid conditions to their liking. This was by far the toughest group in the competition, yet with the possibility of three teams progressing to the second round, we fancied our chances.

We'd been hoping for a five-day period of acclimatisation in Florida but there seemed little chance of that when, after changing at New York, we landed at Orlando Airport in mid-June. Though there was a heavy humidity in the air, we found ourselves in the middle of gale force winds and heavy rain. It was hardly what Jack and his management team expected. For two days it was the same: wet, windy and humid. Jack was panicking. Luckily for him, by the third day, the weather had changed and was more in line with what we'd been expecting. In fact, it was so hot we wanted to spend most our time indoors, out of the sun.

The Irish World Cup party hired an entire floor of the Hilton Hotel in Orlando, with each player getting a room to himself, except Jason McAteer and Gary Kelly who told Jack they were too lonely and would prefer to share. I was happy to have a room to myself. In any case, we didn't intend to spend too long in our rooms. We had a few evenings out at Church Street Station where we met up with television's Des Lynam and my friend Ray Stubbs, the football reporter. The comedian Brendan O'Carroll was there too. Brendan's humour is of the Chubby Brown variety, with plenty of rude jokes, and he was a great guy to have around. Not that he appreciated my presence one night. Brendan had grown a pony-tail at the back of his head for charity and was proud of its length. After a few drinks, I expressed a desire to cut it off. I found a knife from behind the bar and some of the players held Brendan down. Just to make sure the pony-tail would cut easily, Jason and Phil Babb pulled it tight. The pony-tail snapped like a frozen twig and we all fell about laughing. It had taken Brendan six years to grow it. The next time we met the comedian, a few days later, the pony-tail had mysteriously reappeared on the back of his head. 'I managed to have it welded back on,' he said with a smile. Even I didn't have the heart to cut it off again.

That first night with Brendan summed up the mood of the Irish camp. As always, we had tremendous team spirit and we all effortlessly fitted into each other's lifestyles. When twenty-two footballers are together for a number of weeks you have to get on with each other; and you need the odd night out to help ease the pressure. Although we were enjoying ourselves, you could sense an underlying feeling of trepidation. We were due to face Italy in New Jersey on 18 June and if it wasn't the likes of Roberto Baggio who dominated our thoughts, it was the knowledge that eleven members of our squad would not be in the starting line-up. Jack knew we were edgy so he insisted we relax as much as possible. That would often mean going to one of the large shopping malls that seem to be everywhere in Florida. It was at one mall that Andy Townsend, Tony Cascarino and I agreed to get our hair bleached. Andy went first and emerged with blond streaks, I went second and had only a cut and blow, while Tony went in third and had only a cut. 'You bastards,' Andy said when he saw he'd been done up like a kipper. To his credit, he stuck with his blond locks until the end of the tournament.

The Irish squad worked hard in training. There were usually two sessions a day, two hours in the morning, a break for lunch, and an hour or so in the afternoon. Most of the players lost weight, though we were dealing with heat progressively better as each day went on. Some of us even spent time in the gym. And whenever we trained, Jack insisted we drink fluids as often as possible. Florida was so hot and humid you could be dehydrated just sitting around doing nothing. I was injured for a couple of days and missed a few training sessions. But generally, the preparations for the opening game went well.

We flew to Newark two days before the kick-off against Italy, though our seven o'clock in the morning flight was too early for most of us. We stayed at the beautiful Sheraton Tara Hotel just outside New York, which was close to the Giants Stadium in New Jersey. I knew the day before the match that I wouldn't be in the starting line-up. Jack decided to play with a lone striker, Tommy Coyne, in a 4–5–1 formation. I was disappointed, but I felt confident I would get into the action at some point. When we were led out into the stadium for the match we couldn't believe how many Irish fans were there. We were under the impression that Italian fans would dominate but that couldn't have been further from the truth. Of the 76,000 there, two-thirds of them must have been from Ireland. I don't think I've seen so many Irish football shirts in my life. The noise was deafening when the match began.

Ireland began confidently and there were only eleven minutes on the clock when Ray Houghton controlled a loose ball with his chest and lobbed the Italian goalkeeper Pagliuca. Ray was always scoring important goals. I feared an Italian onslaught but it never came. Ireland seemed to grow in stature and could have added to the scoreline when John Sheridan hit the top of the crossbar with a fierce shot. I was sent on as a substitute for the hard-working Tommy Coyne and enjoyed the last few minutes of the match. I'd have liked more action – I felt Jack should have put me on earlier – but I still played a part in Ireland's most famous World Cup victory. When the final whistle heralded our 1–0 victory, the prevailing emotion was one of satisfaction in a job well done. We had beaten one of the best teams in the world and, what is more, deserved it.

Tommy was in a hell of a state after the game. He had lost too much fluid during the match and made the mistake of trying to replace it too quickly. On our flight back to Orlando, he was spread across three seats with ice packs all over his body. Tommy's condition certainly gave credence to Jack's view that players should be allowed water during matches. FIFA were not impressed when water bags were constantly being thrown from the Irish bench to the players. Tommy didn't train for the three days after the Italy match. The rest of us celebrated with a few drinks on the way back to Florida. Jack insisted that we enjoy ourselves and relax, and we did exactly that. It was a famous win. Our plan had been to get a draw against Italy and hope for the victory against Mexico that would surely put us through to the second phase. Victory in the opening match put us ahead of schedule.

With six days between the game against Italy and the game against Mexico, Jack arranged a number of days out for the players. We went to the Hard Rock Café in Orlando, Universal Studios and Sea World. One day, Jack took us all to Cocoa Beach, near Cape Canaveral on the coast. Ronnie Whelan and I went to a Star Trek convention one evening and I don't think I've seen so many overenthusiastic people in my life. I couldn't believe how men and women could take a television programme so seriously. We joined in the spirit of it, of course, and acquired a set of Mr Spock ears each. There was a time that night when I couldn't stop laughing, though I suppose you had to be there to appreciate how crazy it really was. A few of the players had their wives over in Orlando at that time but there was no chance of Joan and the kids joining me. Paul and Joanne were still at school and were not scheduled to break up for the summer holidays until early July. When you are away from your family for so long you are bound to feel lonely. Joan and I spoke on the telephone every day, of course, but I wanted her in America with me.

The six-day preparation for the Mexico game seemed to take forever and it came as some relief when the day finally arrived. Not that the weather provided much comfort. I opened the curtains and took one look at the scene outside. There wasn't a cloud in sight and though the air conditioning was on in my room, I could tell it was going to be a hot day. That's fine if you are sunbathing, but not when you are playing Mexico in the World Cup. Mexico might be famous for underachieving at international level but they are notoriously difficult to beat in hot conditions. It gave them an advantage even before the match kicked off.

The Citrus Bowl in Orlando was an excellent stadium, shaped like a horseshoe, with fans on only three sides. Like everything in America, it was larger than life. Unfortunately for the fans there was no cover, so the heat was bound to pose problems for them, too. Most to suffer was Steve Staunton, who was fair-skinned and blond-haired. Steve would frazzle even when walking in the sun, which raised question marks over the prospect of him playing for ninety minutes in such hot conditions.

For the second successive game, Jack left me out of the side, though this time I suspected I might enjoy more of the action. Tommy Coyne had covered much ground against Italy but the conditions in Orlando against Mexico would be even more difficult. And so it proved. Mexico were comfortable from the kick-off, even if we did give a good account of ourselves for the first forty minutes or so. Then it started to go wrong. Luis Garcia scored with a low shot from twenty yards to give Mexico a one-goal lead.

In the second half, the Citrus Bowl was a cauldron; a microwave oven without the luxury of an 'off' switch. Jack decided it was time to throw Jason McAteer and me into the action, hoping to unsettle the Mexicans. Jason had the advantage of youth and mystery – few outside Ireland and Britain had heard of him – while I had the advantage of experience and reputation, good or otherwise.

But things don't always work out as you plan them. Not only did Mexico score a second goal as we were warming up on the touchline – Luis Garcia again, with another low shot – but a routine substitution turned into a farce, thrusting me reluctantly into the limelight as an anti-hero. At two goals down it was looking ominous and Jack knew it. He was going crazy, kicking water bottles all over the place, and swearing at anyone who happened to be nearby. Jason was sent on to replace Steve Staunton, while I was given the go-ahead by Jack to replace Tommy. But a communication breakdown between a World Cup official – an Egyptian with a lifetime's supply of self-importance – and everybody else meant I wasn't legally allowed on to the field. I didn't know this, of course, so when Tommy came off I went on, or I tried to. This Egyptian with a blue hat and a yellow coat pulled me back, manhandling me in the process. My temper blew up and using every swear-word in my vocabulary – which is an achievement, believe me – I made the Egyptian aware of my sentiments. Acrimony poured out of me. I was uncontrollable. I even screamed in Spanish, just to make sure the Mexicans in the vicinity were aware of the injustice. Composure? Forgiveness? Understanding? There was no time for any of that. For the forty-five seconds it took me to declare war on one football official, we were playing Mexico with ten men, through no fault of our own.

Fifteen minutes later, in the eighty-fourth minute of the match, I scored: a downward header from twelve yards following Jason's clipped cross. The Mexican goalkeeper, Jorge Campos, less a human being than a blinding feast of colours, failed to deal with the bounce. The Irish supporters rose to their feet as one and made the most incredible noise. Ireland were back in the match and suddenly the draw we needed looked viable. Sensing time was against us, I ran into the goal to retrieve the ball, just to make sure the Mexicans were not tempted to delay the restart of the match. I found out later that goal was Ireland's one hundredth in World Cup history. My haste was futile. Eight minutes later, the referee blew the whistle to signal full time. We had lost and I feared for the first time that we might not progress to the second round. But a delighted Tony Cascarino put his arms around me.

'Well done, Aldo,' he said. 'Your goal means we only need to draw with Norway in our next game to qualify for the second round.' It wasn't long before Tony's words hit home. Even in defeat, my goal had effectively given us a draw.

After exchanging shirts and kind words with Hugo Sanchez,

the former Real Madrid striker, I sought the comfort of cold air in the dressing-rooms. Nobody was talking. I stripped off and wrapped a wet towel around my body. Bliss. I took as long as possible in the shower. I suppose it's a kind of masochism, where aching muscles and stinging cuts give pleasure. I came out of the shower cubicle, sat down, and allowed the air to dry me naturally.

In Orlando, it was 1.44 p.m. when the touchline débâcle took place. In Liverpool, it was 6.44 p.m. Joan was watching the match on television. Along with more than one billion viewers (yes, billion) around the world, she saw the full extent of my anger. And she knew something I didn't: the cameras had zoomed in on me to emphasise the incident in all its technicolour glory. The bad language was audible to even the weakest hearing aid. The hate in my face was visible to those who chose to close their ears. At some point in the dressing-room – I don't remember when – I sensed the media were waiting for me. They might have been on the other side of the ground yet I could almost feel them congregating, waiting for my immediate reaction to events that might take a week to analyse.

Inevitably, I was summoned by the World Cup press officer on duty that day. On walking into the media room, the press moved towards me. They wanted Jack as well but he had the advantage of knowing it was always like that. And then the circus began. Dozens of journalists gathered around me to ask about the touchline incident and the importance of my goal. Camera lights flashed at me. Television crews followed me. Tape recorders and microphones were thrust under my nose, some so close I could have eaten them without having to adjust the position of my head.

I learned later that my picture was prominently displayed in newspapers in most of the 200 or so countries and dominions of the world. The touchline scene was shown on television news programmes throughout the day. For a few hours at least, and much against my will, I was among the most famous people in the world.

The following day, however, I was handed a £1,000 fine by

FIFA for my 'bad behaviour', and for his insistence that the players be allowed to drink water during matches, Jack was fined £7,000 and banned from the touchline for our next match. This was where FIFA were bang out of order. When I was warming up as a substitute, I could see fans being stretchered out of the stadium. Apparently they had fainted in the heat. So if fans sitting down could be affected by the conditions, it must have been a lot worse for the players sprinting around for ninety minutes. There is no doubt about it, games should have been staged later in the day. I can understand that television schedules dictated the kick-off times but this was missing the point. The pursuit of television money put players' lives at risk. Asking us to perform under pressure in the fierce midday heat was a short-sighted decision by people who have probably never even kicked a ball.

In the aftermath of the Mexico game, Irish fans back in Dublin arranged a series of collections to help pay the fines that FIFA had imposed on Jack and I. We'd heard that the money raised exceeded £100,000 and were delighted to discover it had been donated to charity.

When we flew off to Newark two days later for the game against Norway in the Giants Stadium, we felt confident. All we needed to do was keep a clean sheet and we were through to the second round. And if I had to back one side to stop anyone else from scoring it would be Ireland. We had defended well so far and in Paul McGrath and Phil Babb had two of the outstanding defenders in the tournament. Norway, who also found the conditions uncomfortable, had beaten Mexico in their opening match but had lost to Italy. They needed to beat us to stand any chance of progressing.

I was given a boost when Jack gave me a place in the starting line-up. Deciding to rest Tommy Coyne was probably wise, while Jack knew I would be in a confident mood after my goal against Mexico. Our spirits soared when we discovered the temperature in the Giants Stadium was two or three degrees cooler than in the Citrus Bowl. But it didn't help the quality of the match. Norway, though full of decent players, hardly played like a team going out for victory, while Ireland didn't produce their most convincing display. The goalless draw seemed inevitable, even if there were some difficult moments for Ireland. My own display was also below par and, after a couple of half-chances, I was replaced by David Kelly late in the game. It was at least good for David to have a taste of World Cup action, but I felt a more convincing display up front would have given me a great chance of being an automatic selection for our second-round game. I didn't know it then, but my appearance against Norway would be my last in the World Cup.

Results elsewhere conspired to send us back to Orlando on 4 July for a game against Holland. I had figured in all of Ireland's previous eight World Cup matches and I was bitterly disappointed not to get even a chance as a substitute. I half-expected to be omitted from the starting line-up, but not to be given a chance late in the match as a substitute hurt me. It was by far the worst moment of my Irish career under Jack. By half-time we were two goals down and chasing the game. Two uncharacteristic defensive errors handed goals to Dennis Bergkamp and Wim Jonk. Wim's goal was particularly galling because his shot was weak but somehow slipped through Pat Bonner's hands. With little to lose, Ireland played well in the second half and Paul McGrath had a goal mysteriously disallowed. But the luck wasn't with us that day. I felt things might have been different had I been given an opportunity mid-way throught the second half. I don't like to question Jack's methods and neither do I like to blow my own trumpet. But this was one occasion when I should have been thrust into the action when time was running out. That was all forgotten afterwards, however. We drowned our sorrows in the only way we knew how: with a good old Irish knees-up. We partied until the early hours and, if disappointed by our departure from USA '94, at least enjoyed the freedom to relax after six weeks under the microscope.

Joan and the kids were in America by then so I had the people who mattered most around me. When Joan first arrived I planned a prank to wind her up. I had false studs put in my ears and nose, grew a goatee beard, and planned to shock her with my new look. Joan's face was a picture when she set eyes on her gypsy-looking husband. It was only when I revealed the studs were merely magnets that she managed to force a smile, but I could tell she was worried. My goatee had to go, too. Joanne didn't like it. I had vowed to keep it until we were knocked out of the World Cup so, from Joanne's point of view, it was a good job we didn't reach the final.

Holland lost to Brazil in the quarter-final and Brazil went on to beat Italy in the final on 17 July in the Rose Bowl. It wasn't a great final and, after a goalless draw, Brazil won on penalties. Unlike the new world champions, Ireland had managed to beat Italy in ninety minutes, something which brought its own satisfaction.

The Ireland players were invited to a civic reception in Phoenix Park, Dublin, following our defeat against Holland but I declined it. I wanted to stay in America with my wife and kids. When the rest of the players left the Hilton, there was a great void. After spending the best part of six weeks with thirty or so familiar faces, suddenly the hotel seemed empty. I didn't really know how to cope at first and suffered a sense of loss. I'd promised the kids a five-day holiday around the Walt Disney World complex, which proved to be physically and mentally draining for me. I tried to hide my discomfort, of course, because I was anxious to give the kids a good time. The following week we went to Clearwater for a seven-day break. This would be my holiday. For the entire week I planned to do nothing but sit in the sun, something that nearly proved costly. On one occasion, while I sunbathed I noticed two sharks swimming menacingly towards Paul who was, in his innocence, paddling in the water. I've never moved so quickly in my life. I grabbed Paul and threw him on to the sand, letting out a huge sigh of relief in the process. We returned to England the day of the World Cup final.

Overall, it had been a good World Cup. There seemed to be more emphasis on attack than in Italia '90, with better matches, and a more carefree spirit. It ensured a good atmosphere in and around the stadiums. The Americans rarely fail when it comes to big events and they turned this World Cup into something memorable. Italia '90 was typically European and, in a sense, was played in familiar circumstances. USA '94, in organisation and atmosphere, was something new to most teams, fostering peace and friendship among competing nations and giving the game the boost it needed. The downside was the shooting of Andres Escobar, the Colombian defender, who was murdered allegedly for scoring an own goal in his team's crucial game against the USA in Los Angeles. That shook up the Irish squad and upset us. It was only a game of football, for goodness' sake. Another disappointment was the scandal surrounding Diego Maradona. He was found guilty of taking illegal substances and was kicked out of the tournament. This was upsetting to anyone who cares for the game of football. The finest player of his generation, Diego was ultimately good for the game. His mastery of the ball was breathtaking, his skill remarkable, but there were blemishes on his career, blemishes that, alas, put question marks against his integrity. I never played against Diego, one of the few regrets in my own career.

Comparing the Irish sides of Italia '90 and USA '94 is a difficult exercise. Although a number of players turned out in both tournaments, what we had was essentially different teams competing in different circumstances. Both Irish teams were talented and had the ability to go further in the tournament. Because the 1990 side went a round further, you have to say that gives it the edge. But the 1994 team underachieved, had a stronger squad, and, with luck, could have won the tournament. Yes, we would have faced Brazil in the quarter-final of USA '94, and perhaps we would have lost. But I reckon we would have given them the fright of their lives.

Against expectations, USA '94 did not spell the end of international football for Jack's so-called old guard. Paul McGrath, Tony Cascarino, Ray Houghton and Andy Townsend vowed to carry on. I have to admit I considered retiring from international football myself, but a conversation with Kevin Moran convinced me I should make myself available for selection. 'Aldo,' he said, 'always keep the door open.' And I did just that, making it clear to Jack Charlton I wanted to be considered for Ireland's qualifying matches for the 1996 European Championships. There was an added incentive: Euro '96 would be staged in England, something that would suit Ireland, its fans and its band of English-based players. Our group consisted of Northern Ireland, Austria, Portugal, Latvia and Liechtenstein so we felt confident we would occupy one of the top two places. We seemed to have the perfect mix of experienced players with wise heads and younger ones with more energy. Phil Babb, Jason McAteer and Gary Kelly were very much the present and were talented enough to suggest our future was in safe hands.

I was delighted to be called into Jack's squad for the opening qualifying match against Latvia in September 1994. Sensing Jack might be looking to the future, I thought my age would count against me, but sure enough, my name was among those selected for the trip to Riga. I still had my critics, of course, but they were usually from England. The Irish press stuck by me, as they had done for the previous eight years. Loyalty is an overused word in football but that is exactly what the Irish people and journalists showed me. Even when I went nineteen games without an international goal they preferred to look at the positive aspects of my game, giving me the kind of boost money cannot buy, and making me feel important at a time when my self-esteem could have taken a battering. How many other groups of supporters or media people would have stuck by me? Very few. I desperately wanted to give the Irish people something by which they could remember me; something that would make them pleased they remained loyal.

I began the Euro '96 qualifiers with fourteen international goals to my credit, just six away from equalling Frank Stapleton's record. If Jack was prepared to keep picking me, I reckoned the Republic of Ireland scoring record was a realistic target. That is why I was delighted to score twice in Ireland's 3–0 win against Latvia, a country against whom I always seemed to do well. We followed that up with a 4–0 win against Northern Ireland in Belfast. Much had changed politically since the World Cup game at Windsor Park and the atmosphere was actually quite pleasant, a welcome contrast to the eerie feeling of 1993.

The day before the match, however, Jack could see I was struggling. I had a painful foot injury where bone was rubbing against bone and this was making training difficult.

'I am not playing you tomorrow, Aldo,' Jack said. 'I am playing Tommy Coyne.'

'Why aren't you playing me?' I replied.

'Because I don't think you're fit.'

'Jack, I've never felt better – and I'm scoring goals for Tranmere.'

Three times Jack told me I wasn't playing only to change his mind. I found out later that he asked Andy Townsend about me. 'You've got to play Aldo,' Andy told Jack, 'because he'll always get you a goal.' So Jack decided to put me in the starting line-up. The problem was I couldn't see how I was going to get through the ninety minutes without enduring pain. I asked Mick Byrne, the Ireland physiotherapist, to give me a pain-killing injection before the match.

'You can't do that, Aldo,' Mick said.

'Listen, Mick, I need an injection,' I replied. 'But this is between me, you and the doctor. Tell Jack and I'll never speak to you again.'

Mick relented and I had one injection. But when I tried to warm up an hour or so before the kick-off, I was in agony. I couldn't run properly. Jack came out on to the pitch and I ran straight back off. Mick saw me and ushered me into the toilets, locking all the doors so Jack couldn't come in. It was there the doctor gave me another injection which, fortunately, allowed me to play the first hour without discomfort. I scored again, taking my tally to seventeen goals in sixty-two appearances, but by the end of the match I was in pain again. The injury caused me to miss six matches for Tranmere, but given the importance of the first goal, I have to say the injection served an important purpose.

It meant I was unavailable for the friendly against England in Dublin in February, a match that started but never finished. After David Kelly had given Ireland the lead, a small section of fans rioted, giving the referee little choice but to abandon the game. Sitting next to England and Arsenal striker Ian Wright, I was particularly saddened. I had been at Hillsborough in 1989, seen people die at close quarters, and was convinced football hooliganism was a thing of the past. It hit me hard that fans should want to riot at matches. A football game should be an occasion where anybody – man, woman or child – could feel comfortable and safe. But this was a throw-back to the disgusting scenes of the mid 1980s when riots at matches were more commonplace. I was depressed on the flight from Dublin to Liverpool the following day.

The key game of our Euro '96 qualifying campaign – or so it seemed at the time – was the one at home against Portugal in April 1995. Victory would make us hot favourites to qualify from our group, while even a draw would be considered useful. In the event, we won 1–0, going to the top of the group, with the seemingly simple task of beating Liechtenstein in Eschen in June to come. And it was simple. We bombarded the Liechtenstein goal with around forty shots, most of which were on target. The match was so one-sided it was embarrassing, but the final score was 0–0. To this day I wonder how we failed to score. I'd played in many remarkable football matches in my time but never one like this. Shots were bouncing back off the woodwork, hitting defenders on the goalline, hitting the goalkeeper. We would still be searching for an opening goal today if the referee hadn't blown his final whistle. But it was no joke. We threw away two vital points against opponents the Ireland Under-15 team would have beaten. Suddenly, qualification for Euro '96 was out of our hands.

Defeat against Austria in Dublin really put us under pressure. The day before the Austria game, Jack took the squad to Harry Ramsden's fish and chips restaurant, which surprised me. We stuffed ourselves with food and, when we tried to train later in the day, I had all the movement of a crippled elephant. But the day got worse. My mother and father had come over from Liverpool for the match and they were introduced to Jack. They knew all about him, of course, but were grateful for the chance to meet him in the flesh.

'Ah, good to see you both,' Jack said to my parents. 'But you've come a long way for nothing. Aldo's not playing.' Even I didn't know I'd been omitted at that point, which baffled my mother and father, and made me wonder what was going on. My father might have said something a few years before but this was a rare case of him showing diplomacy. I didn't even come on as a substitute, something which annoyed me. I suspected it was my father's one and only chance to see me in action for Ireland. My mother had seen me play in the 1990 World Cup, but my father's fear of flying meant he couldn't see much of me in international football. The game itself was terrible from Ireland's point of view because, after Ray Houghton had given us the lead, we conceded three late goals.

We needed a big win against Latvia at home to boost our chances but the game was much tougher than in Riga the previous season. The Latvians had learned how to play against us, while we were suffering a confidence crisis. The game stayed at 0–0 for what seemed like an eternity, until Steve Staunton was brought down in the eighteen-yard box for a penalty. When I picked the ball up to take the kick I was as nervous as I had been taking the penalty for Liverpool against Wimbledon in the 1988 FA Cup final. As I put the ball on the spot against Latvia, all you could hear was the slight wind whistling in your ears. A virtual silence had enveloped Lansdowne Road and I was beginning to feel the tension. A miss was unthinkable. Fortunately, I hit a good penalty and scored to give us the lead, making it one of the biggest goals of my Ireland career. Four minutes later I scored with a powerful header following an excellent Steve Staunton cross. It was my nineteenth goal for Ireland, putting me one behind record-holder Frank Stapleton. Late in the game, I was put through on goal but miscontrolled the ball as I tried to evade the challenge of the goalkeeper. I was tired and might have scored had the chance come earlier in the match. The record would have to wait another match but at least Ireland won 2–1.

We went to Portugal in November 1995 needing a victory to be sure of progressing to Euro '96, while a draw would still have been good enough depending on the results of other groups. Defeat and we would be forced into a play-off with another team. We stayed just outside Lisbon but there were no training facilities available to us. Instead, we tried to play football near the swimming pool in our hotel, which turned into a farce. It had been raining non-stop for four days prior to our arrival in Portugal and the forecast suggested there would be no change. It meant our scheduled training session in the Stadium of Light the day before was ruined. I felt sorry for the 20,000 Irish fans who made the trip. They were drenched even before we kicked off against Portugal and they probably wished they hadn't bothered by the end. After keeping it tight early on, I had a couple of goalscoring chances in the match and should have scored with at least one. But once Portugal scored they took control, winning with as much comfort as the 3–0 scoreline suggests.

Even in defeat we finished runners-up in our group, which meant a play-off game against Holland at Anfield. From a personal point of view it was an incredible irony. I'd enjoyed so many great occasions at Anfield and here was a chance for yet another one. If Ireland won, we would be through to Euro '96; if we lost, it would probably be my last international game. And, of course, if I managed to score, it meant I would equal the Ireland scoring record. The permutations were endless and I revelled in the pre-match preparations, expressing great delight when Jack confirmed I would be in the starting line-up. As I went out on to the pitch for the warm-up, I witnessed one of the greatest atmospheres in Anfield's history. I'd been to all the great Liverpool occasions at Anfield – against St Etienne in 1977, against Bruges the year before, and against Leicester in 1973 – yet the Irish fans and the Dutch fans produced a remarkable sea of colours and a wall of noise that proved inspirational. Unfortunately, it was Holland who benefited most. They were the better side and took advantage of a below-par Irish display to win 2–0. In truth, our performance made Holland look better than they really were. I had been substituted by the time Patrick Kluivert scored the second goal for the Dutch, confirming their place in Euro '96 and ending Jack's reign.

After the match, Jack went out on the Anfield pitch to thank the Irish fans for a decade of support. It was an emotional experience for all concerned. It really was the end of an era. There was no-one quite like Jack. He could bring out the best in even average players, while the more seasoned professionals were anxious to do well for him. The Irish fans took to him from day one and, understandably, he was made an honorary Irishman long before we were qualifying for World Cups. Jack made Irish men and women proud to have a football team. A number of players owed their international careers to him and I have to say he is one of the greatest figures in my own life. How many other managers would have kept faith with a man who had failed to score in his opening nineteen internationals? When I was criticised, Jack merely pointed out that I had done the job asked of me. Once I started scoring regularly for Ireland, I was pleased, not only for myself, but for Jack, because it proved his instincts were correct. He always believed I could do a job for Ireland, and I valued the role he played in my career as an international footballer.

It was unfortunate that the Jack Charlton reign should end in defeat but football, alas, has little room for sentiment. The stark reality was that our failure to qualify for Euro '96 was of our own making. I believe the tournament would have been richer for Ireland's, and especially the fans', presence. Had the team performed to its potential, we would have strolled into the European Championships. But we played badly at key times, most notably against Liechtenstein when we couldn't even score one goal never mind ten. A team that draws 0–0 with Liechtenstein can't expect to be qualifying for major tournaments. Jack accepted that and politely stepped aside. He was replaced by Mick McCarthy, the one-time Irish skipper, who had produced some young, talented players at Millwall and had turned the London club into a free-flowing football team.

Jack's departure gave me another opportunity to consider my own international future, and again Kevin Moran intervened with some wise counsel, 'Aldo, always keep the door open,' repeating his words of two years before. So for the second time in two years, I heeded Kevin's advice. I made it clear to Mick that I wanted to be part of his plans and welcomed any opportunities to equal and then hopefully beat Frank Stapleton's scoring record. I was still a goal behind Frank when I was called into Mick's squad for the friendly against Russia in Dublin in March 1996, but it wasn't the night for Irish strikers. We lost 2–0 against a very good team. I was surprised to be included but I sensed Mick was worried about dispensing with his experienced players too quickly. Two weeks later, I took over as manager of Tranmere Rovers. Suddenly I had more on my plate than just playing and this was bound to be a factor as I contemplated my future as an international footballer. I celebrated my thirty-eighth birthday in September 1996 and wondered how long I could go on playing for Ireland.

When I was named as a substitute for Ireland's opening World Cup qualifier against Macedonia in Dublin on 9 October 1996, I suspected Mick was already looking to the future. We were 3–0 up when I was thrust into the action. The Irish fans were great that night, cheering me every time I went near the ball, hoping I would get the one goal that would give me a share of Frank's record. In truth, however, I didn't even come close to scoring in the ten minutes I was on the field. I believe Mick could easily have given me most of the second half without affecting the balance of the side or our performance. The game was won, after all. My attentions now turned to Ireland's World Cup game against Iceland in December.

Mick's influences had already been noted by this time. He was right to bring in younger players at the expense of older ones, but he was reluctant to let us go out drinking. He wanted to be more disciplined than Jack, a state of affairs that surprised me given that Mick benefited more than most from Jack's methods. A week before a match, Jack would let us relax over a pint. With Mick, this was out. I think we were allowed a pint on the Saturday before a Wednesday night match, which was hardly worth the effort. I am all for discipline, but players should be allowed a release. There is already much pressure on players and a quiet drink can be a good thing. Mick didn't agree, however.

Not long after the Russia game, I was contacted by the FAI who informed me that the ancestry rules had changed. To play for Ireland now, I had to acquire Irish citizenship, something I had not done up to that point. It was a belated move by FIFA, but one with which I was in agreement. I went into a court room with an FAI official. There were about twenty-five people in attendance and in front of them, I had to swear my allegiance to the Republic of Ireland.

'Mr Aldridge,' the judge said, 'you don't know how delighted we are that you are now an Irish citizen.'

'Well, not as delighted as I am,' I replied.

The people present burst into applause and I could feel the hairs on the back of my neck stand on end. Few people really appreciate how proud I was to be so much a part of Irish life. Growing up in Liverpool, I was never really patriotic towards England. I loved Liverpool and will always have strong affections for the city in which I was born, but I love Ireland too. The day I became a citizen of Ireland was a special one for me and my family. I often ask Paul, my son, who he would play for if England and Ireland come in for him. 'Ireland, Dad,' he always says. I like that.

I was called into the squad for the Iceland tie and we all met up a week before the game. I didn't see this as a problem with Tranmere. In my absence, Dave Philpotts and Ray Mathias were more than capable of running affairs. I offered my assistance to Mick, something he chose to reject. That was up to him. He had to do his job as he saw fit, but at least he knew I was available if required. Inevitably, I was a substitute against Iceland. I could accept that. Mick probably thought I would be more useful coming on fresh, late in the game. The score was still 0–0 at half-time, by which time I realised Mick had got it wrong tactically. As a result, Iceland's ten outfield players would comfortably retreat when they lost the ball. The time ticked away; still there was no prospect of Mick giving me a taste of the action, something I could not understand. Though most of the Lansdowne Road crowd was silent, some people were chanting my name, hoping I would be allowed an opportunity to play some part. But Mick did not agree. Instead, with twenty minutes remaining, he sent on Alan Moore, the Middlesbrough striker. I was devastated. Five minutes before the end of the match, I made my decision to retire as an international footballer. I'd had enough of Mick messing me around. When the final whistle heralded a 0–0 draw, I walked on to the pitch for one final look at Lansdowne Road. I had a lump in my throat but I knew the time was right to quit. The fact that I didn't equal Frank's record was only a minor blow. I showered quickly in the dressing-room and approached Mick.

'That's it for me, Mick,' I said. Mick looked shocked and said nothing. On the team coach afterwards, it was his turn to approach me.

'What's up, Aldo?' he asked.

'I am finished, Mick. I am retiring.'

'Fine. But why?'

'Mick, bloody hell. I've been away from Tranmere for a week, which wouldn't be too bad if I was here to play for Ireland. But there we are, drawing 0–0 with Iceland, the crowd are chanting my name, and you put Mooresy on instead of me. The crowd would have been lifted had I been sent on to the field and, in turn, that would have lifted the players. It would surely have changed the nature of the game in our favour and I might have got on the end of something and given us a 1–0 win.'

'Oh, I never thought of that.'

Even I wasn't prepared for that response from Mick. My respect for him as a manager diminished in the time it takes to utter six words. I decided to wait a few days before announcing my decision, sensing that there would be a media circus if I announced my retirement immediately. I didn't want the spotlight. On the Friday, I contacted members of the Irish press so they could release the news. The feedback was amazing once the news was circulated. I received faxes, letters and telephone calls. On a radio show in Dublin, one Irish fan was crying when my retirement from international football was discussed. I might have cried too had I not been struck by the realisation that all good things must come to an end.

— 10 —

I THINK I'LL MANAGE

HONEYMOON periods don't last forever. Your only hope is that they last long enough for you to enjoy them. My honeymoon period as manager of Tranmere Rovers began on 12 April 1996 and ended four-and-a-half months later, on 31 August. That was more than enough time to get to grips with my drastic change in direction. And, yes, I did enjoy the period, though I confess it seemed to pass all too quickly. The best memory was perhaps meeting up with the rest of the Tranmere Rovers players for the trip to Mallorca a few days after my testimonial match. Nothing particularly spectacular happened, yet standing at Palma Airport after our arrival and taking a look at the players – *my* players – filled me with a sense of contentment. I reckoned (rightly or wrongly, it didn't matter) that few people could possibly have begun their managerial career with such a great bunch of guys. We were in Mallorca for a holiday we deserved, if only for the seemingly effortless way in which we had avoided relegation.

That one-week break on Spain's beautiful Balearic island allowed me time to reflect and set about forging new relationships with people who were my friends but whose boss I now was. How would the players react to my role as their immediate superior? Would trying to earn their respect mean distancing myself and throwing up barriers? Could I successfully juggle my job as manager with that of player?

Those questions and more danced around inside my brain for a long time. To some questions I had no answers; others, I knew that time would decide. The media, typically, wanted speedy responses to the same questions. In contrast to when I was just a player, the press, though always supportive, now demanded my attention each day. Had I buried myself in the sand on tiny Beachcomber Island, Fiji, journalists would have dug me up and staged a press conference.

On returning to England, I acquired a small office at Prenton Park and found myself confronted with a mound of paperwork. In a short space of time, I had to discuss contract renewals with various players (John Morrissey was immediately offered a new deal), arrange a pre-season programme for the first team (I looked no further than a tour of Ireland), and, of course, cast an eye on new talent.

There was one particular player I knew we needed. I had seen him play for Grimsby Town against Tranmere the previous season and was impressed with his speed and skill. Ivano Bonetti was a left-sided midfielder who had played in the 1992 European Cup final for Sampdoria of Italy against Barcelona. His best days behind him, he had fallen out with Grimsby manager Brian Laws and was available on a free transfer. I wasn't blinded by Ivano's skill, however. I'd heard how Brian was so frustrated by the attitude of the Italian-born player that, on one occasion, he punched him. I was also made aware of how Ivano craved money. On the other hand, I felt I had the strength of character to get the best of out him.

Negotiations seemed to take forever. At one point, I didn't think the deal would go ahead, solely because of Ivano's financial requests. Frank Corfe, the Tranmere chairman, was particularly incensed by the player's wage demands. But in the end, after showing much patience, we got our man. Inevitably, Ivano brought excitement to Prenton Park. I understand season ticket sales showed a dramatic increase in the week after we signed him. If only I had known what was in store.

As I was still good for twenty or so goals a season, I felt a 4–5–1 formation would bring the best out of the first-team squad. We had an abundance of midfield talent with competition for a place on the right between John Morrissey and Pat Nevin, and in the middle between Ged Brannan, Kenny Irons, Paul Cook and Liam O'Brien. With the right players, a centre-forward guaranteed to score, and an abundance of support from midfield, that system is ideal. The problem was Pat didn't rise to the challenge, while Ged was among a handful of players who would be sold to boost the club's finances. But that was in the future. After a useful pre-season programme, we began the season with a 1–1 draw at Southend United and followed it up with victories against Shrewsbury Town in the Coca-Cola Cup, Grimsby Town and Port Vale. It meant that ten games into my managerial career I had still to taste defeat.

When Tranmere did lose for the first time since I became manager, it hurt more than I'd anticipated. It came against Bradford City on 31 August and signalled the end of my honeymoon period. Despite creating numerous chances, we lost 1–0. I needed to take it out on somebody so I chose the easiest target – the referee. He didn't have a particularly good match but neither did he deserve the sharp end of my tongue. He might not have known how significant the result was.

But by then I had more things to worry about. Ivano Bonetti was proving to be difficult. His genius on the field could never be questioned; it was his attitude off it that was his downfall. The signs that it wouldn't work out were not clear in the beginning, but as time went on I became disillusioned with his inability to conform. It wasn't long before he was ducking training; then he refused to chase back and help defend in matches. It didn't seem so bad when things were going well, but when things went against us, as they did mid-season, Ivano's attitude stood out like a strip-a-gram at a wedding reception. I suspected he wanted preferential treatment but he wasn't getting that from me. It was against my nature and, in any event, I wanted to show the rest of the players that everyone at Tranmere would be treated in the same manner, whether they had appeared in a European Cup final or not. Ivano had problems with a hamstring and so missed a number of matches, but when I made a point of dropping him for our away match against Ipswich Town, he reacted badly.

I remember going for an early morning walk before the match and wondering where things were going wrong, not just with Ivano, but with the whole squad. I made a drastic decision – I dropped Ivano, I dropped myself, I dropped John Morrissey, and I gave some of the younger players an opportunity. In fact, I got myself so wound up about Tranmere's plight that I ended up vomiting in a nearby bush. Perhaps management was getting to me for the first time. I needn't have worried; we won the match 2–0 and turned in one of our best displays of the season.

By the turn of the year, things had deteriorated with Ivano to such an extent that I actually told him I could see why Brian Laws had punched him. My words didn't go down well with either Ivano or his agent. The player left the club later that season. Last I heard, he was involved in a deal to buy Grimsby Town. For sure, I learned lessons from Ivano's spell at Prenton Park and I am man enough to admit I was naive in thinking I could keep him in check. He was a law unto himself and thus did not fit in.

Shaun Teale's days at Prenton Park were also numbered, though for different reasons. I felt he was costing Tranmere too many goals. I began the season by placing Shaun alongside John McGreal, with worrying consequences. After one particularly difficult spell, I asked to see the videos of our most recent matches and they confirmed what I had suspected. Shaun was being exposed by balls coming in behind him, usually from our left flank. My response was to bring back Dave Higgins, who immediately forged a good partnership with John. It was a shame Shaun had to go. He is a nice guy, a great character in the dressing-room, and, at his best, one of the most talented defenders around. But Tranmere acquired him a year or two too late. Shaun still had that tremendous left foot and he rarely lost anything in the air, but, alas, his pace had deserted him and that proved costly. He moved on to play in Hong Kong and has since joined Motherwell in Scotland.

I was learning the hard way. After a reasonably successful

beginning to the season, we were showing the unpredictable form that had dogged John King in his later years as manager. In the Coca-Cola Cup we lost to Oldham Athletic, which was doubly disappointing. Not only should we have beaten the Manchester club but we needed a good run in the competition for financial reasons. We drew 2–2 at home and lost 1–0 in the replay at Boundary Park. Leading 2–1 in the game at Prenton Park, we had a chance to score and make it 3–1. That opportunity went begging and Oldham immediately equalised. They were drawn to face Newcastle United in the following round, a money-spinning tie that would have suited Tranmere. I knew Frank Corfe was upset when he made some pointed comments about our defeat.

My own form was as good as I could have expected, but I was anxious to delegate work to my assistants, Ray Mathias and Kevin Sheedy. So while Ray was dashing around the British motorway system in search of talent, I was keeping myself fit and making sure the first-team squad were falling in line with my plans. With two goals in the 3–0 defeat of Ipswich Town on 30 November, I had taken my tally for the season to fourteen. Tranmere were well placed in the play-off zone, but there was no hint of what was around the corner.

December was a terrible month for the club. We lost 2–0 at Reading, 2–0 at Stoke City, 3–0 at Barnsley and 2–0 at home to Wolves. I vowed after that run that we would never again play three successive league games away. The defeat at Reading put us under pressure and we never recovered. A 1–1 draw against Huddersfield Town on Boxing Day halted the slide but our promotion hopes were damaged.

Dave Higgins showed his versatility on New Year's Day when we played West Bromwich Albion at the Hawthorns. Trailing 1–0 on an ice-bound pitch, Danny Coyne, our goalkeeper, was hurt in a collision. With no replacement on the substitutes' bench, Dave went in goal and made a number of good saves. At the other end of the field, I scored twice and we won 2–1. It was a great team performance, probably the most memorable of that campaign.

Our season effectively ended on 14 January 1997 when we lost 1–0 at Carlisle United in the FA Cup. Late in the game, I was sent off for swearing at a linesman. I was incensed.

'Well done,' I said sarcastically to the referee afterwards. 'You can tell all your friends in the pub tonight that you sent off John Aldridge. Bloody hell, this is a man's game and players are swearing all the time. If a player was sent off every time he swore there would be no game left.'

I fined myself £1,000 and took the first-team squad out for a meal with the money. That was an example of how keen I was to lead by example. I never liked being sent off as a player but now, as player-manager, it affected me more.

The club's financial plight also affected me. I knew I had to sell some of our younger players to bigger clubs but I hoped I would be able to spend some of the money generated. We sold Alan Rogers to Nottingham Forest for £2 million, and Ian Moore to the same club for £1 million. Ged Brannan left to join Manchester City for £750,000. At first, Frank Corfe seemed ready to accept £1.5 million for Alan until I intervened.

'No,' I said. 'He's worth more than that. We're not taking less than two million quid for Alan Rogers.' It was similar with Ian. Frank contacted me on my carphone one day.

'John,' he said, 'we need £400,000 quickly. Would you sell Ian Moore for £400,000? I think Everton want him.'

'No, I won't sell him for that.'

In any event, Everton lost interest and Nottingham Forest came in with a £750,000 bid. Again Frank was going to accept it; again I rejected it. We held out for the million. Ged might have left Tranmere for French club Strasbourg on a free transfer had an agent got his way but luckily Frank Clark, the Manchester City manager, offered us an acceptable fee for the player. John McGreal also looked set to move to France but we persuaded him to sign a new contract. There was no way John was leaving us.

I had Ray and Kevin checking out the form of players such as Mick Mellon of Blackpool and Karl Connelly of Wrexham, but in the event I was not able to splash out on either of them. I'd have liked some sort of budget but, according to Frank, this was impossible. I had to bring in players on free transfers. Andy Thorn was one to come. An experienced defender, he had played for Wimbledon against Liverpool in the 1988 FA Cup final. He was well known for giving nothing less than one hundred per cent effort, and he could read a game well. I knew Andy had bad knees but I believed he was a risk worth taking. He wasn't a great runner – Dave Bassett, his Wimbledon manager, said Andy had dyslexic legs – but he made up for this with his brain. He was a good thinker and I can't speak too highly of him.

Next to arrive was Lee Jones, a striker from Liverpool. Lee didn't appear to have much of a future at Anfield and he was training with us at a time when I was keen to sign him. Liverpool made life difficult for me at first and Peter Robinson called him back. Then, after we acquired the striker on loan, Liverpool seemed reluctant to sell him on a permanent basis. In the end, knowing they might lose the player for nothing at the end of the season, they agreed to sell him to Tranmere for £100,000. It was one of the best pieces of business the club had done. Selling Ian Moore for £1 million and replacing him with Lee for a tenth of that fee was a good deal. Lee's effect was immediate. He scored goals and quickly became a favourite among the supporters. I was not as successful in my bid to bring in Liverpool's Dave Thompson on loan. As with Lee, Liverpool made things tough for me, and Dave instead went on loan to Swindon Town the following week, making me wonder what I had done wrong.

Our results continued to be mixed, however. While there were memorable victories, like the 3–1 win at Portsmouth and the 2–1 win at Oldham Athletic, there were frustrating defeats against Wolves, Port Vale and Queens Park Rangers.

We were not in danger, of course, so when first-division champions Bolton Wanderers came to Prenton Park on the final day of the season, we were in the position to deny them two major milestones. They needed a victory to finish the season with a hundred points and needed two goals to finish up with a hundred goals. In a sense, they deserved to be successful on both counts. They were easily the best team in the division and deserved to return to the Premier League, but we were not planning to help them. In forcing a 2–2 draw we prevented Colin Todd's men from reaching a hundred points. I scored one of our goals – finishing the season with twenty – but what delighted me most was Lee's equaliser which came from a move we had been practising in training. At the final whistle, a majority of the 6,000 Bolton fans present started singing 'John Aldridge is a wanker, is a wanker', to which I responded by indicating, with my fingers, that Bolton would be coming back down to the first division. I didn't want Bolton to be relegated, of course, I was merely giving the fans a taste of what they had given me. It didn't go down too well. Colin criticised me in the press the following day, suggesting he thought I was too big to let fans' insults hurt me. The insults didn't hurt me; I merely believed that if people can have a go at me, I can have a go back. I contacted Colin to let him know how I felt. I had played alongside him at Oxford United and respected him enormously. A brief chat settled this minor disagreement and I could look forward to a welcome break.

Incredibly, it was the third successive season the first-division champions ended their campaign by playing Tranmere at Prenton Park.

I took the players to Spain for a holiday and looked on as the lads enjoyed their time out of the spotlight. I always believe players should have as much fun as possible when the pressure is off, just as I believe they should go out and enjoy themselves after a match. If you work hard in training and in matches, it follows that you should play hard on holiday. The ability to let off steam is one reason, I believe, that I was still playing right up until my fortieth birthday.

It was during this holiday that I realised how much I was distancing myself from the players. The previous year in Mallorca, I was still one of the lads; but now things had to be a little different. Whether you like it or not, a manager has to make difficult decisions. To maintain respect there has to be a distance between yourself and the players. It is a fact of life at a football club. I knew that. The players did, too. To be fair, I have rarely had trouble and most of my players have shown me a lot of respect.

That summer I flew to Mauritius for an exhibition football tournament. I was sitting on the beach one day, casually reading a list of players who were available on a free transfer, when I noticed that Wolves were releasing full-back Andy Thompson. I immediately contacted Dave Philpotts, one of my assistants, who had faxed me the list.

'Get Andy Thompson on the phone and tell him Tranmere want to sign him,' I said. Watford were also chasing the player but it was Tranmere who secured his signature.

That was also the summer I decided the 1997–98 season would be my last as a player. It was a difficult decision but one, as a manager, I had to make. I was maintaining a good goalscoring rate but I knew something nobody else did: my body wasn't right. The effects of eighteen years of professional football were taking their toll. If I needed proof, it would come at around four o'clock every morning. For as long as I can remember, I always have a cup of tea before I go to bed which, in turn, means I always get up in the early hours of the morning. There were times during the 1996–97 season when I would wake up, try to head for the bathroom, and realise I couldn't walk properly. It was worse after matches. Though I kept it to myself, I was often in pain for a day or two after playing. I never trained on a Monday and I often missed training on a Tuesday, too. I never wanted to give up playing but I had to listen to my body. If I'd carried on, I could have ended up crippled and addicted to anti-inflammatory pills.

With this in mind, I signed David Kelly from Sunderland. The one-time Republic of Ireland striker was still a friend and I knew, if he was fit, he was guaranteed to score twenty goals a season. David wasn't a long-term answer, of course, but as I intended to reduce my appearances, he would prove to be a good partner for Lee Jones up front. I also knew David would be good for morale. He is a great character to have around the dressing-room. I always called him golden bollocks because things seemed to work out well for him, as they did with this move to Tranmere.

While I was able to strengthen the squad with the likes of David and with Andy Parkinson, a young striker from Liverpool,

I was still under pressure to reduce the wage bill. There was some natural wastage, which helped. Andy Thorn was forced to retire. He had done a great job for Tranmere but had to face up to the inevitable: his knees couldn't take it any more. Gary Stevens, the former England international, also retired injured. In the summer, Pat Nevin moved to Kilmarnock, Eric Nixon moved to Stockport, and Tony Thomas moved to Everton. By the end of September, Paul Cook had joined Eric at Stockport.

So much changed at Tranmere around this time. Although it wasn't planned that way, only a few players who had been brought in by John King were left. In a little more than a year, the face of the first-team squad had changed. Of the twenty-four players who played for Tranmere in the 1997–98 season, half of them were given their debuts by me; only eight players from the John King era ended the season.

And what a strange season it was. For the most part we were fighting against relegation, but I put that down more to bad luck than bad play.

We began the season with a 2–1 defeat at West Bromwich Albion which was notable only for David Kelly's debut goal. We bounced back with a 2–1 win over Queens Park Rangers at home the following Friday and drew 1–1 with Manchester City. Then something went wrong: we lost five successive matches. Losing to Hartlepool 2–1 in the Coca-Cola Cup wasn't too depressing because we won the tie 4–3 on aggregate. Losing 2–0 at home to Middlesbrough was half-expected because Bryan Robson had assembled a strong side. It was the defeats against Birmingham City, Bury and Swindon Town that bugged me. Equally worrying was our failure to score regularly so I was delighted when we beat Notts County 2–0 in the Coca-Cola Cup and Reading 6–0 in the League.

My appearances on the field were few and far between. When I came on as a substitute in our 2–0 home win against Norwich City on 14 October it was only my fifth appearance of the season. I didn't start a match until 14 November when we won at Bradford City, and that was only because David Kelly was injured. It was the first of three successive matches which I began, and I scored twice. I also began the game against Stockport County in December which was an ill-tempered affair. I'd heard stories that Gary Megson, the Stockport manager, had ordered his players to hurt me in the match. Apocryphal or otherwise, the mere suggestion of danger put me in the wrong mood. Even though I scored and we played reasonably well, we contrived to lose 3–1.

We beat Stockport 3–0 at Prenton Park later in the season, the match which ensured our survival. We had been battling to avoid relegation for the most part and there was a time, at the turn of the year, when I was genuinely worried. While we were defending well, we were struggling to score. We made the history books by drawing five successive league matches 0–0. Including cup ties, we went seven games without conceding a goal. I don't know why we were underperforming because we had a strong squad. We finally signed Mick Mellon from Blackpool and he was joined by other younger players.

The FA Cup brought greater rewards. After a 3–0 win at Hereford, we beat high-flying Sunderland 1–0 in the fourth round. Young Andy Parkinson scored the goal and was in stunning form on a memorable day at Prenton Park. We drew Newcastle United in the fifth round, a dream tie that would ensure we made a decent amount of money from a full house at St James' Park. Alan Shearer scored the only goal of the match but we more than played our part in a tight game.

Our younger players were at last making names for themselves, so it was no surprise when Alan Mahon attracted interest from further afield. Leeds United were believed to have been interested at one stage, while he continued to be involved in the Republic of Ireland Under-21 set-up. On one occasion, however, his involvement with the Under-21 squad caused me problems. Ian Evans, the coach, contacted me one evening.

'I'd like to take Alan Mahon on the international five-day ruling,' he said.

'Oh, would you,' I said. 'Actually, Alan's playing for Tranmere against Bradford on Friday night.'

'No he's not. I want him here in Ireland on Friday morning.'

243

'Come on. He can play Friday night and then meet up with you on Saturday. After all, the game for Ireland is not until next Tuesday.'

'Sorry. I want Alan on Friday morning.'

I slammed down the telephone receiver. I accepted that Alan wouldn't be able to play for Tranmere against Bradford but consoled myself with our 3–1 win. The following Tuesday, however, Alan was left out of the Ireland match. I couldn't believe it. Anger inflated within me like a balloon ready to burst. It was one of the most disgraceful managerial decisions I've come across. To my way of thinking, Ian Evans showed a total lack of courtesy and judgement and I don't envisage the circumstances in which I will speak to him or deal with him in any way.

But despite difficult times such as those, Tranmere finished the 1997–98 season in fourteenth position. It hadn't been an easy campaign but we survived the loss of key players and emerged with a new identity. There seemed to be a string of talented youngsters waiting to make their mark in the first team. Older players, such as myself, were finally accepting that time had caught up with us.

Alan Mahon wasn't the only youngster to make a name for himself. Andy Parkinson was maintaining his impressive form, while goalkeeper Steve Simonsen emerged from the reserves to become one of our prized assets. Steve's form took every-one at Prenton Park by surprise and he had barely played a dozen matches when I was tipping him to play for England one day. It may have seemed a rash prediction but I still believe Steve will win full honours for his country. Alas, he won't be a Tranmere player when he does. Steve's departure to Everton in September 1998 was as messy as it was inevi-table. It was a complicated deal, too, and it will be some time before we realise how much money it was worth to Tranmere. What it did to my health was more apparent at the time. When media speculation concerning Steve's future was at its height, I realised our goalkeeper hadn't turned up for a train-ing session. I immediately contacted him on his mobile tele-phone.

'Steve, what are you doing? Where are you?'

'I'm on my way to Bellefield to train with Everton.'

'You're what? But you're not an Everton player yet. You still play for Tranmere Rovers. And I don't have a goalkeeper at the moment.'

'Well . . .'

'Get yourself back here at once.'

Eventually, Frank Corfe and Peter Johnson managed to sort out the affair and Steve became an Everton player.

Soon after, Frank quit as chairman. He claimed he was booed by a section of the Tranmere fans and he immediately put his majority shareholding up for sale. What we didn't know at the time was that Frank was having his own financial problems. All I knew was that life at Prenton Park was becoming difficult. With no money to spend on players, the team bottom of the table, and morale as low as I'd known it, I twice offered my resignation. I couldn't see a future at Prenton Park.

Out of the uncertainty came Fred Williams, who replaced Frank as chairman and provided much stability at a difficult time in Tranmere's existence. I liked Fred a lot and sat down with him to discuss key issues. A fund for attracting players was vital and Fred promised me cash. Getting the team off the bottom of the table was my problem and I worked hard, gave the players confidence, and watched them enjoy an impressive unbeaten run. I was proud to win the Football League manager-of-the-month award for October. With the threat of divorce over, I can once again enjoy my marriage with Tranmere Rovers.

— 11 —

IN THE NAME OF
THE FATHER

I ALWAYS knew I would one day have to look at my father as
he lay in his coffin. It was a thought that lurked at the back of
my mind, even when I was a child growing up in Garston. But
having thirty-odd years to familiarise yourself with a particular
situation is often no preparation at all. When the moment came,
in March 1998, I was devastated. Seeing his name on the coffin
lid before the funeral shook me up big time.

But the real sense of loss came five weeks later at Prenton
Park. Sitting in the dressing-room before my final match as a
footballer, I was reading an article extolling my contribution to
the sport. The article ended by saying the only thing missing
from my swansong was the presence of my father. I could feel
myself welling up.

Bill Aldridge died after failing to regain full consciousness
following an operation. He'd had a second stroke. His first,
in 1991, took away much of his spirit and personality. But I
remember the words of a friend, Jeff Carr, who spoke to me
during the aftermath of the first stroke.

'John, if you get five good years out of your father you'll have
done well.'

They seemed blunt words at the time but I realised how apt
they were. My father had seven years between his first stroke
and his second. They were not his best seven years and he was
a mere shadow of his former self. But I always enjoyed having

him around. Even today I sometimes wake up in the middle of the night, frantically searching for the light switch to check to see if he is there. Silly, really, but he was such an influence on my life that I cannot accept he has gone. I really do half expect to see him turn up somewhere to offer words of wisdom. Nobody backed me like my father, especially in the early days when parental guidance was the most inspiring thing available to a child. His dedication was worth more than every penny I've earned and every goal I've scored.

I was right to fear the worst when my mother telephoned me to say my father had been taken ill, but I didn't realise the full extent of how he had deteriorated until I came face to face with him at the hospital. I am not even sure if he recognised me; he certainly didn't know my name. He kept calling me Betty. Though his mental state was clearly cause for concern, the doctor wanted to operate on his stomach. Apparently, gangrene had set in. When I left him that Friday afternoon it was the last time I saw him up and around.

I got another telephone call over the weekend, this time from my sister Jean. The operation hadn't been successful and my father was now alive thanks to a life-support machine. Occasionally it would be switched off when he showed signs of recovery but we had to face the stark reality: the machine was the dominant force in his life. Once it was switched off for the last time he politely stepped aside to leave us with the memories.

I was determined to give my father the send-off he would have wanted. His funeral in Liverpool was packed with relatives and friends, people of all denominations, as if to emphasise his own feelings on religion. My mother and I are Catholic but my father, though Protestant, refused to embrace religion. He didn't care. If you could drink a pint and tell a story, that was enough for him.

After Tranmere's 3–1 win against Bradford City, I went to the hospital to talk to him. He couldn't hear me, of course, but I wanted to thank him for the victory and tell him how things were going. He would have understood. In a strange sort of way, I felt his presence, as I did a few days after he died when we travelled to Stoke City and won 3–0. That was a hard day and the Tranmere players helped pull me through it.

It was more difficult for my mother because she had fewer people around her. Even now she can barely utter a sentence without mentioning my father. She speaks with affection of the way he would hide cigarettes around the house to make sure he always had access to one. He would even hide cigarettes in his clothes. My father was an advocate of cigarettes. He toned down his drinking after his first stroke but he never saw the need to limit his intake of nicotine.

I took my mother and father too much for granted, never seeing them as often as I should have. The family is the most important thing in your life yet sometimes it takes the death of a loved one for you to realise just how important relatives really are. These days I make sure I see my mother more regularly and I hope in twenty years or so, my own children learn from my mistakes.

Family bereavements are terrible things. Joan suffered the loss of her father in the summer of 1996. Tommy and Bill were good friends and often went out together. They would spend hours exchanging stories and jokes. Like my father, Tommy always gave me confidence. If one of my managerial decisions went wrong, it was always somebody else's fault, never mine. If things hadn't worked out on the football pitch, blame another member of the team. Whenever I was down, a few hours in the company of Tommy and my father would cheer me up. Tommy's death cut Joan up for a time. It came out of the blue, at a time when we were feeling happy with life. I didn't understand it. Tommy seemed so fit, he was the last person you would expect to die suddenly of a heart attack. At least Joan never took her father for granted. It is to her credit that she was close to him throughout, and she remains close to her mother, Nelly.

Someone else who died too early was Tommy Cain, my uncle. Married to Auntie Josie, Tommy treated me well when I was a child, often taking me to Liverpool matches and making sure I always had a taxi home. He wasn't a blood relative but he acted like one. He was one of the most generous men I've known. A good singer and as gregarious as my father, Tommy was someone everyone in the family looked up to. When I found out he had been run over by a bus, I was terribly upset. The news came through as the Republic of Ireland were preparing for the 1988 European Championships. I was in Finniston House, Dublin, a day or two before our flight to West Germany for the tournament. Taking time off to attend the funeral was out of the question and, for a time, I was full of remorse. The irony of Tommy's death was that he was on the road helping somebody whose car had broken down when the bus hit him. Life can be so cruel. Tommy might still be alive had he ignored a member of the public in need.

I'd have loved the two Tommies to have been around for Tranmere's game against Wolves on Sunday, 3 May 1998. But the fact that my own father wasn't there was my main source of distress. I vowed to score in my final match as a lasting reminder of what his influence had given me. There was never a doubt in my mind that I would sign off with a goal.

In the event, I scored twice in our 2–1 win and should have had a hat-trick, but throughout the game, I was aware of my father's absence. Part of me was looking towards the main stand where he used to sit to see if he was there. Everything I did that day, I did for him. It was only the second time that season I played an entire ninety minutes, but if my body was suffering it didn't tell me. I felt as fit as I did when I played my first match, for Newport County back in 1979. There was a spring in my step.

I lapped up the applause afterwards, did a lap of honour, and spent the rest of the evening drinking. Billy Hamilton, my striking partner at Oxford United, had come to see my final match. I think he was the only person more drunk than me by the end of the night. It was only when I sobered up the following day that I realised I was no longer a professional footballer. My nineteen-year career, along with my 476 goals, was consigned to the history books. I was now a manager and an ex-footballer.

I'd had time to get used to it. I didn't play much of the 1997–98 season and, if the truth be known, Tranmere were no longer paying me to play. I had signed a new deal the previous summer which only took into account my role as manager. The drop in wages meant I was essentially an amateur footballer, playing games when my full-time job would allow.

I hung up my boots with pride. I had scored more goals than Jimmy Greaves, produced a greater ratio at Liverpool than Ian Rush, and won more international caps than George Best. I was the only Scouser to have played in two World Cups, I succeeded in Spain where many foreigners had failed, and I came within one goal of equalling the all-time Republic of Ireland goalscoring record. Most importantly, I didn't let anybody down.

The facts say I was successful but I don't feel I have had the credit I deserve. Perhaps had I played for a London club, the national press would have embraced me as a great goalscorer. But I am appreciated in the two places that matter most to me: Ireland and Liverpool.

I am not content to rest on my laurels, however. I don't want to stop achieving things in football. I have developed a strong affection for Tranmere and I hope that when I do leave the club it will be in better shape than when I first arrived. There is potential at Prenton Park and I believe that, if money to spend on players is forthcoming, a place in the Premier League is within our grasp these next few years. The infrastructure is in place and, with one of the best youth academies in England, we know we are well on the way to creating something good.

As for Ireland, it is no secret that I have ambitions to manage the nation's football team. My ten-year international career gave me more pride than I can express in words and I want more of it. There is nothing like being part of a World Cup or a European Championship, and if I can lead an Irish team to the finals of one of these tournaments, it would be my finest achievement.

I still find it hard to believe that people want to talk to me even though I am no longer a footballer. In Dublin it is especially noticeable but the people there are so genuine you cannot help but enjoy the attention. It is similar in Liverpool. Even Evertonians come up and shake my hand, and whenever they do I am reminded of the time I went to get the snip. I was sitting in a chair, talking to the doctor about football, when he pulled out a large syringe which contained a transparent substance.

'This jab is to numb the area,' he said, trying to calm my nerves by stating the obvious.

'That's fine, Doc,' I replied as I felt the stinging sensation.

'I support Everton, myself. I'm sorry.'

'That's OK.'

'But I'll tell you this,' he added. 'This is the first time an Evertonian has had you by the balls!'

My father would have appreciated that story. He would have gone down to the pub, gathered his friends around him, and told it with clarity and timing to squeeze the maximum humour out of it. In a sense, I am no different from Bill Aldridge; just an ordinary family man with the same insecurities that dog us all.

POSTSCRIPT

I AM over the fact that I no longer earn my living by playing football. Retiring hurt at first but, like dealing with a death in the family, your best friend is time. It really is the greatest of healers. At first I wasn't sure how I would deal with life after professional football; wasn't sure if any career would give me that same rush of adrenalin, the buzz that comes with people chanting your name and urging you to do well. In that sense, I have dealt with the end of my playing days better than I expected.

Interesting, then, that I have twice contemplated coming out of retirement to play again for Tranmere Rovers. The first occasion was in September 1998, the second in September 1999. In each case Tranmere were bottom of the first division table; in each case we were struggling to score goals. Over a pint in the Gardener's Arms, Woolton, my friends would convince me that I could, after all, score the goals that would keep Tranmere in the first division. A few pints later and I would be agreeing with them. The surge of energy at a time like that is immense. It takes the morning light and a glass of cold water to make you realise that defying age, and the physical consequences that come with getting older, is a futile exercise. In truth, I could no more play football in the first division than I could master the details of the jet engine. For me, now, earning a living from football means giving other players their opportunity, signing new players if the present ones are not up to scratch, and trying to combine the two within specified financial guidelines. My playing days are confined to light-hearted games for the Tranmere backroom staff against the Sunday League teams of friends. It is not the stuff of dreams, but it's a kick-around, and I've got to be grateful for the smallest of mercies.

When football gets too serious you need that release from the pressure that can threaten to blow your mind. Yes, my hair is getting greyer. Those Sunday morning kick-arounds do more than keep the weight off my stomach; they help keep me sane in times of frustration. I have to be honest – the times of frustration have far outweighed the times of contentment since I gave up playing football full-time and concentrated on managing Tranmere.

A five-day period in September 1999 sums up why I feel so vulnerable but, equally, why I must carry on in a bid to see the job through and repay the faith people have shown in me. I will never walk away for there is too much work to do.

We faced Coventry City in the Worthington Cup at Prenton Park with few neutral observers giving us much of a chance for victory. Tranmere were bottom of the first division, Coventry were maintaining their respectability in the FA Carling Premiership, one of the top leagues in the world. Logic suggested that the best we could do would be to scrape a draw, yet somehow it all came right and, with the help of a David Kelly hat-trick, we won 5–1. That was around about the time I was convinced we were incapable of scoring goals. Suddenly to score five, and against one of the top twenty clubs in Britain, taught me a lot about the players in my squad. Gordon Strachan, the Coventry manager and a former player against whom I'd enjoyed many battles, said afterwards: 'This defeat is an embarrassment – and I'm not trying to take anything away from Tranmere. It's a humiliating experience, a stigma that will stay with us.'

If only I'd known that I would be expressing similar sentiments the following Saturday. At home to Portsmouth, I insisted that we maintain our standards. I wanted us to show that the game against Coventry was the beginning of an improvement in our league form. The response was incredibly disappointing. At the start of the second half we were four goals to nil down and looking like a team incapable of putting five goals past a Premiership team. We rallied, scored twice, and avoided the further embarrassment of a fifth Portsmouth goal. But we still lost 4–2 and in doing so turned in some of the worst performances I'd seen in some time. I knew what Gordon Strachan must have been going through.

After enjoying my best moment as manager of Tranmere, I was forced to contemplate the effects of my worst moment. Never has the result of one football match deflated me so much as that defeat against Portsmouth. Management was beginning to take its toll. Yes, I was the first player to miss a penalty in an FA Cup final; yes, I was a Liverpool player that night Arsenal beat us 2–0 at Anfield and thus secured the English championship. But in those days I could console myself in the knowledge that I had the power to bounce back. It was in my own hands. Now, as manager of Tranmere, my ability to bounce back is, in a sense, in the hands of the players I select. My control of the situation ends when the referee signals the start of the match.

So what a time it was for Lorraine Rogers, the new chief executive of Tranmere, to arrange a meeting with me. There we were, bottom of the table, and, depending on which newspaper you read, seemingly on the road to oblivion. Someone else might have expected the sack; not me. I was convinced that, under the circumstances, I was doing a reasonable job. I suspected Lorraine thought the same way so I was not too surprised when she began the meeting by offering me a new contract. Support hardly comes stronger than that. Rock bottom and suddenly I am offered a new contract. It is moments like those when your confidence comes back with a force that makes you want to work twenty-four hours a day just to repay someone else's faith. With that kind of backing, I am as certain as I will ever be that I will succeed as manager of Tranmere. It may take time, but I will play my part in the revival of this football club.

I think people sometimes forget that we are still holding our own – just – in the first division. The way people talk, you would think we had been relegated or had gone bust. When you consider how many of our best players we have had to sell since I took over as manager from John King, it is fair to say that we are something of a minor miracle. The fact that we are hanging on, fighting for our lives under ridiculous circumstances, says a lot for our perseverance. Such a quality will stand us all in good stead.

In our return match with Coventry we lost 3–1 but we went through to the next round of the Worthington Cup with a 6–4 aggregate victory that few people would have thought possible when the draw for the competition paired the two sides together. It wasn't the victory that impressed me most that night, however, it was the response of the Tranmere supporters. They knew how upset I was with our defeat against Portsmouth and they responded in a manner that brought a lump to my throat. All night they chanted 'Aldo, Aldo' and left me in no doubt about what they thought of me. How can I fail with such backing? The Tranmere fans, especially those who follow the club to away matches, are as good as you get. They supported me when I was a player when the times were mainly good. Now, as a manager, when times have been more difficult, they have shown how loyal they really are.

Like all managers, I get the abusive letters from people who would rather be negative, while the local press has published a few letters from supporters who have felt the need to criticise me. I can live with that. Dealing with it is easy because I know the majority of Tranmere fans are on my side and, equally comforting, I know that Lorraine Rogers is working in my best interests and in the best interests of the football club.

For the record, I delayed signing that new contract. I didn't feel the timing was right.

When this book was first published, Mick McCarthy, the Republic or Ireland manager, is believed to have objected strongly to my interpretation of our disagreement in December 1996, although I have only heard that through a secondary source. I have not seen Mick since and I suspect there would be little in the way of conversation even if we did come face to face. Mick is welcome to confront me and discuss the issue but I think this is unlikely.

I care not how much I offend Mick, but, paradoxically, I wish him well in his job with the Ireland team. My love for Ireland has not diminished in the years since I stopped being an international footballer and, just because I've had disagreements with one man, that doesn't mean I should pray for his downfall. If Mick matches, or even eclipses what Jack Charlton achieved as manager, that is fine by me. No Irishman was more disillusioned than I when the side let in a late equaliser in Macedonia, denying Ireland an automatic spot for Euro 2000. I have Irish blood and I am not going to allow a disagreement with the Ireland manager take away my affection for this unique nation and its football team. I also believe that in Robbie Keane, Ireland have unearthed a player of rare quality. There are few better strikers in the Premiership at the moment and Robbie has the ability to achieve everything the game has to offer.

The book played its part in reuniting me with some old friends. Howard Goddard, my former team-mate at Newport County, contacted me and came to see me after a Tranmere match. We swapped jokes and discussed the days when we were both younger, fitter and faster. We lamented the fortunes of Newport and welcomed the club's revival as a non-league club, hopefully one that will become a professional outfit.

Around about the time I retired from international football, in December 1996, I was under the impression that the Football Association of Ireland had a policy that handed out testimonial matches to players who had exceeded fifty caps or had represented the Republic for ten years or more. I naturally assumed that I would be presented with such a match, as did Ray Houghton, who would have passed on both counts. In fact, so did quite a few others and by way of compromise I let it be known that Ray and I would stage a joint testimonial at Lansdowne Road, Dublin. We provisionally set the date for May 1999 and waited for official approval, but nothing was forthcoming. Time moved on, still nothing seemed to be happening, and it dawned on us that the FAI may not be interested. It seemed to me that we were an embarrassment to them, though nothing was said to confirm that.

I toyed with the idea of staging an unofficial game. After all, no one could stop me from hiring out Lansdowne Road for my own match. I even got as far as listing players to be invited but it all fizzled into nothing. The lack of a match hurt, for sure, but the fact that the FAI seemed to be uninterested in me was far more upsetting.

Of course, I had the option of taking the matter to court, having been advised that I might have a good case, but I didn't really see the point. I had to accept that you don't get everything you want in life, even the things you feel you deserve. Whether I get a testimonial for Ireland in the future is a matter for the FAI. I am too busy to worry about it now. Ireland players have always had a good relationship with the fans and they are why Irish football has inspired feelings of affection around the world, and why tournament organisers want Ireland to be among the competing nations. When I went to Dublin to help promote this book the fans came in their hundreds to support me. They hadn't forgotten me – and that will always remain a valuable source of confidence.

Tranmere Rovers is a selling club, has been for some time now and might be for a long time yet. It is a fact of my life and a fact of Lorraine Rogers's life. So it was no surprise when, having returned from holiday in the summer of 1999, I was informed that the club were about to accept an offer of £450,000 from Huddersfield Town for the services of Kenny Irons, a midfield player of composure and skill. Deep down I was disillusioned but I could not complain. You cannot fight the facts of economics. Not only was I losing a quality player – certainly the most consistent player in my time as manager at Prenton Park – but we were giving him away for less than I considered to be his market value. Had Tranmere not been so desperate for money, I believe we might have sold Kenny for twice as much, but the fact is this – without that money we might no longer be in business. It was, by all accounts, a fine dividing line between surviving and going under. Kenny had played more than 400 times for Tranmere and, having been carefully nurtured as a youth at Prenton Park, become part of the fabric of the club. When the club enjoyed the good times, Kenny was part of it. When Kenny played well, Tranmere played well.

It was similar with John McGreal. The defender – my first captain when I was appointed manager – had the potential to go far in the game and it was inevitable that we would also have to sell him. The need was as pressing as it was with Kenny, though for different reasons. John would have been out of contract at the end of the 1999–2000 season and we would have been forced to let him leave for nothing. At least selling him a year earlier, as indeed we did, to Ipswich Town, we were able to earn £770,000 out of the deal.

Liam O'Brien, a midfield player, left us to return to Dublin; John Morrissey, a winger and Tranmere's longest-serving player, went on a free transfer; and Danny Coyne, the goalkeeper, left for free when he failed to sign a new contract. So much was changing at Tranmere it was difficult to keep up. Suddenly, time was as important a commodity as money.

I was able to bring in new players, firstly signing defender Steve Yates from Queens Park Rangers. I paid £250,000 for Wayne Allen, a striker, and I also managed to acquire Tony Grant, a player similar in style to Kenny Irons, on loan from Everton. We're hoping that Alan Mahon, a young Irish player with pace and skill, will agree to sign a new contract at Tranmere and that, believe me, would be a relief. On his day, Alan is one of the best players in the first division. We did not want to lose him, certainly not for less than his market value. That is not in Tranmere's best interests. The experience with Kenny and John McGreal taught us to be more ruthless.

Of course, if Tranmere are to be successful, our youth policy becomes vital. It is getting harder for Tranmere to attract quality schoolboys, with bigger clubs offering bigger incentives. But we have been at the forefront of developing young players and that has to continue. What does not help, however, is outside intervention. We had one player, a youngster with vision, skill and strength, who looked as though he was on the verge of something big in football. Unfortunately, a club larger than Tranmere, a club with greater resources, realised the player's potential and managed to acquire his signature, much to our chagrin. We complained, of course, and received an apology and small compensation – nothing compared to what the player will be worth when he makes the grade. This, alas, is what Tranmere are fighting against. Ten years ago we were able to set up a youth policy with strong foundations. Now, even that is difficult because the competition has increased. It makes my task even more difficult.

I sometimes ask myself a question: if I am improving as a manager – as I believe I am – why does the job seem to be getting more difficult? It is a question to which I have no answer but the subject nevertheless intrigues me. You really do learn more about life, and about yourself, when you go through the tough times than when you go through the good times.

Fulfilling my lifetime ambitions to play for Liverpool and to play in the World Cup have left me priceless memories but didn't make me much stronger. Going to Newport alone, at the age of twenty, made me stronger. Hillsborough definitely made me stronger, made me appreciate what is really important in life. If I am to succeed in management, I will take refuge in the lessons that life at the bottom of the first division provide. As an education it has been vital. It just isn't much fun going through it.

John Aldridge

Born: 18 September 1958 in Liverpool
Married: Joan Corlan, 21 June 1980
Children: Paul (born 1981), Joanne (born 1985)
Height: 5 feet 11 inches
Weight: Ranging from 11 stone (1980) to 12 stone 3 lbs (1998)

CAREER DETAILS

Teams, appearances, goals

Newport County (1979–84): 213 games, 90 goals

Oxford United (1984–87): 141 games, 90 goals

Liverpool (1987–89): 104 games, 63 goals

Real Sociedad (1989–91): 75 games, 40 goals

Tranmere Rovers (1991–98): 287 games, 174 goals

Republic of Ireland (1986–96): 69 games, 19 goals

Total: **889 games, 476 goals**

Honours list

League Division One championship medal (1987–88)

League Division Two championship medal (1984–85)

FA Cup winners' medal (1988–89)

League Cup winners' medal (1985–86)

FA Charity Shield winners' medal (1988)

Welsh Cup winners' medal (1979–80)

League Division One runners-up medal (1988–89)

FA Cup runners-up medal (1987–88)

Oxford United presented John Aldridge with a special medal for his involvement in the 1984–85 League Division Three championship-winning side, even though he didn't play enough games to win an official medal from the Football League.

Hat-tricks

Newport County (4)

Oxford United (5)

Liverpool (3)

Real Sociedad (0)

Tranmere Rovers (9)

Republic of Ireland (2)

Total hat-tricks: **23**

World Cup finals appearances

Ireland v England (Cagliari, Italy, 11 June 1990): 1–1

Ireland v Egypt (Palermo, Italy, 17 June 1990): 0–0

Ireland v Holland (Palermo, Italy, 21 June 1990): 1–1

Ireland v Romania (Genoa, Italy, 25 June 1990): 0–0

Ireland v Italy (Rome, Italy, 30 June 1990): 0–1

Ireland v Italy (New Jersey, USA, 18 June 1994): 1–0

Ireland v Mexico (Orlando, USA, 24 June 1994): 1–2

Ireland v Norway (New Jersey, USA, 28 June 1994): 0–0

Debuts

Newport County (H v Lincoln City, 29 September 1979): 1–1

Oxford United (A v Walsall, 4 April 1984): 1–0

Liverpool (A v Aston Villa, 21 February 1987): 2–2

Real Sociedad (H v Osasuna, 24 September 1989): 1–0

Tranmere Rovers (A v Brighton, 17 August 1991): 2–0

Republic of Ireland (H v Wales, 26 March 1986): 0–1

INDEX

Ablett, Gary 75
Adams, Tony 56, 71, 104
Addison, Colin 34–5, 37
Adidas 49
Adidas Golden Boot 45, 77
Alaba 122, 125, 129, 143
Albania 206, 209
Aldershot 27, 62
Aldridge, Bill (father) 1–9, 18, 20, 25, 28, 38–9, 73, 171, 226–7
  ill-health and death 178–9, 247–52
Aldridge, Joan (wife) 10–11, 25, 46, 54, 56, 65, 73–4, 79, 97, 171, 216, 219, 221–2
  engagement 18
  marriage 30
  move to Spain 115–20, 122–3, 126, 132, 178
Aldridge, Joanne (daughter) 46, 54, 94–5, 216, 222
Aldridge, John
  apprentice welder 12
  birth 2
  career
    hat-tricks 27, 44–5, 87, 89, 105, 182–3, 203, 208, 262
    statistics 261–2
    testimonial match 33, 197–8, 202
    Ireland 51, 145–75, 203–32, 251, 261
    fined by FIFA 219–20
    Liverpool 65–114
    signs for 9–10, 59–63
    Newport County 23–40, 261
    signs for 19
    Oxford United 39, 41–63, 80, 261

signs for 41
Real Sociedad 98,
    115–44, 261
    signs for 109–110
Tranmere Rovers
    233–45, 251, 261
    manager 26, 85,
        198–202, 233–45,
        253–6, 258–60
    signs for 142–4,
        177–8
Hillsborough disaster
    91–9, 164
Irish citizenship 231
Irish Sportswriters
    Player of the
    Year 206
meets the Pope 172–3
schooldays 3–4,
    8, 10–12
Aldridge, Paul (son) 33,
    46, 54, 95, 171, 216,
    222, 231
Allen, Wayne 259
Altrincham 16
Anderson, Viv 54, 88
Anfield 6–7, 95–6
Arconada, Luis 141
Argentina 174
Arrowsmith, Alf 6
Arsenal 47, 53, 71, 77,
    88–9, 101, 103–4,
    107, 113
Ashurst, Len 17–19, 24–7,
    28, 30–2, 34, 39

Ashurst, Robin 17–19
Aston Villa 19, 51, 66,
    146, 190–2
Athletic Bilbao 126,
    134–5, 137
Atkinson, Dalian 134,
    136–40, 191
Atletico Madrid 136, 139
Austria 226
Azurdia, Doctor Mike 195

Babb, Phil 212–14,
    220, 224
Banks Road School 3–4
Barcelona 123–4, 126–8,
    137, 139–40
Barclay, Patrick 73
Baresi, Franco 207
Barnes, John 69, 71–3,
    75–7, 79, 82, 87–8, 103
    England 159–60, 167
    Hillsborough 93
    PFA Player of the
        Year 81–2
Barnsley 44, 194, 237
Bassett, Dave 239
Beacroft, Graham 141
Beardsley, Peter 44,
    69–71, 75–9, 88, 103,
    106–8, 112–13
    England 159, 167
    Hillsborough 92
Beasant, David 78
Belgium 150, 153
Bengoechea 135

Bennett, Gary 196, 198
Bennison, Johnny 8
Bergkamp, Dennis 221
Best, George 36, 81
Bingham, Billy 211
Birmingham City 49, 186, 193, 242
Blackburn Rovers 113
Blackpool 185
Blue Union 13–14
Bolton Wanderers 76, 195, 239
Bonetti, Ivano 234–5
Bonner, Pat 153, 159, 172, 174, 207, 213, 221
Booth, Dennis 38
Boronat, Marco 119–20, 124–5, 130, 133–7
Bosnich, Mark 191
Bournemouth 36
Bradford City 235, 242, 248
Brady, Liam 147, 150–1, 155, 162, 165
Brannan, Ged 185, 190, 197, 235, 238
Brazil 153, 221
Brentford 89
Briggs, Gary 45, 72
Brighton and Hove Albion 179–80
Bristol Rovers 181, 187, 196
British Leyland 15, 19–20
Brock, Kevin 44, 46, 59

Bruges 12, 228
Bruton, Mike 26
Bulgaria 152–3, 155
Burnley 31, 34, 43, 44
Burrows, David 101
Bury 242
Butragueño, Emilio 130, 163
Byrne, John 56, 205
Byrne, Mick 147, 168, 171, 225

Cadiz 126
Cain, Tommy 249
Cambridge United 185
Campos, Jorge 218
Canada Dock 15
Cantwell, Noel 162
Cardiff City 34, 36
Carl Zeiss Jena 32
Carlisle United 89, 238
Carr, Jeff 247
Cascarino, Tony 162, 165–6, 212, 214, 218, 223
Case, Jimmy 14
Castellon 137
Celta Vigo 125
Charles, Jeremy 53
Charlton Athletic 87, 89, 105, 184, 193, 201
Charlton, Jack 51, 146, 149–50, 152, 155–60, 162–4, 205, 223–9, 257
   World Cups 167–73, 203, 212–20

fined by FIFA 220

Chelsea 53, 67, 86

Cheshire Lines 15

Chettle, Steve 77

Chilavert 127

Clark, Brian 23–4

Clark, Frank 238

Clarke, Wayne 75

Clemence, Ray 49

Clough, Nigel 53, 190

Connelly, Karl 238

Cook, Paul 235, 242

Corfe, Frank 194, 198, 234, 237, 238, 245

Corlan, Joan *see* Joan Aldridge

Corlan, Nell 33

Corlan, Tommy 33, 249

Coventry City 71, 254, 256

Coyne, Danny 187, 196, 237, 259

Coyne, Tommy 188–9, 212, 215, 217–18, 220–1, 225

Crystal Palace 112, 115

Czechoslovakia 149

Daily Mirror 45, 59–61, 117

Dalglish, Kenny 50, 53, 61–2, 65–89, 97–8, 102, 105–6, 108, 112
  Hillsborough disaster 93–4, 96–7
  testimonial 131

Dalglish, Marina 97–8

Daly, Gerry 148

Davis, Paul 71

Delaney, John 42

Denmark 206, 208–9, 211

Derby County 47, 75, 183–4, 186, 195, 197–8

Desayev 130

Diana, Princess 78

Dixon, Lee 103, 204

Donadoni, Roberto 174

Dunga 153

Dwyer, Phil 36

Dysart, Mark 10

Echo Cup 8

Egypt 167, 170, 172

Elliot, Paul 182

England 156, 159–60, 167, 169–70, 172, 204–5, 225

Ensor, Tony 110

Escobar, Andres 223

European Championship (1988) 156–61 (1992) 204–6

European Cup (1985) 150

European Cup (1992) 127

Evans, Ian 243–4

Evans, Maurice 47–8, 53–7, 60, 62–3, 84

Evans, Roy 107

Everton 35–6, 47, 53–4, 67, 73, 75, 77, 83, 99, 101–2, 148

FA Charity Shield 87, 107

FA Cup finals
  (1977) 14
  (1988) 77, 182
  (1989) 101
  (1992) 113
FA Youth Cup 13
Fairclough, David 13
Fashanu, John 87
Ferguson, Alex 83–4, 88
Finney, Tom 76
Flamenco 131
Ford, Richard 38–9
Frickley Athletic 17
Futcher, Paul 183
Futre, Paolo 138

Galvin, Tony 160
Garcia, Luis 217
Garnett, Shaun 185, 190–1
Garston Woodcutters
  13–15
Gascoigne, Paul 84, 167,
  204, 210
Germany 172, 206
Giles, Johnny 162
Gillespie, Gary 72, 75–6
Givens, Don 169
Goddard, Howard 26–9,
  257
Goicoechea 125, 127, 209
Goodyear, Clive 78
Goole Town 16
Gorriz 119
Grant, Tony 259
Graydon, Ray 43

Greaves, Jimmy 187, 251
Grimsby Town 46, 181–2,
  189, 192–3, 201, 235
Grobbelaar, Bruce 50,
  75, 104
  Hillsborough 95–6
Gubba, Tony 52
Gullit, Ruud 161, 167, 172
Gwyther, David 29, 35

Hagi 172
Halifax Town 25, 181
Hall, Eric 57
Hamilton, Billy 44, 46,
  49–50, 54, 55, 250
Hand, Eion 51, 146
Hansen, Alan 66, 71, 75,
  79, 82, 102
  Hillsborough 95–6
  Scotland 150
Hardwick, Steve 46
Harford, Mick 27
Harnan, Kevin 15
Hartlepool 242
Hebberd, Trevor 46, 53
Hereford 243
Heysel Stadium disaster
  50, 150
Higgins, Dave 181–2,
  236–7
Hill, Brian 78
Hill, Dave 73
Hillsborough disaster
  91–9, 164, 226
  Taylor report 97

Hoddle, Glenn 187–8

Holland 160–1, 167, 170–2, 220–1, 227–8

Holly Park 16, 17, 20

Horner, Dolly 24

Houghton, Ray 53, 54, 69, 72–3, 75–6, 79, 104, 191
  Hillsborough 92, 96, 164
  Ireland 146–8, 154, 156–7, 159, 161, 163–4, 166, 170, 204, 207, 208, 209, 212, 213, 215, 223, 227, 257–8

Huddersfield Town 37, 44, 237

Hughes, Mark 191

Hughton, Chris 205

Hull City 38, 89

Humphries, Joby 15

Hungary 163–5

Hunt, John 60

Hunt, Roger 6–7, 77

Iceland 149, 231

Independent 73

Ipswich Town 85, 183, 200, 236

Ireland 19, 51, 79, 145–75, 203–32, 251, 256–8, 261
  Euro '88, 156–61
  Euro '92, 204–6
  v Albania 206, 210
  v Austria 226
  v Belgium 150, 153
  v Brazil 153
  v Bulgaria 152–3, 155
  v Czechoslovakia 149
  v Denmark 209–10
  v Egypt 170
  v England 159, 169–70, 225–6
  v Holland 171–2, 221, 228
  v Hungary 163–5
  v Iceland 149, 231–2
  v Israel 155
  v Italy 173–4, 207, 214–15
  v Latvia 208–9, 210, 224, 227
  v Liechtenstein 226, 229
  v Lithuania 210
  v Luxembourg 154–5
  v Macedonia 230
  v Malta 164, 166, 168
  v Mexico 128, 216–19
  v Northern Ireland 162, 166, 209, 210–11, 224
  v Norway 157, 220–1
  v Poland 150, 157, 204
  v Portugal 208, 226, 227–8
  v Romania 172
  v Russia 230
  v Scotland 150, 152
  v Spain 163–4, 209–10
  v Switzerland 206
  v Tunisia 162–3
  v Turkey 169, 203, 205
  v USA 206, 208

v USSR 159–60
v Wales 51–2, 146,
    148, 206
v West Germany 165
World Cups 128, 130,
    161–2, 166–75, 203,
    212–23
Irons, Kenny 185, 188,
    190, 201, 235, 258–9
Israel 68, 155
Italy 173–4, 207, 214–15,
    221

Johns, Hugh 27
Johnson, Peter 141, 177,
    194, 245
Johnstone, Craig
    66, 72, 85
Jones, Gary 197
Jones, Kenny 199, 202
Jones, Lee 239–40, 241
Jones, Tosh 14
Jones, Vinnie 78, 83, 182
Jonk, Wim 221
Juventus 50, 150

Keane, Robbie 257
Keane, Roy 208–9
Keegan, Kevin 13, 184,
    186, 200–1
Kelly, David 155, 209,
    221, 225, 241–2, 254
Kelly, Gary 213, 224
Kendall, Howard 134
Kendall, Mark 35

Kennedy, Alan 50
Kennedy, Mick 149, 151
King, John (Altrincham) 16
King, John (Tranmere
    Rovers) 17–18, 141,
    143, 178–81, 184,
    190–2, 195–9, 255
Kluivert, Patrick 228
Koeman, Ronald 123

Langan, David 44, 46, 51,
    146, 153
Larranaga 125, 135
Latvia 208, 210, 223–4,
    226–7
Laudrup, Brian 209
Lausanne Sports 133, 135
Lawler, Chris 6
Lawrenson, Mark 66,
    84, 152
Laws, Brian 100–1,
    104, 236
Lee, Gordon 19
Lee, Sammy 75, 121
Leeds United 45, 104, 142,
    177–8, 183
Leeson, Mr 12
Leicester City 12, 53, 189,
    193, 200, 228
Lewis, Ray 92–3
Liechtenstein 225–6, 229
Lincoln City 27
Lineker, Gary 53, 80, 159,
    170, 205
Liverpool 6–7, 47,

49–51, 53, 55, 129, 148, 156, 261
Coca-Cola Cup 113
FA Cup final
   (1977) 14
   (1988) 77, 102, 192
   (1989) 101–2
   (1992) 113
Hillsborough disaster 91–9
schoolboys 8
signs JA 9–10, 59–63
v Arsenal 71, 77, 103, 107, 113
v Aston Villa 66
v Atletico Madrid 85–6
v Brentford 89
v Bruges 12, 228
v Carlisle United 89
v Celtic 97
v Charlton Athletic 87, 89, 105
v Chelsea 67, 86
v Coventry City 71
v Crystal Palace 112, 115
v Derby County 75
v Everton 73, 75, 77, 83, 99, 101–2
v Hull City 89
v Israel 68
v Juventus 50, 150
v Leicester City 12, 228
v Luton Town 67, 72, 89, 108
v Manchester City 77
v Manchester United 14, 80, 83, 87–8
v Millwall 89
v Newcastle United 84, 89
v Norwich City 73
v Nottingham Forest 76–7, 80, 82, 100–1
v Oxford United 52, 72
v Queens Park Rangers 101
v Real Madrid 109
v Real Sociedad 86, 121, 131
v St Etienne 13, 228
v Sheffield Wednesday 88
v Southampton 6, 67
v Stoke City 77
v Tottenham Hotspur 76, 89
v Watford 75
v West Ham United 71, 103
v Wimbledon 76–8, 85, 87, 101–2, 156, 182, 239
Liverpool County FA 16
Logrones 125, 134
Lorimer, Peter 45
Lownes, Steve 38
Lukic, John 103
Lumbreras 133
Luton Town 58, 67,

72, 89, 108, 187, 189, 194
Luxembourg 154–5
Lynam, Des 213

McAteer, Jason 212–14, 217–18, 224
McCall, Stuart 102
McCarthy, Mick 229–30, 231–2, 256–7
McDonald, Bobby 46, 49
Macdonald, Malcolm 80
McFerran, Phil 15
McGrath, Paul 49–50, 149, 160, 165, 191, 208, 213, 220–1, 223
McGreal, John 236, 238, 259
Mackay, Gary 156
McLoughlin, Alan 211–12
McMahon, Steve 35, 68, 75, 78–9, 83, 102
  England 170
  Hillsborough 96
McNamara, Alfie 2
McNamara, Anne (half sister) 2
McNamara, Betty (mother) 2–3, 145, 178, 226–7, 248
McNamara, Denny (uncle) 6
McNamara, Jean (half sister) 2, 248
Macedonia 229–30, 257

Mahon, Alan 243–4, 259
Malaga 126
Maldini, Paolo 174
Malkin, Chris 185, 196
Mallorca 141
Malta 164, 166, 168
Manchester City 58, 77, 242
Manchester City Youth 13
Manchester United 14, 47, 49–50, 52, 56, 80, 83, 87–8, 192
Manolo, Manuel 163
Maradona, Diego 209, 223
Marsh, Mike 108
Marshall, Ian 54
Martindale Cup 8
Martindale, Dave 179
Mathias, Ray 200, 231, 237
Maxwell, Robert 39–42, 45–8, 53, 57–63, 148
Megson, Gary 243
Mellon, Mick 238, 243
Mexico 128, 216–19
Michel 164
Middlesbrough 195, 242
Milk Cup 51–3
Miller, Brian 34–5
Mills, Mary 145
Millwall 89
Mirandinha 153
Molby, Jan 67, 88
Monkou, Ken 182
Moore, Alan 232
Moore, Ian 196–8, 238–9

Moore, Johnny 14
Moore, Ronnie 196,
    199, 201–2
Moran, Kevin 151, 161,
    163, 166, 168, 208, 213,
    223, 229–30
Morrissey, John 179–80,
    188, 234–6, 259
Muir, Alec 189
Muir, Ian 196
Mullery, Alan 80
Mungall, Steve 188

Neal, Phil 50
Nevin, Pat 184, 189, 190,
    194, 235, 242
New Heys School 8, 10–11
Newcastle United 47,
    51, 55, 182, 184, 186,
    237, 243
Newport 19, 31–3, 76,
    257, 261
    v Aldershot 27
    v Bournemouth 36
    v Burnley 31
    v Cardiff City 36
    v Everton 35–6
    v Halifax 25
    v Huddersfield 37
    v Hull City 38
    v Lincoln City 27
    v Northampton
        Town 27
    v Port Vale 26
    v Portsmouth 28

    v Rochdale 29
    v Shrewsbury Town 30
    v Stockport County 27
    v Walsall 29
    Welsh Cup 29–30
Nicol, Lee 99
Nicol, Steve 71, 75, 83,
    102, 104
    Hillsborough 92
Nike 49
Nixon, Eric 179, 181–2,
    190, 193, 197, 242
Nolan, Ian 184, 190–2, 194
Northampton Town 27,
    51
Northern Ireland 162,
    166, 209, 224
Norway 157, 220
Norwich City 51, 73, 242
Nottingham Forest 53,
    76–7, 80, 82, 100–1, 183,
    190, 238
    Hillsborough disaster
        91–9
Notts County 242

O'Brien, Liam 190, 192,
    200, 235, 259
O'Carroll, Brendan 214
Oldham Athletic 45, 190,
    197, 237, 239
O'Leary, David 104,
    149, 172
Omar, Brian 201
Osasuna 120–1, 127, 136

Oxford Mail 46
Oxford United 72, 76, 80,
  84, 261, 262
  sells JA 9, 59–63
  signs JA 41
  v Aldershot 62
  v Arsenal 53
  v Aston Villa 51, 146
  v Barnsley 44
  v Birmingham City 49
  v Burnley 43
  v Everton 53–4
  v Grimsby 46
  v Huddersfield
    Town 44
  v Leeds United 45
  v Liverpool 49–52, 55
  v Luton Town 58
  v Manchester City 59
  v Manchester United
    49, 56
  v Newcastle United 51
  v Northampton
    Town 51
  v Norwich City 51
  v Nottingham Forest 53
  v Oldham Athletic 45
  v Portsmouth 51
  v Queens Park
    Rangers 52, 56
  v Rotherham United 43
  v Sheffield Wednesday
    54
  v Southampton 58–9
  v Tranmere Rovers
    183–4, 186,
    189
  v Watford 63
  v West Bromwich
    Albion 49

Pagliuca 215
Paisley, Bob 13, 80–1
Parkinson, Andy
  241, 243–4
Parry, Les 189
Partizan Belgrade 135
Pearson, Jim 49
Perkins, Russ 15–16, 18
Peterborough 187
Phillips, Les 49, 53, 56, 59
Philpotts, Dave 231, 241
Poland 150, 157, 204
Polster, Tony 129–30
Port Vale 26, 201, 235, 239
Portsmouth 28, 47,
  51, 239, 254–5, 256
Portugal 208, 225, 227
PSV Eindhoven 105

Queens Park Rangers 52,
  56, 101, 239, 242
Quinn, Jimmy 211
Quinn, Niall 151, 172,
  204, 208, 209, 210

Ratcliffe, Kevin 102
Rayo Vallecano 128
Reading 47, 180,
  195–6, 237

Real Madrid 109, 117, 124–5, 128, 137, 142
Real Madrileno 122, 124
Real Oviedo 121, 134–5
Real Sociedad 98, 109, 261
  v Athletic Bilbao 126, 135, 137
  v Atletico Madrid 136, 139
  v Barcelona 123–4, 126–8, 137, 139–40
  v Cadiz 126
  v Castellon 137
  v Celta Vigo 125
  v Flamenco 131
  v Lausanne Sports 133, 135
  v Liverpool 85–6, 121, 131
  v Logrones 125, 134
  v Malaga 126
  v Mallorca 141
  v Osasuna 120–1, 127, 136
  v Partizan Belgrade 135
  v Rayo Vallecano 128
  v Real Madrid 124–5, 128, 137, 142
  v Real Madrileno 122, 124
  v Real Oviedo 121, 134–5
  v Real Zaragoza 127, 132–3, 172
  v Sabadell 125
  v Sevilla 126, 129–30
  v Sporting Gijon 125, 136–7
  v Tenerife 125, 166
  v Valencia 125
Real Zaragoza 127, 132–3, 172
Relish, John 37
Rhoades-Brown, Peter 43–4, 46, 56
Richardson, Kevin 130, 134–6, 140, 191
Rimmer, Warwick 185
Roach, Dennis 105, 109–11, 116–17, 138
Robinson, Michael 174
Robinson, Peter 61–2, 68, 108–11, 113, 239
Robson, Bobby 81, 156
Robson, Bryan 242
Rochdale 29
Rogers, Alan 238
Rogers, Lorraine 255, 256, 258
Romania 172
Rotherham United 43
Runcorn 17, 183
Rush, Ian 44, 61, 62, 66–7, 69, 74, 85–9, 102–3, 105–8, 113, 251
  with Juventus 57–8, 85
  Wales 148

Sabadell 125
St Andrews 189

St Etienne 13, 228
San Sebastian 116–17, 126, 143
Sanchez, Hugo 128, 218
Sanchez, Lawrie 78
Sansom, Kenny 159
Saunders, Tom 9
Schillaci, Salvatore 174
Scifo, Enzo 150
Scotland 150, 152, 156
Setters, Maurice 157
Sevilla 126, 129–30
Shankly, Bill 12, 75, 113, 196
Shearer, Alan 243
Sheedy, Kevin 35, 149–50, 168, 170, 174, 209, 237
Sheffield, Hillsborough disaster 91–9
Sheffield Wednesday 54, 88
Sheridan, John 210, 215
Shilton, Peter 67, 80, 159
Shoot 45
Shotton, Malcolm 46
Shrewsbury Town 30, 235
Sillett, John 71
Simonsen, Steve 244–5
Sinclair, Trevor 185
Smith, Alan 103
Smith, Jim 40, 42–4, 46–7, 51–2, 198
Smith, John 60–1, 68, 109–11
Somerton Park 24, 37

South Liverpool FC 13, 15–17
Southall, Neville 102, 148
Southampton 6–7, 58, 67
Southend United 195, 235
Southport 16
Spackman, Nigel 75–6, 107
Spain 163–4, 208–11
Speedie, David 193
Sporting Gijon 125, 136–7
Stafford Rangers 107–8
Standard-Triumph car factory 12
Stapleton, Frank 29, 149, 156, 168, 224, 227, 230
Staunton, Steve 164, 191, 204, 208, 209, 217–18, 227
Steel, Jim 180, 182
Stevens, Gary 73, 194, 242
Stockport County 27, 242–3
Stoke City 77, 195, 237, 249
Strachan, Gordon 254–5
Stubbs, Ray 214
Suarez, Luis 164
Sun 57, 69, 81, 97
Sunday Express 80
Sunday League 13–15
Sunderland 39, 46, 183, 185, 193, 201, 243
Sutton, Steve 76
Swindon 180, 187–8, 242
Switzerland 206

Taylor, Gordon 82
Taylor, Graham 204
Taylor report on
    Hillsborough
    disaster 97
Teale, Shaun 196, 198, 236
Tenerife 125, 166
Thomas, Michael 103
Thomas, Tony 190,
    192, 242
Thompson, Andy 241
Thompson, Dave 239
Thorn, Andy 78, 239, 242
Timofte, Daniel 172
Todd, Colin 240
Toshack, John 24, 117,
    121, 139–40, 142–3, 178
Tottenham Hotspur
    52, 76, 89
Townsend, Andy 191,
    208, 213, 214, 223, 225
Tranmere Rovers 18, 85,
    113, 233–45, 253–6,
    258–60, 261
    Anglo–Italian Cup 186
    signs JA 142–4, 177–8
    v Aston Villa 190–1
    v Barnsley 194, 237
    v Birmingham City 186,
        193, 242
    v Blackpool 185
    v Bolton Wanderers
        195, 239–40
    v Bradford City 235,
        242, 248

v Brighton and Hove
    Albion 179–80
v Bristol Rovers 181,
    187, 196
v Bury 242
v Cambridge United 185
v Carlisle United 238
v Charlton Athletic 184,
    193, 201
v Chelsea 182
v Coventry City
    254, 256
v Crystal Palace 189
v Derby County 183–4,
    186, 195, 197–8
v Grimsby Town 181–2,
    189, 192–3, 201, 235
v Halifax Town 181
v Hartlepool 242
v Hereford 243
v Ipswich Town 183,
    200, 236
v Leeds United 183
v Leicester City 189,
    193, 200
v Luton Town 187,
    189, 194
v Manchester City 242
v Middlesbrough
    195, 242
v Newcastle United
    182, 184, 186, 243
v Norwich City 242
v Nottingham Forest
    183, 190

v Notts County 242
v Oldham Athletic 190, 197, 237, 239
v Oxford United 183–4, 186, 189
v Peterborough 187
v Port Vale 201, 235, 239
v Portsmouth 186, 239, 254–5, 256
v Queens Park Rangers 239, 242
v Reading 195–6, 237, 242
v Runcorn 183
v St Andrews 189
v Shrewsbury Town 235
v Southend United 195, 235
v Stockport County 243
v Stoke City 195, 237, 249
v Sunderland 183, 185, 193, 201, 243
v Swindon Town 187–8, 242
v Watford 186, 197
v West Bromwich Albion 195, 237, 242
v West Ham 186
v Wimbledon 195
v Wolverhampton Wanderers 186, 195, 237, 239, 250

Trewick, John 46
Tunisia 162–3
Turkey 169, 203, 205
Tynan, Tommy 26–9, 32

UEFA Cup 130
United States 206–7
Uruguay 148
US Athletic 201
US Cup 206–7
USA (football team) 206, 208
USSR 159–61, 229

Valencia 125
Van Basten, Marco 161, 167
Van Breukelen 172
Vaughan, Nigel 36
Venison, Barry 70, 75
Vialli, Gianluca 207
Villabona 125

Wales 51–2, 146, 148, 206
Walker, Des 170
Walsh, Gary 80
Walsh, Paul 66–7
Walsall 29
Wark, John 85, 201
Warriner, Steve 24
Watford 62, 75, 186, 197
Welsh Cup 29–30
Welsh League 23
West Bromwich Albion 49, 195, 237, 242

West Germany 165, 174

West, Gordon 18

West Ham United 53, 71, 103, 186

Whelan, Ronnie 75, 79, 102, 164
Hillsborough 96, 164
Ireland 157, 160, 166, 168, 208

Whitehurst, Billy 55–6, 58–9, 89

Whiteside, Norman 83

Wilkinson, Howard 142, 177

Williams, Dai 77

Williams, Fred 183, 245

Wimbledon 76–8, 85, 87, 101–2, 156, 182, 195, 239
FA Cup final (1988) 77, 102, 192

Wise, Dennis 78, 182

Wolverhampton Wanderers 186, 195, 237, 239, 250

World Cup
(1982) 162
(1986) 148, 150, 162
(1990) 109, 130, 162; Ireland 166–75, 193, 203
(1994) 112, 128; Ireland 212–23

Wright, Ian 226

Yates, Steve 259

Yeats, Ron 65

Young, Eric 78

Zubizarreta 123–4, 209